HITS, HEATHENS, AND HIPPOS:

Stories from an Agent, Activist, and Adventurer

MARTY ESSEN

Praise for *Hits, Heathens, and Hippos: Stories from an Agent, Activist, and Adventurer*

"*Hits, Heathens, and Hippos* proves life is mostly luck and a little timing with many laughs along the way. Marty Essen has demonstrated that life is what you do while you decide what you are going to be when you grow up. This is a great book about a life of ventures, friends and a few lessons about winning and losing."
　　　　　　—Governor Brian Schweitzer (Democrat, Montana 2005–2013)

"Marty Essen's latest book, *Hits, Heathens, and Hippos*—which includes a funny story from my days working with his talent agency—really drew me in. His descriptions of our old Minneapolis stomping grounds, and our mutual hometown of Duluth, brought back a lot of forgotten memories, and it was a pleasure to delve into his recollections through his colorful storytelling. Even if you're not in the music business, Marty's stories will fascinate you!"
　　　　　　　　　　　　　　　—Phil Solem, The Rembrandts

"These days it's imperative to be reminded that one's dreams can still be made manifest through a combination of fortitude, aptitude, and a good-humored willingness to fail miserably. Marty Essen's aptly titled new book, *Hits, Heathens, and Hippos* is a glorious romp through the pathos, triumph, and sheer absurdity of a small scale rock and roll universe, one that nonetheless, has all the trimmings of the big one."
　　　　　　　　　　　　　　—Peter Himmelman, musician

"Marty Essen's book, *Hits, Heathens and Hippos*, takes you on a comedy journey that never ends. It's a wicked funny ride. And I know funny."
　　　　　　　　　　　　　　—Karen Pickering, comedian

Praise for *Endangered Edens: Exploring the Arctic National Wildlife Refuge, Costa Rica, the Everglades, and Puerto Rico*

"Join photographer extraordinaire Marty Essen and his intrepid wife Deb on their adventures through four *Endangered Edens*. You'll be treated to funny stories, unforgettable characters, and striking images. But most of all, you'll come away with new appreciation for special places, and their wild inhabitants, under threat today. May this book inspire its readers to protect them!"

—Sy Montgomery, author, *The Soul of an Octopus*

"A magical, fun journey through some of the world's hidden and not so hidden *Edens*, as seen through the eyes of a true wildlife aficionado and author whose writing makes the pages come alive and vibrate with the sound and pulse of nature. A book that once started is impossible to put down."

—Dr. M. Sanjayan, senior scientist at Conservation International and television host

"*Endangered Edens: Exploring the Arctic National Wildlife Refuge, Costa Rica, the Everglades, and Puerto Rico* is impressively informative and a lot of fun. Ideal for the armchair traveler and certain to be an enduringly popular addition to community library collections."

—Midwest Book Review

"I highly recommend that everyone join author Marty Essen and his wife, Deb, as they explore our planets' *Endangered Edens*. After reading about these last great wild places, you will surely be tempted to visit them and more importantly protect them for future generations to enjoy."

—Cindy Shogan, executive director, Alaska Wilderness League

Praise for *Time Is Irreverent*

"Highly recommend. It's fun, clever, cool, witty, surprising, political, sexy, everything a sci-fi book should be. And as someone who's also written a sci-fi-time-travel-humor novel, I love that Marty Essen doesn't break the time rules he sets up from the start—so many sci-fi authors do, and as far as I'm concerned, that's just lazy writing. Not the case here! Yes, his characters learn and adapt and grow, but the foundation of his rules remain intact always. To repeat: fun, witty, surprising, sexy. Highly recommend."

—Jeff Abugov, writer, producer, director

"*Time Is Irreverent* is a delightful romp that scores solid satirical points about religion, human nature, sex, the Trump administration, and a great deal more."

—Tom Flynn, editor, *Free Inquiry* magazine

"Ironic, original, hysterically funny, deftly crafted, and an impressively entertaining read from first page to last, *Time Is Irreverent* by Marty Essen is an especially and unreserved recommended for community library Science Fiction & Fantasy collections. It should be noted for the personal reading lists of dedicated science fiction fans that *Time Is Irreverent* is also available in a digital book format."

—Midwest Book Review

"*Time Is Irreverent* is a well-written, well-paced novel peopled with solid, likeable characters. Marty Essen is a talented author who has managed to wrap several complex threads into a light, enjoyable narrative. I hope he will continue writing in the sci-fi genre and I look forward eagerly to his future works."

—Charles Remington, Readers' Favorite Book Reviews

Praise for *Time Is Irreverent 2: Jesus Christ, Not Again!*

"*Time Is Irreverent 2* is a madcap blasphemous comedy of the most delightful sort. Recommended for those whose tastes incline that way; if you loved *Time Is Irreverent*, run, don't walk, to consume this perfect sequel."

—Tom Flynn, editor, *Free Inquiry* magazine

"An excellent follow-up to the original, and this from someone who typically hates sequels! All the same great characters and more, plus Jesus—although not your mama's Jesus. The funny is funnier, the crazy crazier, and the politics even more in your face (in the good way!). If you loved the first, you've got to read the second. Well done, Marty!"

—Jeff Abugov, writer, producer, director

"For those aficionados of entertaining, optimistic sci-fi, who have been avidly waiting for another *Time Is Irreverent* adventure—your wait is over. Marty Essen has produced a fine follow-up to his first time traveling escapade and I hope that the likeable characters he has created will get many future outings. A great addition to a currently gloomy, pessimistic genre. I do not hesitate to recommend it."

—Charles Remington, Readers' Favorite Book Reviews

Published by:

Encante Press, LLC
www.EncantePress.com
SAN: 850-4326

Cover and interior layout by Tugboat Design
Cover photo by Marty Essen

Publisher's Cataloging-in-Publication data

Names: Essen, Marty, author.
Title: Hits, Heathens, and Hippos: Stories from an Agent, Activist, and Adventurer / Marty Essen.
Description: Encante Press, LLC, 2021.
Identifiers: LCCN: 2020924514 | ISBN: 978-1-7344303-2-5 (pbk.) | 978-1-7344303-3-2 (e-book)
Subjects: LCSH Essen, Marty--Travel. | Americans--Foreign countries--Biography. | Voyages and travels. | Social activists--Biography. | Businesspeople--Biography. | Environmentalists--Biography. | BISAC BIOGRAPHY & AUTOBIOGRAPHY / Personal Memoirs | BIOGRAPHY & AUTOBIOGRAPHY / Adventurers & Explorers | HUMOR / Form / Essays | TRAVEL / Essays & Travelogues
Classification: LCC CT275.E7375 2021 | DDC 920--dc23

10 9 8 7 6 5 4 3 2 1

Dedicated to:

All the musicians and entertainers I have worked with over the years, especially Brian Kenney, Phil Solem, Peter Himmelman, André Cymone, William Ellwood, Paul Metsa, Jeff Victor, Al Wolovitch, Andy Kamman, Eric Moen, Tom Riopelle, Richard Wieser, Palmer Harbison, Mark Steele, Mary Ott, Diane Goldberg, Gavin Morrison, Gary Harpole, Lisa Collins Harpole, Jeff Brown, Gregory Ragsdell, Danny Allen, Scott Moore, David Cullen, Jill Haley, Mark Oppenlander, Peter Sittler, Brian Bart, John Bolin, Brian Lorenson, John O'Neil, Tammy Thomas, Stan Nyborg, Brad Kittelson, Doug Berglund, Frankie Gordon, John Wellvang, Brian Dynes, Jeff Hauschildt, John McKenzie, Frosty Atkinson, Pancho Torres, Ed Garido, Robert Nieto, Ernie Palestino, Cesar Berra, Jerry Gomez, Peggi Blu, Jeff Sutherland, Kelly Anderson, Boyd Bowdish, John Neilson, Mike Converse, Steve Guillaume, Leslie Peters, Alan Lutkevich, Miriam Colacci, Vinny Peterson, Lonnie Hammer, Scott Mattila, Greg Allen, David Cormier, Randy Barnette, Scott Gumz, Russ Guldeman, Scott Haugen, Tim Monson, Rudy D'Agostino, Steve Harrison, Jesse Bastos, Peter Kay, Jeff Born, Tim Braun, Bill Strohm, Ricki Koenig, Buck Reeves, Eric Castles, Dave Armstrong, Peter Banfield, Pete Meados, Larry Preston, Bradley Joseph, William Hill, Jeff Parlow, Randy Zwarte, Mick Furlo, David Sainden, Mitch Viegut, Peter Phippen, Jon Douglas, Ace Gyro, Traciana Graves, Naomi Grossman, and Damona Hoffman.

Special thanks to:

My intrepid wife, Deb Essen, for her support, suggestions, and neck rubs.

CONTENTS

INTRODUCTION

I have a good, but not perfect memory, and some of the events I write about in this book took place decades ago. I covered them as accurately as I could, and scrapbooks I maintained during my years as a talent agent and manager helped me out. Nevertheless, I probably got some things wrong, and like biographical movies or religious texts, I occasionally condensed events. Additionally, when I featured dialogue, rather than strive for word-for-word accuracy, I recreated it the best I could to reflect my memory of the conversation. Sometimes I used false names. Reasons for that include not remembering the names of some people and masking the identity of those who might object to what I have to say about them. I have marked false names with an asterisk, like this*. Most importantly, I wrote this book to entertain and hope my stories put a smile on your face.

CHAPTER 1

The Little Blond-Haired Kid

"I loved going to church as a child. I would snuggle in between my mother and father, listening for the moment when Rev. John Reppe, of Bethlehem Lutheran Church, would begin talking about a man he admired almost as much as Jesus. The minister would saunter to his lectern, gaze over the congregation, and say something like this: "Today we turn to the Epistle to the Philippians, where Paul writes, 'Look out for the dogs, look out for the evildoers, look out for those who mutilate the flesh.'"

I was too young to understand much of what Pastor Reppe said, but I did know this: once again, he was quoting the strongest and wisest man in the world, my hero, my father, Paul Essen—and the entire congregation was hanging on his every word!

* * *

Life began for me in the Minnesota town of Two Harbors, located on Lake Superior, twenty-five miles north of Duluth. I was the youngest of three siblings; my mother, Marcie, was a housewife, and my father was the owner and president of one of the two banks in town. My father's bank was the Commercial State Bank, and the other was Satan's Savings and Loan, or something similar to that. In addition to believing my hero-father was *the Paul* Pastor Reppe quoted so often, I also believed he was the richest man in town. That belief would be shot down years later, when I learned that running a bank in a town of a little over four thousand people wasn't all it was cracked up to be.

I lived in Two Harbors only through kindergarten, but those years were rich with small town experiences. When I think back about it now, I'm amazed at just how much freedom I had to roam. Usually I was with the local mortician's son, Brent, or Luann, the girl I was determined to marry when I was older—like ten. Both lived just down the street from me. No part of town was off-limits to us, including Lake Superior, where we would spend hours on the pebble beach searching for agates, or uptown, where we would check out the water tower to make sure it wasn't leaking. And, naturally, we would tiptoe into the mortuary attached to Brent's house, where we'd ultimately chicken out before seeing any dead people.

Haircuts in Two Harbors were also unaccompanied. My father would simply hand me a few dollars and say, "Walk over to the barber's after school. Tell him to give you a *butch*." Hmm. . . . Now there's a word that's evolved over the years.

Family entertainment in northern Minnesota meant *Captain Kangaroo* in the morning, leaf-viewing automobile rides in the fall, and skating in the winter. Then, during the summer, we'd spend weekends at our cabin on Stone Lake, where we would swim, fish, and my brother would shut me inside the hide-a-bed. In retrospect, I was lucky to have lived through playing hide-a-bed-sandwich. People have actually suffocated doing it. Me? It just gave me a lifetime of claustrophobia.

Other family fun at the cabin included watching our neighbor, Lenny, put-put by on his motorized DDT fog machine. Back then, few people in the woods of northern Minnesota understood the dangers of DDT. All anyone knew was that after Lenny made his rounds, mosquitoes and biting flies disappeared for several days. Years later, my mother claimed that after reading Rachel Carson's *Silent Spring*, she always called everyone inside when she heard Lenny's contraption coming down the gravel road. While I don't doubt that, I still have vivid memories of watching the man riding his machine. Perhaps that's why I always sleep dead insect-style, with my arms and legs tucked in.

Of all the cabin activities, hunting for frogs, snakes, and turtles was my favorite. I adored wildlife and always carefully released everything I caught after showing them to my mother, who would pretend to be impressed. Sadly, as I grew older, the vast majority of those creatures disappeared from Stone Lake. Kid-logic told me they had all become craftier hiders. Now, of course, I know DDT did them in. As for Lenny? He lived to be ninety.

* * *

After I triumphantly aced kindergarten, my parents announced that we were moving to Fort Collins, Colorado. The year was 1968, and at the time, I didn't understand that the move was an attempt to save their marriage. I was just excited to see the mountains. The eleven-hundred-mile drive, in our 1963 Buick station wagon, went something like this:

Me (age six): "When will we see the mountains?"

Mom: "It will be a while, dear. We aren't even out of Minnesota yet."

Paul Jr. (age eleven): "Diana just stuck her tongue out at me."

Diana (age thirteen): "I did not!"

Me: "Pauly and Diana are squishing me!"

Paul Jr.: "Stop calling me 'Pauly.' I'm 'Paul' now."

Me: "I see the mountains!"

Dad: "Those are hills, son. We won't see the mountains until late tomorrow."

Paul Jr.: "Diana just wiped a booger on me!"

Mom: "Stop it! All of you."

Dad: Turns on the radio and frantically searches for Johnny Cash.

Me: "I think I see the mountains."

* * *

Shortly after moving into our new house, both of my parents enrolled at Colorado State University, and we lived off the money my father received from selling the bank. My mother would ultimately earn her master's degree and become a licensed psychologist. My father would earn his bachelor's degree, with the intention of transferring to a seminary and becoming a minister. Unfortunately for my father, learning Latin and feeding a family of five prevented him from reaching his dream. Instead, he went back into banking, having to settle for a loan officer position beneath his talents. He didn't pout about being overqualified for the job, however, because he had recently upgraded himself from being a standard Christian to being a new and improved born-again Christian. Banking provided him the perfect opportunity to "share the good news."

Although I never had the opportunity to watch him work, I imagine his customer interactions went something like this:

Customer: "Hi. I'd like to apply for a loan."

Paul: "Certainly! Please sit down."

The customer sits.

Paul: "Are you looking for a home or auto loan?"

Customer: "Home loan."

Paul: "And how much are you looking to finance?"

Customer: "One hundred and twenty thousand."

Paul: "Oh, that must be a nice house. Don't forget to invite Jesus."

Customer: "What?"

Paul: "I'm sorry. I was like you not too long ago. I bought this beautiful house, but it just felt empty until I asked Jesus to come inside— and into my heart."

According to my mother, the bank threatened to fire my father several times for his on-the-job preaching.

As for me, I graduated from *Captain Kangaroo* to *Batman* and had an entirely new list of creatures to catch and release. At the time, the population of Fort Collins had yet to explode (going from 35,000 when I lived there to roughly 170,000 in 2020), so I had lots of creeks and open spaces to explore.

The street I lived on was wide and quiet, with gutters that would become tiny streams whenever it rained or someone ran a sprinkler too long. My G.I. Joe found those gutters especially hazardous, since he'd have to navigate those streams in his tiny boat while fighting lighter-fluid-pissing monsters that breathed fire. Sometimes poor G.I. Joe would get quite hot under the collar during those adventures. So hot, in fact, he melted.

Lighter fluid was also a key ingredient to the tennis ball cannons my friends and I made. We'd cut the ends off soda cans and attach a few together with duct tape, and when we added the final can, we left on the bottom end and punched a hole low in its side. After that, it was just a matter of inserting a tennis ball, squirting some lighter fluid into the hole, and applying a match. The explosion would shoot the ball high into the air. Later, after sky balls lost their excitement, we upped the game. One set of friends would team up in the middle of the street, fifty or so feet away from the other set. Then one boy would hold the tennis-ball-loaded cannon on his shoulder and aim—like a bazooka—while the other stood behind to pour in lighter fluid and ignite. (Please don't try this. It's dangerous!)

Our tennis ball cannon fights soon became bottle rocket fights, since those didn't require teams and, I don't know . . . they seemed safer. Those battles required real skill, because after lighting the fuse, we'd have to hold onto the end of the stick long enough so that when we flung the firework, like a baseball, the propellant would ignite at the exact moment necessary to shoot the rocket directly at an opponent.

Yes, I still have both of my eyes.

My days as a budding pyromaniac came to an abrupt end when I started a fire that shot along the dry grass beneath the wooden fence in my backyard. I burst into tears as I grabbed the garden hose and put out the fire in a panic. Had I delayed for even a moment that fire would have spread beyond the reach of the hose.

* * *

After I turned nine, my family moved to a smaller house a few blocks away. There I had a new neighbor, Bruce, who was a few years older than me. He had access to a treasure even better than a can of lighter fluid: *Playboys!* He acquired the magazines from his father's dresser drawer, and we carried them up into the garage attic of my house. We were both too young to do anything other than stare at the pictures, but stare we did. Back then, *Playboy* magazines were mildly risqué, showing only women's breasts and a hint of pubic hair. The mystery of what was beyond the hair was a source of great frustration for me. I even tried holding the magazines at an angle, hoping that somehow it would help me see between the model's legs. It didn't work.

One female who was happy to demonstrate the cycle of life for me was a black widow spider I caught in the window well outside my sister's basement bedroom. Unlike other creatures I caught and released, putting this one back where I found it seemed unwise. Instead, I sealed her into a jar and carried her to the attached garage. There I cared for her until she presented me with just short of a billion pin-head-sized babies. That created an unanticipated problem. I had been feeding the black widow moths and grasshoppers, but they were way too big for the babies. I looked for some mosquitoes, but those insects only show up when you *don't* want them. Finally, I decided to throw in some small moths and let the spiders sort things out.

I carefully unscrewed the lid and tossed in the meal. It was at that moment I screamed for the very first time the most versatile word the world has ever known: *"Fuuuck!"*

A million or so of the baby black widows had been crawling on the underside of the lid. Now they were crawling on me. I violently shook my hands and brushed the babies off as I danced around the garage in a panic. Then I screamed for the first time another, slightly less versatile word: *"Shiiit!"*

I had forgotten to put the lid back on!"

Did I mention that my parents were clueless that I was harboring black widow spiders in the garage? Using a piece of cardboard and a putty knife, I wrangled as many spiders as I could find back into the jar before doing what any nine-year-old boy would do. I confessed to Mom.

Perhaps aided by her psychology training, my mother was amazingly cool about the ordeal. First, she inspected me; then she walked from the kitchen into the garage and inspected the spiders.

"You know what you have to do," she said.

"I won't kill them," I replied.

"You don't have to kill them. You just have to get rid of them—far away from the house."

Those black widows were lucky I had another friend, Andy, who was a few years older than me. His father was as good at unwittingly whetting a boy's curiosity as Bruce's father had been. He was a herpetologist, and down in his basement he had dozens of terrariums containing native reptiles and amphibians. Since Andy and I frequently snuck into the basement to view all those critters, I knew exactly what I wanted when my friend offered to make a trade for the spiders. That beautiful coral snake in the corner terrarium would make a fine addition to the Essen family garage!

* * *

Epilogue: No, I didn't bring home a deadly coral snake. Instead, I settled for my second choice—the cutest little horned toad you've ever seen. Even my mother thought it was cute. And if you are wondering how I escaped sickness or death from all the baby black widows crawling on my hands: even if they had tried to bite, none would have been big enough to break my skin. That was a fact I wouldn't learn until many years after the event.

CHAPTER 2

Religion Gone Bad

After four years in Colorado, my mother announced that we were moving to Duluth, Minnesota—and my father wasn't joining us. What had I missed while I was out playing with fire, looking at *Playboys,* and searching for reptiles? I took the news of the divorce as hard as any child could. My parents had done an outstanding job of keeping their disagreements behind closed doors, and even when they told me the divorce was permanent, I couldn't believe it. I had never seen my father cry before, and his bursting into tears that day ripped my heart out. The divorce was my mother's decision and she held firm.

Many years later, my mother would share details with me on why she had to leave, including some overly personal ones that I wish she had kept to herself. No, my father wasn't a wife-beater, a closet alcoholic, or anything like that. Mostly she left him because his old-fashioned, rigid conservatism clashed with her modern feminism, and she despised him for it. His upgrade to born-again Christian status was the final push that sent her over the edge.

In the coming pages, I will share multiple stories about my father's Jesus-obsession overwhelming my relationship with him too. But for now, let's go to Duluth, a hillside city on the western shore of Lake Superior. When we moved there, in 1972, the city had a population of just under one hundred thousand.

My mother was one gutsy lady. She had no job and did poorly in her divorce case—an incident she blames on a misogynistic judge who was determined to punish her for being a feminist. Consequently, she could only afford a tiny apartment in an old house on a busy street. Our accommodations were just a kitchen, a living room, and a small, mostly open space between those two rooms that became my brother's and my bedroom. My brother claimed the top bunk and relegated me to the bottom bunk, and my mother and sister shared a pullout couch in the living room.

My memories of our cramped living quarters are generally positive. At ten years old, I can equate my feelings to those of a family dog that couldn't care less about where it lived—as long as it was with its pack. Being with my people and getting to make a phone call to my father once a week was all I needed. Well, that and the transistor radio I held to my ear each night listening to baseball games.

Soon my mother got a job as a psychologist at the Human Development Center, and a month after that she was able to rent an entire house for us. That house, in a middle-class part of town called Woodland, had us styling. There I started fifth grade and my mother fought off advances from our lecherous landlord, who was the spitting image of professional wrestler Vern Gagne. A year after that, we moved into a house of our own in a neighborhood called Hunters Park.

Fifth and sixth grade were easily the most miserable years of my life. Each was at a different school, and I found it so hard to fit in that I got stomach cramps every morning before trudging off to school. The teasing I had to put up with for being new and different was relentless. One of my worst days happened in sixth grade, when two kids punched me, dragged me to the ground, and kicked me in the eye. I don't know which was more humiliating, going back to school the next day with a big shiner or having to explain to my teacher that the two kids who beat me up were a year younger than me.

My life began looking up the summer after sixth grade. I had my first girlfriend, Karen. She was taller than me and lanky. And that summer, she let me do something I had dreamed about since ogling the models in that first *Playboy* magazine: she let me touch her breasts! Sure, at that age, they were little more than bumps, but it took nothing away from the experience.

As that summer progressed, we both worked up the nerve to take things even further.

"Okay, on three," I said.

"One, two, three!" we called out in unison.

We pulled down our pants—and I was humiliated again!

Never did it occur to me that Karen would have pubic hair. At twelve, I was still bald.

I yanked up my pants.

Later, in an effort to regain my dignity, I bragged to one of my buddies, "Karen and I went all the way!"

In retrospect, that was a shitty thing to do. But I really did think that showing each other our private parts was what going all the way meant. In my defense, neither my born-again Christian father nor my feminist psychologist mother was informative on the subject of sex. It wasn't until my discovery of *Penthouse* magazine and Xaviera Hollander's *The Happy Hooker* column that I learned that *going all the way* meant much more than mere nakedness.

* * *

The three most transformative years of my childhood would follow those first two miserable years in Duluth. But before I go there, let's go back roughly three years, because my story wouldn't be complete without discussing my father becoming a born-again Christian and how it affected my life. We had always been a Christian family, so even when my father talked about going to seminary and becoming an ordained minister, it didn't seem like a big deal.

That's because my father had yet to inform me that going to church and being a good person was no longer enough. Now that he had received his upgrade, he had new information for me: I wouldn't be "saved" until I became a born-again Christian, and for that to happen I had to ask Jesus into my heart. Once that occurred, Jesus would take care of me, tell me how to serve him, and give me eternal life. Another benefit was that once I was born again, I would no longer have any difficulties understanding the Bible. Jesus would reveal the truth to me! In the meantime, since my father was already enjoying his upgrade benefits, God would work through him to provide me with all the biblical interpretations I desired.

I was too young at the time to think "cult," but that's what being born again turns Christianity into. During a particularly rocky time in my parents' marriage, my father took his car and drove alone into the mountains. There, in his depression, he had his born-again experience and returned home a changed man. From that moment, until his death at age eighty-four, Jesus consumed his life.

And his obsession affected the lives of everyone around him.

My father was never at a loss for stories to tell about contemporary miracles from Jesus. One of his favorites to repeat was about Jesus working through a faith-healing evangelist to fix his nagging back problems. That evangelist had determined that the cause of the problem was that one of my father's legs was longer than the other one. He instructed my father to sit in a chair on the stage, parallel to the audience, and rest his outstretched legs in the evangelist's hands. When the evangelist prayed, the shorter of my father's legs instantly grew. It was a miracle! He was healed.

For years, I wasn't quite sure how to respond to my father's leg-growing story. Then I spent some time researching the phenomenon and learned that it was a common evangelists' trick. The leg, of course, doesn't really grow. Instead, the evangelist surreptitiously pulls on the heel of the shoe to create the illusion for the audience, and the power of suggestion convinces the person being "healed" that it grew too. And if you are wondering how that power of suggestion could have such a lasting effect, look no further than acupuncture. Even though millions of people swear by it, scientific studies show no difference in results between real and sham acupuncture. It's all a placebo effect!

Even if my father wasn't actually *the Paul* Pastor Reppe quoted so frequently in his church services, or any of the other fabulous things my young mind gave him credit for, he was still my childhood hero. I desperately wanted to please him. Unfortunately, no matter how many times I asked Jesus into my heart, no one other than me ever occupied my body.

So I faked it.

After my parents divorced, I could only see my father one week a year. This was mostly because he married another woman, quit his job at the bank in Fort Collins, and moved with her to Orlando, Florida, where she quickly divorced him. (She would marry and divorce my father again, but both marriages were so short that I never met the woman.) Rather than move back to Colorado or Minnesota, he stayed in Florida to sell Successful Living books and other Jesus-oriented paraphernalia.

Sometimes during our annual visits, I would accompany my father on his rounds, as he drove from supermarket to supermarket refilling the bookracks he had there. Another time, I accompanied him to a local fair, where he sat behind a table, hawking his Jesus-wares, while I recruited for him by walking the grounds, handing out "Jesus Christ, he's the real thing" pins that ripped off the Coca-Cola slogan and logo.

As I neared my teens, my unease with Christianity grew stronger, and my embarrassment in my father's behavior overrode my desire to please him. During the short times we had together, he'd often take me out to eat. It was never anything fancy—usually someplace that sold hamburgers. Nevertheless, each time before taking my first bite, I'd steel myself for the inevitable, "Dear Lord. We thank you for this . . ." prayer he would deliver in a voice loud enough for everyone in the restaurant to hear clearly.

I wanted to die!

I learned to anticipate when he was going to pray. Then I'd stand up and say, "I have to go to the bathroom."

"Oh?" he'd reply with a startled look in his eyes. "I'll wait."

"No. That's okay. Start without me. I'm going to be a few minutes."

Of course, suddenly having to go to the bathroom before restaurant meals only led to just as awkward make-good events later at his apartment. Those happened at bedtime, when he'd ask me to get down on my knees and pray with him. I'd get a knot in the pit of my stomach, dreading those sessions. My father was a gentle man, so there was never anything physical about his coercion, but in retrospect, the mental pressure he applied bordered on abuse.

Aside from those uncomfortable moments, where my father acted as my personal evangelist, our annual visits were loads of fun. Since he lived in Orlando, we visited practically every amusement park and tourist attraction within a half-day's drive of his apartment. Considering that he wasn't making much money with his Christian book business, I don't know how he was able to afford everything we did.

He even found a way to make Space Mountain the most terrifying ride in all of Florida. If you're unfamiliar with Space Mountain, it's an indoor roller coaster at Walt Disney World, where pretty much everything is in the dark other than occasional lights that give the illusion that you're about to hit a beam or a wall.

We climbed into a roller coaster car, with me sitting in front of my father. I looked back and smiled—more excited than scared. He responded with a smile significantly more nervous than mine.

The car lurched forward.

I giggled in anticipation.

We raced down a lighted tunnel and wheeled around a corner.

Everything went black!

"Heavenly Father, please put a protective shield around us . . ." my dad began, his words loud enough for me to hear.

From there, I don't recall exactly what he said. All I remember is that he prayed through the entire ride—his voice rising on the curves and dips, and lowering on the straightaways. Without his praying, Space Mountain would have been just a dark, over-hyped roller coaster. With his praying, it was terrifying. After all, my hero wouldn't pray for our safety without a good reason.

Would he?

* * *

After I became a teenager, I saw my father even less than once a year. He'll continue to appear sporadically throughout these pages, kind of like he did in my life, but for now let's return to the summer of 1974.

About the time I was going "all the way" with Karen, my mother began dating Vern Simula, a professor at the University of Minnesota Duluth (UMD). He was a classic liberal-bordering-on-radical professor, and in what seemed like the blink of an eye, he became my stepfather. I can summarize my feelings for him like this: I liked him in the early years; I resented him when I was in high school; I was ambivalent about him when he divorced my mother; I lost contact with him for years after that; and now, as I write this, I think of him as one of my all-time favorite people. His joining my family, as he did, was difficult for everyone involved. Sometimes it's easier for people to appreciate one another after the passage of time.

Aside from courting my mother, Vern was involved in creating a new alternative school, called "Open School." The school served roughly 250 students, from first grade through twelfth grade. I jumped at the opportunity to attend, mostly because I dreaded going to the local junior high, where kids from both of my previous grade schools would be attending. At Open School, I joined a group of students where everyone was new, and there weren't any long-established cliques.

Open School was true to its name. Credit hours replaced grades, students worked at their own pace, and the only real division was that sixth grade and younger students were separated from those who were seventh grade and older. Consequently, many of my classes during the three years I was there were with students substantially older than I was.

Those older students treated me as an equal, and working at my own pace eventually gave me enough credit hours to move up two grades if I desired. I passed on that option, however, because I knew that later on I'd want to graduate with students my own age.

Then, after I finished ninth grade, Open School closed for good. While the closing was mostly due to conservative politics, the school had a different feel during its final year. That was because teachers and counselors from other schools had started using it as a dumping ground for failing and disruptive students. Vern, and everyone else who had worked so hard to found the school, hadn't accounted for the possibility that a school created to help self-motivated students excel could also be corrupted to make unwanted students disappear. In fact, midway through my ninth grade year, I had already decided to transfer to Duluth East High School for tenth grade.

That said, for me and many others, Open School accomplished everything it was supposed to accomplish. The work-at-your-own-pace concept was especially helpful in preparing me for a lifetime of self-employment. Conversely, I'd be willing to bet that few, if any, of the students who took the slacker approach went on to careers working for themselves.

Just as important as the academics was that the school introduced me to a liberal, activist, pro-environment mindset that would last a lifetime. Considering how my first try at activism turned out, I'm glad I wasn't easily discouraged.

Try number one happened during a current events class, when a student pointed out a newspaper article about a snowmobile group

16

meeting with politicians and the media at the Duluth Arena to stop a bill that would ban snowmobiles from the Boundary Waters Canoe Area (BWCA). None of us thought allowing snowmobiles into the BWCA was a good idea.

"We should go down there and protest!" someone suggested.

"The meeting begins in two hours," I said, thinking we'd never have time to prepare.

"I can drive anyone who wants to go," our teacher said. "But first you have to make some signs."

And that's where the plan went downhill. The school only had a limited selection of supplies we could use for making signs. Most of the newbie protesters opted to write their messages in tempera paint. That would've been okay—had they waited for the paint to dry before nailing the signs to boards and holding them up. The paint ran so badly, their messages were barely readable. I, and a few others, used a magic marker for our messages instead. Our signs looked better. Though they were a bit faint, because the only marker we could find was low on ink.

With no time for a redo, we raced down to the arena and began our protest. At first things seemed to be going okay. Then some of the snow-mobilers noticed our pathetically constructed signs and began snick-ering. Even worse, our photo appeared in the newspaper the following day. Back then, I felt humiliated. Now, I'm proud of what we did. Our group of teenaged rebels had actively contributed to a movement that ultimately led to the passage of the BWCA Wilderness Act of 1978. To this day, that piece of legislation is still protecting the BWCA's lakes, land, and wildlife from snowmobiles.

After that, my teenage activism grew more direct. Partway into my second year at Open School, there were already rumblings that the Duluth School Board was going to shut us down. Since elections were coming up, my best friend, Reid, and I wanted to help candidates who would be on our side. We didn't have money to donate and were too young to vote, so we volunteered for door-to-door literature drops instead.

Soon the two of us grew bored with lit drops and wanted to try something else. There had to be something we could do that would be more effective and more exciting.

Commencing Operation Steal-A-Sign!

We knew that taking yard signs was wrong, but so were the conservative candidates who were determined to shut down the school we loved. And if we put the signs back after the election, were we really stealing?

We worked under the cover of darkness and only took a few signs each night. Those we hid in my mother's garage, unsure if we would actually return them post-election or leave them there indefinitely. Within a few weeks, we had an impressive collection and had to work hard to find offending signs within walking distance.

Once we nabbed our signs, we couldn't just carry them home out in the open. We had to take the backstreets or walk along Tischer Creek. On one of those nights, we were slinking along the creek where it passed behind Glen Avon Presbyterian Church. The parking lot between the church and the creek was buzzing with activity, because some youth event inside had just gotten out.

"Hey!" yelled one of the boys.

"What are you doing?" yelled another.

Reid and I dropped our signs and ran. A gang of Presbyterians— perhaps two years older than we were—had the angle on us and quickly apprehended us.

Four of the boys hauled us onto the parking lot, while a couple of the girls retrieved our signs. Initially, I was only mildly nervous. After all, these were good Christian youths. Once we explained our honorable mission, they'd give us their blessing and send us on our way.

Or maybe not.

"We're just trying to save our school," I said.

A husky boy smacked me in the stomach with the hard cast he wore on his forearm.

I doubled over, gasping for breath.

"You're putting them back!" he declared.

"Okay," I wheezed.

"We're going with you to make sure you do it!" another boy blustered.

Neither Reid nor I put up a fight, but our cooperation didn't matter. Four boys and two girls escorted us through the dark streets as if we were Jesus carrying his cross to Golgotha. And whenever we didn't carry the signs in front of us properly, cast-boy clubbed us in the back of the head or in the stomach.

Once we replaced the signs and apologized to the homeowners, I thought our night of terror was over. But no! The leader of The Presbyterian Gang demanded to know if we had any other signs. The threat of another clubbing forced us to confess.

So off we went to my house.

The leader rang the doorbell and my mother answered. At that point, I should have yelled for her to call the police, but my mother has always been frail from childhood polio, and she was home alone. I couldn't risk any harm coming to her. Instead, as the leader ratted us out, I hoped my mother could read my facial expressions, which were telling her that these clean-cut teenagers weren't choirboys.

She was clueless.

We opened the garage and grabbed four more signs—at least no one saw where we hid the others. Then back onto the dark streets we went—knocking on doors, apologizing, replacing the signs, and taking more beatings. And if you're wondering how Reid and I knew which houses to go to, I honestly can't remember. It's not as if we kept careful inventory. All I know is that we survived the night without any serious injuries, and when we returned to those houses a few days later to reacquire the signs, we never carried them anywhere near the church.

CHAPTER 3

Minnesota's Youngest Disc Jockey

I can point to four events that changed my life: sitting in on a class I wasn't taking at Open School; cancelling my registration at the University of Wisconsin-Green Bay to stay in Duluth and attend UMD; being at the front desk of my talent management agency when the woman I would marry walked in to have a meeting with my partner; and telling a newspaper reporter that I was heading to the Amazon Rainforest. If any of those events had failed to happen, you would not be reading this book. So I guess, in a small way, those events changed your life too.

I will get to all those events before the last page, but for now, I'm only going to share with you the first one. It happened when a teacher mentioned to me that Russ Blixt, a disc jockey from WEBC, was stopping by her class to talk about careers in radio. I had a different class during that period, but I cut it so I could listen to Russ. His talk fascinated me. Especially at the end, when he said, "The radio station is looking for some students to answer request lines, and eventually the program director hopes to select someone from that group to take on the high-paying job of research director."

I immediately volunteered. At the time, I was just thirteen, and WEBC was among the last AM radio stations playing top-40 rock before FM took over. Each day, after school, I'd walk the two miles to the radio station to work my shift. My job as a *phoney* involved answering request lines and calling people at random to ask them to rate song samples I played over the telephone. Within a few months, I earned the research director's position and had a staff of teenaged phoneys under my direction.

The high-paying part of the position never came, mostly because child labor laws prevented the radio station from putting me on the payroll. I didn't complain, however, because I couldn't imagine any kid my age having a job that was more fun. I got to hang out with all the DJs, help them run the mobile sound system at dances, ride with them as their spotter when we gave prizes to drivers with WEBC bumper stickers on their cars, and if I wasn't with a DJ, sometimes I'd accompany the engineer to nearby Superior, Wisconsin, where the radio station's tower was located. For nearly four years, the entire staff was my second family, and they never treated me like a kid.

I take that back. One DJ did give me the kid treatment, but he was new and it only happened once. He and I were alone at the radio station on a Friday night, when we got knocked off the air.

I ran into the control room and shouted, "I can fix it!"

"What are you, like fifteen?" he said sarcastically. "If you wanna help, get me the engineer's phone number."

"But I can get us back on—"

"Don't touch anything! Get out of here!"

I recited the engineer's pager number and dejectedly departed.

I waited at my desk for ten minutes. When we were still off the air, and the engineer had yet to make contact, I cautiously entered the studio and said, "Please, let me help."

The DJ raised his hands in surrender and said, "If you break anything. . . ."

I smiled and hurried to the tower control panel, located just behind where he was sitting. I entered the reset code I had memorized when watching the engineer do the same thing months earlier. Then I crossed my fingers, hoping my memory was correct, and I didn't accidentally activate an ejector seat, self-destruct, or something worse. We were back on the air within minutes.

During my first three years at WEBC, the radio station gave me a couple of albums a week and concert tickets in lieu of money. Sure, it was a hell of a deal for them, but had they been able to pay me, I probably would have turned around and spent most of the money on albums and concert tickets anyway.

* * *

I could fill multiple chapters with stories from my years at WEBC, but I'm going to limit myself to just a few of my favorites.

First, I believe I will always hold the record for being the youngest disc jockey in Minnesota history—at least at a commercial radio station. Back then, the FCC required that all DJs get a Third Class Broadcaster's License before going on the air (a requirement they dropped years later). The test for the license wasn't easy. It even required math.

Once a year, a representative from the FCC came to Duluth to give the test. When WEBC's general manager, Bob Porter*, promised to give me an on-air job running Sunday morning church tapes after I turned sixteen, and he could legally pay me, I contacted the FCC. To my delight, their annual local test would take place shortly before my birthday. I gathered all the test materials and studied hard. Although the math was beyond my level, it didn't worry me too much, because I reasoned that if I aced everything else I could still achieve a high enough score to pass.

And it almost worked. I failed by just two points.

For most applicants, failing meant having to wait at least three months before the FCC would allow another try. Since I was so close to passing, I gained a waiver, which allowed me to retake the test without waiting. Then I buckled down and learned the math (mostly calculating day versus night transmitter power settings and antenna angles for AM radio stations). For my second attempt, I had to travel to the FCC's office in Minneapolis. I wasn't old enough to drive, so I took the train. That just added to the adventure of going to the big city for the first time alone. I don't remember the score on my second test, but I do remember the only thing that mattered: I passed!

A week or so later I turned sixteen, and the following Sunday I went on the air as Minnesota's youngest radio announcer. Sure, it was just church tapes, but I still got to turn on the microphone at the top of every hour and announce, "You're listening to fifty-six WEBC Duluth-Superior!" And—hot damn!—I got paid minimum wage.

A few weeks after that, I graduated to what was most certainly the longest regular radio shift in Minnesota history. I worked from midnight on Saturday night until two in the afternoon on Sunday. At this point, I should mention that I matured late in life, and my voice had not yet fully changed. Even if I knew that the Puberty Gods would ultimately make it up to me by making me look younger than my contemporaries on the other side of life, I wouldn't have given a shit. That I didn't have deep DJ pipes was a constant source of frustration for me.

While WEBC's program director could let my youthful voice pass for a top-of-the-hour ID on Sunday mornings, when only a few people were listening, he felt uncomfortable with my voice for a regular air shift, which would require talking between songs and expose me to a much larger audience. He solved that problem by recording some stylized "Music Machine" announcements to insert between songs, while still allowing me to give station IDs live. In many ways, it was like popular automated radio stations are today. Fortunately, midway between the ages of sixteen and seventeen, the Puberty Gods had mercy on me, and my voice matured enough that I could perform as a full-fledged DJ without Music Machine help.

Going nocturnal one night a week to work a fourteen-hour-long shift was exhausting, so at six a.m., when playing music gave way to playing church tapes, I would set an alarm and try to doze on the studio floor until the top of the hour, when I had to change tapes and give the station ID. Then, at ten a.m., it was time for *American Top-40* with Casey Kasem. That show required me to be more alert, because it arrived on four LP records, and I had to insert commercials five times each hour.

Before long, I got to know most of the other all-night DJs in town. Hey, at three in the morning, nothing beats the loneliness of an empty radio station like a conversation with your competition. Sometimes we'd select an obnoxious novelty song and all agree to play it at the same time. Knowing that hundreds, perhaps thousands, of radio listeners in the Duluth-Superior area were frantically switching between stations, only to hear the same obnoxious song wherever they went, had us howling.

There was also a huge rivalry between WEBC and WAKX-FM to win the top-40 market. That meant lots of semi-friendly vandalism of each other's studios. No one ever did any permanent damage. Usually it was a good window soaping or toilet papering, followed by lots of giggles. Radio was for kids—both the young and those who refused to grow up.

WEBC's GM, Bob Porter*, was a huge man in his mid-forties. He had always been nice to me, but as soon as I got my driver's license, he started going out of his way to offer me the use of the radio station's luxury company car.

"Be careful around Bob," more than one DJ warned me. "He likes 'em young."

I was aware enough to know there were men who preyed on adolescent boys, but I was also confident I could outrun Bob if necessary. And besides, the band Styx was coming to town for a WEBC-sponsored concert, and he was going to let me chauffeur them around in the company car!

The reality of potential danger hit me when Bob invited me to ride with him on an errand, drove me down a residential street, and abruptly stopped the car. He just sat there for a moment, breathing heavily. Had he grabbed me, being faster on my feet wouldn't have done any good. Whether he talked himself out of the crime, decided I wasn't his type, or it was something perfectly innocent, like indigestion, I will never know. All I know for sure is that he started driving again and left the radio station for good shortly thereafter.

The general manager who took Bob's place wouldn't let me near the company car. Although that was something I mourned at the time, deep down I knew I was better off with a more aloof GM than one who might have been fighting to resist temptation—and could have added another life-changing event to my list.

* * *

I had turned sixteen in February 1978, and during late May of that year, Cindy, a nineteen-year-old strawberry blonde, started hanging out at the radio station. I guess you could call her a groupie. Ted, a DJ in his late twenties, had the serious hots for her. He was a good guy, but there was a reason he was in radio, not TV. I also lusted after Cindy, but since I was so much younger than she was, I considered her out of my league.

One thing Ted had in his favor was a spotless Corvette, which he'd give us rides in (one at a time, since it was a two-seater). Affording such a car on a DJ's paycheck had to be difficult. Then again, the car was pretty much Ted's entire identity. From the beginning, we made a safe threesome, with Ted too nervous to make a move, me knowing it wasn't worth a try, and Cindy enjoying the role of unattainable hot chick.

During summers in Duluth, there is no better place to be than Park Point—a seven-mile-long sand peninsula that juts into Lake Superior. On a warm evening in early July, WEBC held an event at the park at the end of the peninsula, and the three of us were there.

When the festivities ended, Cindy asked me, "Do ya wanna walk the beach?"

"Sure. Where's Ted?"

"He's already left for the radio station. Come on!" She grabbed my hand.

Yes, my actual hand!

A line of trees and bushes stretched the length of the peninsula, providing privacy for beach walkers. When she pulled me through the greenery, I thought, "Oh, she's only grabbing my hand to be helpful."

Once we popped out onto the beach, she didn't let go.

Then she kissed me.

What happened after that is pretty much a blur.

Up to that point in my life, I had only had a few casual girlfriends, and none were like Cindy. For the first time I was with a real, honest to God, woman.

She even had lady breasts!

No, we didn't do like in the movies and have sex on the beach. I had mostly rejected the years of religious prodding from my father, but abstaining from premarital intercourse stuck with me—*because if I went that far, I would surely go to hell.* All other forms of sexual contact were on the table as far as I was concerned, but like I said, what happened that night was pretty much a blur—except, of course, for those amazing lady breasts.

That was the start of a summer fling Cindy and I agreed to keep secret from Ted. My mother, on the other hand, found out the first time I spent the night at Cindy's house. After Cindy drove me home early that morning, I snuck in the front door to find my mother standing just inside, reciting the exact number of times I kissed Cindy before exiting her car. My mother did not approve! Even so, she didn't specifically forbid me from seeing Cindy, either.

A few weeks later, I was alone at the radio station, doing my all-night show. The studio was arranged so all the controls, tapes, and turntables formed a U around the DJ, with the microphone at the bottom of the

U. As I did every time I was on the air, I kept the lights dimmed for atmosphere, leaving just enough illumination for cuing up records and reading announcements. At the quarter hour, I had to read the weather forecast, coming out of a commercial break.

As I began, I saw a reflection flicker in one of the studio windows. It was Ted, sneaking up behind me! He grabbed the collar of my T-shirt and raked down my back with his sharp fingernails—ripping my shirt and slicing into my skin. I wasn't being attacked by a jealous man. I was being attacked by a werewolf! All the while, I continued delivering the forecast.

Yeah, I was a dedicated employee.

Upon my last word, I toggled off the mic and wheeled around. Ted ran out the door having never made a sound. I guess he too respected the sanctity of a verbally uninterrupted weather forecast. I continued my air shift and reported the incident to management the following day. Ted received a reprimand but kept his job.

From that moment on, he and I went about our business as usual—never speaking of the incident. Cindy and I broke up a month later, and all that remains from that wild and strange summer are fingernail scratches down my back—faded but still visible to this day.

* * *

My time at WEBC concluded in early 1979. During my late-night weekend shift, I spoke frequently with a DJ at a country station, KAOH-FM. He told me about an opening where he worked and said the program director was interested in hiring me. Although there was no question that WEBC had more listeners, KAOH could offer me a perk more appealing than that: a full-time seven to midnight shift!

As a junior in high school, I couldn't imagine a cooler job. Well, playing country music wasn't exactly cool, and neither was switching radio station groupies from strawberry blondes with perky lady breasts to gray-haired, seventy-five-year-old women with . . .

But other than that, it was a dream come true. I made good money for someone in high school, I could do my homework while the music was playing, and I even gained a little appreciation for country music and lonely old ladies.

CHAPTER 4

Cars, Friends, and Theatrical Chases

I'll share more radio stories with you later, but my high school years were more than just spinning records. I had tires to spin too! Midway through my sophomore year, my mother and stepfather moved our family of five to West Duluth. For six months, we lived in a tiny rental house while they searched for a new home to buy in East Duluth. Considering that we vacated a perfectly good house in the Hunter's Park neighborhood of East Duluth to do that, their logic escaped me. Then again, when you're a teenager, what your parents do is seldom logical.

I didn't mind the move too much, however, because I got to live in the attic, where I had lots of privacy. Even more enticing than the attic was that since I still attended Duluth East, my parents had no choice but to let me buy a car.

That first car was a 1955 Oldsmobile Delta 88 in pristine condition. It was built like a tank—and it needed to be because it didn't have seat belts. Vern went with me to buy the car. As he was a highly intelligent professor, I'm not sure why he went along with my choice. What parent would let a sixteen-year-old boy race around town in a car from before the era of seat belts? I guess he either thought the car was as cool as I thought it was, or he secretly wanted to get rid of me.

In retrospect, the lack of seatbelts was probably less dangerous than the stereo system I installed, complete with heavyweight bookshelf speakers, which sat on the backseat. Had I ever gotten into a serious accident, those speakers would have come flying forward like missiles.

I kept the Oldsmobile all the way into college, but near the end of my junior year in high school, it started drinking oil as fast as a teenager drinks cheap beer. I bought a custom cover for it and parked it until I had to sell it for tuition. My next car was a 1967 Ford Mustang. I loved my Mustang, and my Mustang must have loved me, because it protected me when lesser cars would have killed me.

I paid a whole six hundred dollars for that rocket ship. I still remember what the man said when he sold it to me: "Be careful. She's a quicker."

The car looked practically new, both inside and outside, and for as long as I owned it, the engine never failed me. The floorboards, on the other hand, were a different story. After owning the car for a short time, my feet started pushing through the rust. I fixed that by lifting up the carpet and sliding in some thin pieces of wood. Yes, my Mustang had floorboards that were literally boards.

In fact, the entire underside of the car was a mass of rust. That wasn't unusual in Duluth. The city sits on a hill at the edge of Lake Superior, and its extreme winters require lots of car-eating salt to keep the steep roads clear. The previous owner's bodywork and paint job had taken care of the topside rust but did nothing for the underside.

Shortly before I learned just how serious the underside rust was, Reid and I took the Mustang out on the freeway between Duluth and Minneapolis. Stupidity ensued, and I floored the car to see what she could do. I pinned the needle at 120 miles per hour, and the speed kept climbing. When it leveled out, I declared, "One hundred and thirty!" Whether my guess was accurate is debatable—but I'm sticking with it.

A month after that, I slid the Mustang hard into a curb and had to bring it to a mechanic for some front-end work. He looked underneath and declared the car unsafe because multiple components were rusted so badly that the steering could go at any moment. Even as an indestructible teenager, I shuddered at the thought of losing my steering at 130 miles per hour. I had the mechanic replace the worst parts with better parts from a salvage yard and never again dared to push the Mustang faster than 90.

* * *

Even though I had to be creative working around my jobs at WEBC and KAOH, I was deeply involved in the theater at Duluth East High School.

Initially I was in a play, but I soon learned that being on the stage crew was more to my liking. An extra incentive was that our theater teacher, Mr. Canfield, gave all stage crew members permanent hall passes. And later, when my buddy Steve and I worked our way up to co-stage managers, we obtained the set of master keys to the school that came with the position.

Steve, Reid (who had moved from Open School to Duluth East at the same time I did), and all my other theater friends were good students, and we never got into trouble. Or should I say, "We never got caught"? Since we all loved Mr. Canfield, and were eager to please him, any infractions we made were of the minor variety. That all changed when he died suddenly of a heart attack, leaving us without oversight.

What would you do, as a high school student, if you had permanent hall passes and master keys that no adult was aware of? First, let me say that even though we had the ability to unlock any classroom and had access to the school late at night, we never used our keys to steal tests or change our grades. Instead, we set up a "theater students' office" backstage of the Little Theatre, complete with couches and a refrigerator that occasionally contained beer. Seven or eight of us ate lunch there every day.

That luxury lasted for about a half year. Then some student ratted us out, and the principal demanded we remove everything (fortunately, he never looked inside the refrigerator). Undeterred, we simply moved our office into the attic, where the prop closets were located, and did a better job of keeping our secret. The attic door was right across from the principal's office, so getting in and out required a bit of stealth. Even so, we successfully maintained our attic office until we graduated.

Our office never hurt anyone. All it did was allow us to avoid eating in the cafeteria and provide us with a quiet place to study or nap. Oh, and occasionally a private place to make out with girls.

Only once did our free run of the school cause us to misbehave in a damaging way. Golf has never been my sport, but back then, some of us in the theater practiced it a little. Consequently, we had golf clubs and balls hidden backstage. One night, Reid, Steve, and I decided that rather than practicing our putting, working on our driving would be more fun. And where better to do that than directly from the stage? The theater had large chandelier lights hanging from the ceiling, brass railings all around, and sound-dampening tiles on the back wall.

What could possibly go wrong?

We lined up on the stage, giggling at what we were about to do. The sequence went something like this:

Steve hits a drive into the upper seats. No damage.

Reid hits a drive into the back wall, leaving a golf-ball-sized indentation. We all laugh.

I hit a low drive that leaves a dent in one of the brass railings. We all howl.

Steve gets ahold of one and adds another golf-ball-sized indentation to the back wall. We howl again.

Reid slams one into the front seats. We all jeer.

I get under a ball and send it directly at a chandelier. "Oh, shit!" I scream. Somehow the ball passes between the lights without making contact. We all take deep breaths and pat our hearts in relief.

Practice called on account of "You can only push your luck so far."

Thirty years later, I returned to the Little Theatre to perform a show, based on my first book. Steve was there, and together we toured the damage—unchanged over the years. We giggled all over again.

* * *

What happens when you combine my 1967 Mustang with the theater? You get a chase for the ages! From before my time, theater students at Duluth East traditionally held a car chase after each cast party. All I did was up the octane.

I still remember my first chase, as a sophomore. Seniors always led the chase, so Reid and I were positioned near the rear. That chase wasn't ridiculously fast, which was good, because at the time we were in my 1955 Oldsmobile. But what the chase lacked in speed, it made up for in length. Fifteen or so cars followed each other through town, like a caffeinated funeral procession. One of my most vivid memories from that first chase was when the entire line of us ran multiple red lights, while cars attempting to cross those intersections had no choice but to wait until we passed.

The goal of each chase was to lose the other cars, and Ken, who was from one of Duluth's most prominent families, led this one. He drove his parents' luxury car—a Cadillac or something similar—and eventually ditched someone farther up the line. When that happened, Reid and I made the mistake of following the cars he had ditched.

We were out.

The next day, adventures from the part of the chase that continued were the talk of the theater department. Apparently, Ken lost the last of the cars when he raced down an alley so narrow that sparks flew from the doors.

Whether the story of Ken's chase-winning maneuver was completely true was unimportant. His exploits were legendary throughout the rest of that year and the next.

Once Reid and I were seniors, we got to lead the fall cast party chase. Since Reid's old Plymouth Valiant wasn't up to the task, he decided to ride shotgun with me in the Mustang. The two of us were determined to put Ken's legend to shame, and we even prepared by scouting a route ahead of time.

Skyline Parkway runs alongside Duluth's primary hill, providing a stunning view of downtown and Lake Superior. When driving from west to east, the parkway winds through a wooded section of town just before opening up for the best views. There, Reid and I discovered a spot where the parkway veered left, but if we went straight, we'd drop down the hill on a crumbling old road. During the day, that old road was difficult to see. At night, if I cut the lights at just the right time, our pursuers would think we drove off a cliff.

For the cast party, we all got together at a pizza joint on a lonely highway at the edge of town. We enjoyed our meal and initiated the sophomores before lining up our cars to begin the chase. It was time to create a legend that would be the talk of the theater department for the next generation of students and beyond.

Reid raised his hand out the window to signal the drivers. I floored the Mustang!

We raced for perhaps two miles before I chanced a look in my rearview mirror. "Where is everyone?" I asked.

"You blew them away," Reid said.

"So we won?"

"I guess so."

"Well that wasn't any fun."

"I know."

"I'm going back."

"Good idea."

We gathered everybody up and began the chase anew. This time we kept our chase partners in mind and proceeded at a more reasonable pace—slowing down whenever necessary to extend the pleasure of the chase.

Who knew a car chase could be so much like sex?

When it was time for the climax, we led the other cars to Skyline Parkway and executed our disappearing maneuver in perfect form.

We won! We were legends!

"There are still two cars behind us," Reid said.

"Really? Who?"

He looked over his shoulder and studied our pursuers. "Steve is in one car, and Doug and Tim are in the other."

Doug was Reid's little brother and Tim was Steve's little brother. Both were juniors. The five of us had been inseparable that year, and Reid and I obviously didn't keep our secret road quite secret enough.

The chase continued. And no longer was I going to pull back on the Mustang's reins. We lurched right, then left, and headed into a residential neighborhood I hadn't explored before. Here I had to slow down. The streets were dark, and I wasn't about to risk an unseen person or animal emerging from between parked cars.

All the while Reid helped navigate. "Turn left!" he yelled.

I cranked the wheel!

"Dead end!" I shouted.

Our pursuers worked as a team and blocked our way out. It had never occurred to me that Reid and I could actually lose the chase.

Oh, the humiliation!

I U-turned to face the mobile barrier of glass and steel at the end of the street, a half-block away. I pointed and asked, "What do you think, Reid?"

"It would be awesome! We could also get into big trouble."

"I know."

"Go for it!"

I slammed my foot to the floor! As we raced toward our friends, I spun the steering wheel hard to the right to cut across the crested front yard of the corner house.

Did I say "crested"? I hadn't accounted for that.

"Shiiit!" we yelled, as we took to the air!

Granted, it wasn't a jump like in the *Blues Brothers* or *Thelma & Louise*, but we definitely experienced a moment of hang time.

We cheered as we sped off into the night, leaving our friends hopelessly lost in our dust.

The next day what became known as "the move" cemented itself among Duluth East's theater legends—at least for a year or two. And while I loved all the fun, my conscience felt horrible. A few days later, Reid and I returned to the scene of our crime to make sure we hadn't destroyed that poor person's front yard. Much to our relief, no tire tracks were visible. Apparently, the cold fall weather had protected the lawn from damage.

* * *

My final car story doesn't involve much speed, and it started out quite innocently. My mother had a recent-year Chevrolet Impala that she brought to a repair shop near the Miller Hill Mall. When her car was ready, Vern dropped me off at the shop, so I could drive it home. Everything went as planned, until I decided to take a shortcut that routed me through the Target parking lot.

Earlier that day, Duluth had experienced one of the heaviest rainstorms I could remember, and water covered much of the bowl-shaped parking lot. I couldn't tell how deep the water was, but when I saw a Volkswagen Beetle cut across it, I figured it couldn't be too deep. And what could be more fun than splashing through a giant puddle?

I accelerated just enough to make a good splash. As I hit the water, I could feel the car rock as the front tires lifted off the ground. The engine sputtered and stalled. I cranked the engine to no avail. Since the car had electric windows, I didn't dare try them. Instead, I slowly opened the door—like speed would make any difference—and water poured in!

"Shit!" I screamed.

I sloshed over to Target and found a payphone. "Reid, I need you!"

"What's up?"

"I sunk my mother's car in the Target parking lot. I'm gonna be in so much trouble, unless you get here right away!"

"You sunk your mother's car?" he asked with a laugh.

"I didn't know how deep the water was. I watched a VW Bug go through and thought it would be okay."

"VWs float!"

"Yeah, I kind of figured that out."

He laughed again. "This I've got to see. I'm on my way."

"Wait!"

"What?"

"Bring a long rope. You're gonna have to pull me out."

"Will do." He chuckled as he hung up.

While I waited for Reid, I bought a package of paper towels and found some cups we could use for bailing. By the time he arrived, the water had dropped a bit, but he still had to carefully back toward the Impala—just far enough for the rope to reach. Then he pulled the car onto dry land.

Reid was more mechanically inclined than I was, so while I bailed out the interior, he got to work drying out the engine. The process took more than an hour and multiple trips into Target to buy more paper towels, but eventually he got the engine started, and I got the insides all cleaned up. The car was as good as new!

We took the Impala home, parked it in the driveway, and headed to Reid's to listen to music.

I thought that was the end of it, until a hot summer morning, four days later.

My mother stepped through the outside kitchen door and found me at the table eating breakfast. "Marty!" she said. "What happened to my car? It smells moldy, and there are mushrooms growing on the floor."

Oops! I had to think fast.

"I don't know, Mom," I said as I pretended to be shocked by the development. "We've had a lot of rain lately. Did someone leave a window open?"

"No one has driven the car since you brought it home, and all the windows were shut. That's why it stinks so bad."

"Hmm. . . . Now that I think about it, the windows were open when I picked up the car at the repair shop. It must have gotten wet during that big rainstorm."

"And you didn't notice the wet floor?"

"Sorry."

"Okay," she said and headed back out to her car.

One of the advantages I had as a teenager was that I was a polite overachiever who seldom caused problems. No one ever suspected I wasn't an angel. That, of course, was my ticket to get away with almost anything.

* * *

The car-sinking episode didn't resurface until twenty years later, when my mother and I were reminiscing over drinks.

"Remember that time you brought my car home from the mechanic?" she asked. "The floor was all wet, and it sat on the hot driveway for days. I opened the door, and oh God did it stink!"

I chuckled.

She continued. "I had Vern take the car back to the repair shop and read them the Riot Act. When they denied leaving the windows open, he called the insurance company. They agreed to pay for cleaning the interior, but the whole thing was one big headache."

"Mom. There's something I need to tell you. . . ."

I figured that after twenty years, we'd both have a good laugh, but my confession didn't go over well. My mother was pissed at me for days.

Make that years.

From that point on, she brought up the car-sinking incident, adding in my confession, practically every time we had a family get-together.

CHAPTER 5

Goodbye Country Music. Let's Rock!

KAOH fired me! Other than the owner's son and two other people, the entire staff got fired. So it wasn't my fault. The reason for the firings was that the owner, who lived in Michigan, decided to take down the low-rated radio station and start again from scratch. That meant changing the call letters to KQDS, increasing the transmitter power, and bringing in Mark Alan as the station's general manager.

Before moving to Duluth for the job, Mark had managed Tommy James & the Shondells and was the U.S. agent for The Who. He had also been a bigtime New York City disc jockey. Mark was twenty-three years older than me, and initially I knew him only as the intimidating man who fired me. Little did I know that three and a half years later, he and I would move to Minneapolis to become partners in a new talent management agency, and two years after that he would be the best man at my wedding.

But I'm getting ahead of myself.

While losing my job was depressing, I couldn't complain about the new radio station. After a few weeks of radio silence, KQDS 95-FM burst onto the airwaves with a progressive rock format that would soon make it one of the most influential small-market radio stations in America. We were always among the first to play hot new acts, from the Pretenders to U2 to the Cure to Romeo Void to Loverboy to Duran Duran to Joan Jett & The Blackhearts to INXS to Berlin to Joe Jackson to Ultravox to Orchestral Manoeuvres in the Dark to Kim Wilde to the

36

Human League to Huey Lewis and the News. Soon we had an entire wall covered with gold records for our part in breaking the new acts.

Oh, did I say "we"? I was still in high school with a voice to match, but I had one advantage over all the other available part-time DJs in Duluth: I was 100 percent reliable. From the first day I went on the air at WEBC to the end of my radio career, I never missed a shift. That included the times I was sick and had to run to the bathroom to throw up during songs. Fortunately, we always had a can of Lysol nearby to spray the microphone between air shifts!

I joined KQDS when it was only a month old. One of the part-time DJs blew off his shift without warning, and my reputation for reliability earned me a call to be his permanent replacement. I worked every Saturday morning from six to ten and filled in when other DJs got sick or went on vacation.

Though I didn't make much money that first year, I was working at one of the coolest radio stations in the entire country and loving it.

In addition to playing great music, we organized concerts featuring both regional and national acts. When those shows were in nightclubs, my age was seldom questioned when I ordered drinks. After all, I was sitting with DJs and other staff from the radio station. Even when I got carded and limited to soft drinks, the management never kicked me out.

Similar to the people at WEBC and KAOH, no one at KQDS ever treated me like a kid. That felt extra special to me here, because most of the DJs had previously worked at big-city radio stations. In fact, the entire talented fulltime air staff could have easily taken the place of any staff at any radio station in the country and held their own. That also meant the DJs were far more worldly than those I had worked with before—from drugs to outrageousness.

Our biggest star, Big G Walters, had worked with Mark Alan in New York City. The first time I met him, instead of reaching out to shake my hand, he grabbed me by the crotch and said, "Nice to meet you! How's it hangin'?"

Big G wasn't gay, and at the time, I never thought of his grab as anything more than an annoyance. He didn't limit his surprise greetings to me, and they were something everyone laughed off—or at least pretended to laugh off. He claimed they were his test to see how uptight you were. Fortunately, after he got someone once, he rarely got the same person again, because his telegraphed moves were easy to avoid. How times have changed. What was a creepy radio station gag back in the early 1980s would be grounds for immediate termination and a lucrative sexual harassment lawsuit today.

On the air, Big G was a talent to behold. He had a big voice and always found a way to keep his listeners laughing. Even when he made mistakes, he turned them into jokes. For instance, when he started an album track at the wrong speed, instead of quickly toggling from 45 rpm to 33 rpm, like any other DJ would do, he let the song play in its entirety and back-announced it by saying, "That was the latest track from The Speeders."

KQDS was not a place for uptight people to work. Whether it was some outrageous Big G Walters stunt, mooning DJs through the studio window while they were reading public service announcements, or lines of cocaine in the teletype closet, it was all part of the fun. Only once did I put my foot down and say "no" to the fun. The Cove Nightclub, located across the bridge in Superior, wanted a KQDS on-air personality to pudding-wrestle two beautiful women in bikinis for a big Friday night event. Win or lose, they'd pay one hundred dollars. Mark nominated me for the job. Despite all my time working with adults, I was still a teenager with all the insecurities that came with it. Those insecurities couldn't see any positives other than the money. If I lost, people would see me as a wimp. If I won, people would see me as a bully. And though I doubted it would happen with hundreds of people cheering on the match, what if a certain part of my anatomy decided to think for itself and popped up at the wrong time?

Oh, the horrors!

* * *

Early in my senior year at Duluth East, Reid and I discovered a great way to get out of school and do so with the enthusiastic blessings of our teachers and counselors. We took road trips to colleges all over the Midwest. Our trips were a mixture of fun and seriousness, and after we completed our tours, he chose Cornell College in Iowa, and I chose the University of Wisconsin-Green Bay. I made my selection because I planned to go into business, and UWGB had a good program. Also, the atmosphere at the school felt right, and they would let me take a test to bypass freshman composition. I passed that test with ease and was ready to go.

Other than informing my parents and a few close friends, I kept my college plans secret. Since telling everyone at KQDS was going to be painful, I delayed until mid-August before walking into Mark's office to give my two weeks' notice. Radio life had been fun, but now I needed to be a responsible adult, earn a degree, become an accountant or something, get married, and live a typical American life.

What happened next would become the second of my four major life-changing events. No matter how practical it was for me to attend UWGB, I wasn't wired to be practical. I loved everyone at KQDS. I also loved Duluth. So the words that came out of my mouth that day surprised even me. Instead of resigning, I abruptly changed course and asked Mark if I could add part-time advertising sales to my part-time DJ duties. When he said "yes," I canceled my UWGB registration and enrolled at the University of Minnesota Duluth.

Everything was set!

Except for one thing. Vern had divorced my mother a year earlier. When the two were married, we lived in a house one block away from my high school. After the divorce, my mother bought a house back in the Hunters Park neighborhood. That new house was my sixth residence since moving to Duluth at the beginning of the fifth grade. I thought staying in Duluth would spare me another move. That possibility disappeared when I announced my decision to my mother, and a pained look washed over her face. She had already rented my bedroom to another student!

Although I was shocked that my mother would actually kick me out of her house, those feelings soon changed to excitement. In fact, I found a place to live the next day. My new residence was a big orange house on the far northeastern end of London Road. If you're unfamiliar with Duluth's geography, London Road runs along Lake Superior, and once it leaves the city, it becomes a highway that you can follow all the way to Canada. From my new house, I could reach both Lake Superior and Lester River in a two-minute walk.

I shared my new home with four UMD seniors. Since I was the last to move in, I was stuck in a room that was barely big enough for my bed.

And, as you might expect, this was not some luxury lakeside home. It was an old run-down house with bathrooms that were . . . well, I'm sure if one of my roommates was a biology major, he would have been able to discover in them some new lifeform previously unknown to science. Still, other than the bathrooms, the house felt perfect.

I'm not going to spend much time talking about my new living quarters or my roommates, because the events surrounding them weren't all that unusual. We studied, we partied, we watched lots of hockey, we played table tennis on our glassed-in front porch, and when smelting season arrived, we carried beers to Lester River, netted some smelt, and we each partook in the drunken Duluthian tradition of biting the head off the first fish we caught.

During the first semester of my freshman year, I had a few girlfriends, but none were serious. Then one day I drove to the Miller Hill Mall to buy some small appliance for the house. I purchased the item, and as I walked out of the store, a voice behind me called out, "Marty!"

I turned to see two college-aged women smiling at me.

"Do I know you?" I asked.

"It's me, Luann! And this is my roommate, Cheryl."

"Oh. Hi!" I said, wondering how she recognized me after all these years. Luann, as you may remember, was my kindergarten sweetheart from Two Harbors.

As if reading my mind she said, "I wasn't sure if it was you. That's why I waited until you walked by before calling out your name. I wanted to see if you'd turn around."

"Well, I did turn around, and it's great to see you," I said politely while thinking, "How the hell did I walk by you without a second glance? Holy shit, you've grown up—and you're gorgeous!"

We talked for a few minutes before exchanging phone numbers and going our separate ways.

I called her that night, and the next weekend we got together for dinner. I think I was in love (or something like it) before our first course arrived, and I was ready to marry her by dessert. And it wasn't just her big brown eyes, shiny brown hair, and sensuous lips. Conversation came so easily that I believed that our meeting at the mall was more than just chance. We ended up in bed that night, but only went so far, because she still had a boyfriend, and I still had the nagging belief that premarital sex would send me directly to hell. Thus began a weird, sometimes frustrating, multi-month relationship, where I never was quite sure where we were headed. Mostly though, we were close friends with partial benefits.

When I look back at that period in my life, I truly was a product of conflicting influences. Even though I couldn't be the enthusiastic born-again Christian my father wanted me to be, I was too much of a casual Christian to ignore the guilt that came with the religion. Consequently, I could totally relate to Meat Loaf's song, "Paradise by the Dashboard Light." Only it was Jesus, not Ellen Foley, who was flashing the stop sign at third base.

The conflicting influences of my father's conservatism, my mother's liberalism, and my stepfather's ultra-liberalism were all values I had to sort through at that age. For example, other than being liberal on premarital sex that stopped before intercourse and conservative beyond that, I was liberal on equal rights for women, yet conservative on equal rights for gays and lesbians. While I would eventually reject all forms of conservatism and become a strong advocate for LGBTQ rights, back then I said some things that horrify me today. Later I'll introduce you to Nellie Dixon, the lovable, feisty lesbian in my *Time Is Irreverent* series of novels. In many ways, she is my definitive statement rejecting my old conservative-inspired prejudices in the strongest way I know how.

Regarding Luann, our relationship continued to advance over the next few months. We were becoming more than just close friends, and when we weren't together, she was continually in my thoughts. Finally I decided that if having sex with her would send me to hell, well . . . it would be worth it!

We set a date for Friday night. And as I had done many times before, I drove to the College of St. Scholastica (a Catholic college a few blocks west of UMD) to pick her up at her dorm. From there we headed northeast past my house and continued up the North Shore Drive, halfway to Two Harbors. Our destination was Lakeview Castle. In all of northern Minnesota, there wasn't a more romantic place to take a date. Downstairs was a large open room, where KQDS frequently hosted concerts, and upstairs was an elegant restaurant with an unobstructed view of Lake Superior. I knew the owners from various radio station events, so we got the best table in the house.

The evening was magical. We drank a good bottle of wine, and even the food was delicious. (Of all the things Lakeview Castle was locally famous for, good food wasn't one of them.) We would have had no problem talking until the restaurant closed, but neither of us needed words to agree: this was going to be the night.

We walked hand in hand to the car, and once I started the engine, pregame festivities commenced. Finally! I was going to put that silly saving my virginity for marriage superstition behind me. I cranked up Bruce Springsteen—"Ooh, ooh I gotta crush on you!"—and we headed for the big orange house on London Road.

Halfway there, I glanced down at the speedometer and eased up on the gas pedal. At that moment, the only things hotter than the car's exhaust manifold were the occupants of the front seats, and only a speeding ticket could cool things down.

I looked up and slammed on the brakes!

Too late.

Rear-ending the car ahead of us would cool things down too.

To this day, I question whether that accident was truly my fault. Generally, the person doing the rear-ending is presumed guilty. Still, the North Shore Drive was a two-lane highway, and the driver of the lead car admitted to slamming on the brakes when the woman he was with remembered something she left behind. Even if I hadn't been distracted, I might not have been able to avoid the accident.

Fortunately, no one was seriously hurt. I exchanged insurance information with the other driver, pried the fender off my front tires, and limped the car home.

Being a guy, I was ready to pick up were Luann and I left off. And since my car was barely drivable, she would obviously be spending the night.

Being a gal, Luann had a different outlook on the situation. The accident had shaken her up, and her knee had begun to swell. She wanted to go home to her mother in Two Harbors.

An hour later, her mother showed up, and Luann said goodbye. After that, our relationship never rekindled. Nevertheless, the two of us have remained friends throughout the years and still go out to dinner whenever I make it back to northern Minnesota. Other than going to college in Duluth, Two Harbors has remained Luann's home. Occasionally I wonder if things would have been different for us if my father hadn't sold the bank and I had stayed in Two Harbors. Those thoughts aren't thoughts of regret, however. Sure, back then I mourned moving on from the woman who had been both my kindergarten and my college sweetheart. But now, with the advantage of time, I know what happened was for the best. That's because the right woman for me was going to step into my life, just a few years down the road.

CHAPTER 6

College Isn't For Everyone

Somehow, I managed to get through two years at UMD, while also working on the air and in sales at KQDS. Doing so involved gravitating toward night classes and classes I could pass with minimal attendance and lots of cramming. My grades were fine but not spectacular. In fact, my proudest college accomplishment was the only D I ever received.

Open School had been a wonderful life-changer for me in everything except math. The school had a horrible, sadistic math teacher who, like some of the students, had apparently been sent there as a last chance. His way of keeping order was inflicting pain on students with neck pinches and arm bending maneuvers that didn't leave marks. I reported him and then stayed out of his classroom as much as I could. Consequently, once I got to Duluth East High School, I had to play math catch-up.

That D I received at UMD was in calculus—a subject I had to pass if I was going to get a business degree. My first college calculus professor was from some Middle Eastern country, and he spoke incredibly fast with a thick accent few people could understand. By the time I dropped his class, 90 percent of the other students had done the same thing. Then, the following semester, I took the class again with a different professor. I don't remember his name, but he did an amazing job of helping me pass with a flying D.

It was awesome!

That degree, however, was not to come. During my time at KQDS, I had grown close to Mark and impressed him with my sales abilities.

I also grew close to Kurt, the station's program director. Together the three of us, and all the other hardworking people at the radio station, brought KQDS from last in the market to number one in just three and a half years. A victory party ensued!

Then, a few days later, the station's owner fired Mark. The reason for his firing depended on whom you asked. The owner blamed it on Mark's outrageous behavior (you'll see some of that later in my story), and Mark claimed it was because as soon as he led the station to the top, the owner figured he could fill his position with someone cheaper.

Whatever the reason, Mark's previous career as a talent manager fascinated me, and I encouraged him to go back into the business and take me with him.

The forming of our new company, National Talent Associates (NTA), took several weeks. First, I had to convince my mother that I would get far more out of going into business with Mark than I would get out of college. Then I had to convince her to cosign for a loan that would cover my portion of the seed money to start the company. Kurt joined us as a third partner. The deal was that we all put in equal money, Mark would be the president and get half of the profits, I would be vice president and get a quarter of the profits, and Kurt would be secretary-treasurer and get a quarter of the profits. Considering that Kurt and I would be learning the talent management business from a man who had been a major New York City talent agent and manager, it was a good deal for everyone—at least initially.

* * *

Since Mark Alan is going to be a big part of my story for a while, let me help you visualize him. He was a brash New Yorker, and looking back at him now, I see many similarities between him and Donald Trump. But I'm not talking politically—had Mark lived to the year 2016, I'm certain he would have voted for Hillary Clinton. Physically he and Trump were similar, with Mark being a little taller and a little slimmer. Mentally they were even closer, with both having over-the-top personalities, loving attention, and being prone to exaggeration. Like Trump, Mark had numerous phrases that he used repeatedly. His favorites were "Youuu believe it!" and "He/she doesn't have the brains God gave an animal cracker!"

Perhaps the most striking similarity Mark had to Trump was in how he treated his friends. If you were on his good side, he was a generous and hilarious person to be around, but if you were on his bad side—watch out! Unfortunately, I'm unaware of a single person who didn't eventually encounter Mark's wrath—including me. In fact, I went through the great friend/great enemy cycle with him more than once, with us finally ending on good terms shortly before his death from cancer in 2012 at age seventy-three.

* * *

Once we deposited our seed money into the company account, Mark, Kurt, and I moved to Minneapolis. We started work in early January 1983, which put me a month short of twenty-one, Mark at forty-four, and Kurt at twenty-eight. Mark and his wife, Loretta, rented a nice house in a southern suburb, and Kurt and I shared an apartment closer to our office in Golden Valley.

National Talent Associates got off to a quick start, because we already knew much of the Twin Cities' best talent from having them perform at KQDS events and giving them airplay. This was also near the beginning of the Minneapolis Sound heyday that would have Prince, the Replacements, Hüsker Dü, The Time, Soul Asylum, and others hitting it big.

My responsibilities included scouting talent, bringing Mark out to see the most promising acts, going backstage to pitch a meeting with Mark at our office, and, if all went well, booking all the nightclub engagements for the acts we signed. Mark's responsibilities included management duties, which I will detail later, and Kurt's responsibilities included scouting talent with me, booking college engagements, and maintaining the company books.

Our first signing was Sussman Lawrence, a new wave band from the suburb of Saint Louis Park. The entire band was amazing, and I knew them well from both KQDS and UMD concerts. If you were a music lover between the ages of nineteen and thirty-five and lived in any Minnesota town of size during the 1980s, you probably danced to Sussman Lawrence at least once. Their show was easily among the best in the state, and they drew big crowds. If you weren't in Minnesota at that time, you still might know of the band's lead singer, Peter Himmelman, because after Sussman Lawrence, he signed with Island Records and embarked on a solo career that continues to this day. In fact, right now I want you to set this book down and google Peter's song "Beneath The Damage And The Dust." The video features several members of Sussman Lawrence, and the song is simply one of the most likeable pieces of music ever recorded. I challenge you *not* to like it! Peter is now married to Maria Dylan (Bob Dylan's daughter).

Back then, it was common for bands to work with agencies but not have contracts with them. With Sussman Lawrence as our showcase act, we swooped into the Twin Cities, snapped up band after band, and signed them to long-term contracts before other agencies knew what hit them. Kurt and I did this while hitting the clubs in tailored three-piece suits. We hated the suits, but Mark insisted we wear them. It was only after we built up our reputation and our agency that he let us ditch the suits in favor of rock 'n' roll casual.

Soon every talent agency in the Twin Cities despised us—and we loved it! Our pitch to the bands was simple: we'll help you put together a stage show that is second to none, increase your money in the nightclubs, and shop your original material to all the major record labels. In other words, we'd do our best to make them stars, and even if we were unsuccessful, at least we'd increase their paychecks. Mark, Kurt, and I worked our asses off for our clients, and except for the few times when we overestimated the talent, we delivered on our promises.

* * *

Frequenting nightclubs and hanging around bands gave me plenty of opportunities to meet women. Linda was among the first I met after moving to the Twin Cities. I noticed the statuesque blonde when I was scouting a band I didn't particularly like. Rather than make a quick exit, I asked her to dance. From there we started dating.

My mother loved Linda, and so did my father. I think Linda's parents felt the same way about me too. After six months, everyone thought we were going to get married—except me. I had just gotten past the irrational belief that premarital sex would send me to hell when—just my luck—the first big-city woman I dated turned out to be a save-myself-for-marriage, born-again Christian!

What was it going to take for me to get laid on this planet?

In truth, Linda was a sweet girl with many outstanding qualities. I'm not sure if I loved her, but I certainly had strong feelings for her. Had I been sure she was the one for me, I would have waited for sex. In fact, Linda's vow to save herself for marriage wasn't why I ultimately decided to move on. Instead, it was her insistence that I start attending church services and religious concerts with her. Having gone through my childhood fending off religious pressure from my father, the last thing I wanted to do was spend any of my adulthood fending off similar pressure from a girlfriend or a wife.

From Linda, I went in exactly the opposite direction and dated Phyllis, the frontwoman for a cover band I didn't represent. I had mostly been a wine-and-dine, take-it-slow kind of guy, but when Phyllis told me over our first dinner that she supported her music career by being a full-service escort for rich older men, I had no doubt our relationship was going to move fast.

I know what you're thinking, so let me get this out of the way now: finally getting laid didn't cost me a dime.

The whole "going to hell" thing is still to be determined, however.

Phyllis and I were over in a few weeks, and I entered a particularly frustrating stage in my dating life. Even at a young age, my interest in the opposite sex depended greatly on that person's intelligence. Sure, I got dumped my share of times by women who didn't think I met their specifications, but if I was the one initiating the cessation of dating activities, it was usually because the woman I was seeing displayed little or no depth beyond small talk, and it drove me crazy. My poor luck may have reflected the fact that the women I was meeting were in bars or somehow associated with the entertainment business.

That doesn't mean that all such women are unintelligent—far from it. One night I was at a comedy club and had a post-gig conversation with a comedian named Karen Pickering. Although the stories comedians tell on stage are generally far from deep, I reasoned that comedians themselves had to be both intelligent and confident to do what they do. My first impression of Karen was that she confirmed my theory. So in my quest for stimulating conversation, I set up a date with her for the first Saturday night she wasn't booked.

The next day would bring life-changing event number three.

CHAPTER 7

My Best Lie Ever

National Talent Associates was located on the main floor of a four-story office building. My medium-sized office doubled as the reception area, Kurt's tiny office was just beyond mine, and deeper inside was Mark's large office. At first, I didn't like my office, because I worried that people would treat me as a receptionist, not a partner. Later I got used to it, and even enjoyed it, because I was able to meet everyone who stopped by for a visit.

We had recently signed a big regional band, called Fairchild, and as part of getting them ready to showcase to the national record companies, they needed a stage-width backdrop that displayed their name. Sussman Lawrence already had a backdrop, and Jeff Victor from the band recommended the woman who made theirs. Mark had me call that woman to set up a meeting.

That call was one of dozens I made that day, so I completely forgot about it until a familiar-looking woman with short blond hair, wearing a business-casual dress, walked into my office. I informed Mark that his appointment had arrived, but as he always did, he delayed a bit before coming out.

During that delay, the woman stood, examining the promo shots of our bands on the wall. I'm sure we exchanged some pleasant small talk as well, but other than trying to figure out why she looked familiar, all I really remember is staring at the small birthmark on her calf. It wasn't dark or ugly. In fact, it enhanced her fit legs—kind of like a cherry on a hot fudge sundae.

Mark came out to escort the woman into his office, and she flashed a little smile as she passed by my desk.

Oh, my God, she was Princess Diana!

Not really, of course. Her nose and eyes were different, and she was prettier than the princess—especially when she smiled. Still, there was enough resemblance that if you saw her out on the street, you couldn't help but do a double-take.

* * *

I immediately began scheming, and as soon as the meeting ended, I walked into Mark's office.

"What was that woman here to see you about?"

"She's making Fairchild's backdrop."

"Oh, that's right. I couldn't remember which appointment she was."

"What was her name again . . . Debbie something?"

He looked down at his notes. "Deb Bachman."

"When's the backdrop gonna be ready?"

"She says she'll have it done in time for the Cabooze show on Friday."

"Wow, that's quick. Do you have her phone number?"

He looked up and smiled. "You're not going to ask her out, are you? She's way out of your league! Besides, I was thinking of asking her out myself."

"You? You're too old for her! Besides, you're married."

"So?"

I stared him down. "Just give me her number."

He leaned back in his chair, laughed, and clapped his hands. "This is going to be such great entertainment! No way does she go out with you."

"I'll get her to go out with me."

"Yeah, *youuu* believe it! I'll bet you a hundred dollars she turns you down flat."

I shook my head and said, "No, I'm not betting."

He handed me her number and called out, "Kurt! Come in here." He waited for Kurt and then said, "You know that cute girl who was just in here?" He paused to laugh and clap his hands again. "Marty's gonna ask her out on a date!"

Another round of good-natured razzing followed, with Mark doing all the talking and Kurt just smiling and nodding.

Although I knew Mark well enough not to take what he said too seriously, his words shook my confidence. Was she really out of my league? I wasn't quite twenty-two and still felt young for my age. Deb, on the other hand, looked like she was in her mid-twenties and carried herself with the confidence of a cultured woman.

I was so fucked.

* * *

The day before the Cabooze show, I picked up the telephone receiver and started dialing. I set the receiver back down and took a deep breath. Mark was in his office with his door open. He always heard everything.

I waited.

And waited.

The three of us never went to lunch together, because one of us always had to watch the office. Consequently, Kurt and I alternated days having lunch with Mark, and today was Kurt's turn.

When the two of them finally stepped out the door, I picked up the receiver and dialed again.

"University of Minnesota," the receptionist said.

"Deb Bachman, please."

"Who should I say is calling?"

"Oh shit! She's not going to know my name!" I thought before saying aloud, "Um. . . . I'm calling about the backdrop she made."

"One moment." She put me on hold for a few seconds. "She'll be right with you."

"Hello, this is Deb."

"Oh. . . . Hi. You don't know me, but my name is Marty Essen. I'm the guy who was sitting at the front desk at NTA, when you had your meeting with Mark Alan."

"Is something wrong with the backdrop?"

"No. Not at all. I'm just calling to let you know that Fairchild will be debuting your backdrop tomorrow night at the Cabooze."

"Good. Thanks for letting me know."

"Hey! I just thought of something. I'm going to the show tomorrow.

51

If you'd like to see the debut, I'd be happy to pick you up and drive you there."

"I live on the opposite side of town, in New Brighton. It would be a long way for you to drive."

"Oh, no. That's not a problem. I live up that way too."

"Sure. What time?"

"How about seven?"

I wrote down her address and hung up the phone. I did it!

But where the hell was New Brighton?

Meanwhile, at the University of Minnesota: Deb hung up the phone and said to one of her coworkers, "I'm not sure, but I think I just got asked out on a date."

* * *

GPS navigators for cars didn't exist back then, so with a map in hand and an early start, I reached Deb's apartment with only a few wrong turns.

She greeted me at the door and introduced me to her brother and her one-and-a-half-year-old son. Then she answered the obvious question: "I'm recently divorced."

Oh, my! I was relieved that I hadn't accidentally asked out a married woman. But a baby? My experience with such creatures was limited. Mostly I believed them to be terrifying bundles of stinky slobber that cried a lot.

Deb smiled and my terror faded away. "Shall we go?"

I'd love to share with you all the details of what happened next, but frankly much of it is a blur for me. This much I remember:

The backdrop looked impressive and Fairchild rocked the house.

After watching the band for a while, I got up the nerve to ask Deb to dance. When she walked onto the dance floor with me, it served as the signal to both of us that we were indeed on a date.

Then she asked the dreaded question, "How old are you?"

"Twenty-four," I lied.

Now, in retrospect, I have to say to myself, "Brilliant move, Marty!"

I maintained that lie until about a month into our relationship. Deb is three and a half years older than I am, and later she confessed that she had a strict policy of never dating anyone younger than her brother, who is a year older than me.

Between sets, I brought Deb into the dressing room to introduce her to the band. "Hey, everyone," I announced, "I want you to meet. . . ."

Oh, fuck! I forgot her name.

Would my faux pas be fatal? Did she believe me about my age? When I drove her home after the show and put the car into park, I wondered if we were going to have an awkward moment or if she'd just get out.

She leaned over and kissed me.

And it wasn't just a peck—it was a cultured woman kiss!

We agreed to another date, and I floated the entire hour-long drive back to my apartment.

* * *

Suddenly my love life was looking up. I had a special feeling about Deb, and I still had a date scheduled with Karen, the comedian. I lay awake in bed, unable to turn off my brain. Mostly I thought about Deb, but I also thought about Karen. I loved to laugh and wondered if the comedian would be as funny over dinner as she was on stage.

As the morning approached, my thoughts became clear. I couldn't go out with Karen. My decision defied logic—especially for someone who was still days away from turning twenty-two and was new to the big city. Deb could go on a second date with me and decide we were incompatible. If I blew off Karen prematurely, I could soon end up sitting alone in my apartment, singing along with Cat Stevens, "Another Saturday night and I ain't got nobody."

Still, how much fun would I be on a date with Karen if I was thinking about Deb? There was a reason I never had simultaneous girlfriends: I was incapable of being infatuated with more than one woman at a time.

I called Karen later that morning to cancel our date. Her response was far from comedic, and I don't blame her. Who knows? Maybe I ended up as the butt of some joke in her long comedic career (as I type this, she is still working in comedy). If so, good for her. And if by chance she happens to read this and recalls what happened, I hope she understands that what I did had nothing to do with her.

CHAPTER 8

My Life as a Talent Agent

Since much of my story about Deb is intertwined with the story of my life as a talent agent and manager, I'm going to switch topics and talk some more about the entertainment business. I won't leave you hanging for long, however, and will adeptly bring both stories together by the end of this chapter.

First, I want you to forget about every movie you've ever seen that features a talent agent or manager. The politically correct movement has created a long list of people that movies can no longer parody. Talent agents and managers didn't make that list. So, of course, they're often portrayed as the villains. In reality, few performers—whether musicians, comedians, speakers, or actors—would ever make it beyond local notoriety without representation. Sure, some of those representatives are dishonest assholes, but you can find that in any profession. I prefer to think of agents and managers as the heroes of the entertainment industry.

During my lifetime, I would co-own National Talent Associates (NTA) and solely own both Twin City Talent (TCT) and Encante Entertainment, Inc. Some of the acts I worked with had successful careers. Others did not. But one thing is for sure: if you interviewed every performer I have represented in my more than twenty-five years in the business, you wouldn't find even one who claimed I cheated them or didn't work hard for them. I've always believed that I was nothing without my reputation. My two main weaknesses are getting too personally involved with some acts and overestimating the salability and/or talent of other acts. Those weaknesses, however, would apply to many good agents.

In the music business, most successful acts have both an agent and a manager. Sometimes the lines between the two blur and oftentimes more than one person fills the position. At National Talent Associates, Mark's experience dictated that he would do most of the management work, which included putting together stage shows, coordinating the proper look and image for both publicity photos and live performances, shopping for recording deals and negotiating the terms once they were acquired, and arranging for recording engineers and producers. My job was more agent-oriented, which in addition to the scouting and booking duties I mentioned earlier, included working on press and publicity and contacting radio stations for airplay.

As I gained experience, Mark let me branch out and manage a few of our newer bands. And later, when I started Twin City Talent, I signed some acts to agency contracts, where I only handled their bookings, and others to joint management-agency contracts, where I handled their entire careers.

Since management success or failure usually happened over an extended period, and agent success or failure usually happened immediately, I enjoyed my management duties much more than I enjoyed my agent duties. That was because before the national drinking age was raised to twenty-one, even bands without major label recording contracts could make a respectable living by traveling from bar to bar— if they had a good agent.

The pressure I felt to keep multiple bands working full-time on the road was enormous. There were times I'd look at a band's calendar and see an opening I had no idea how to fill. If a band was finishing a multi-night gig in Raleigh, North Carolina, I couldn't very well book them in Denver, Colorado, the next night. The tours had to be routed with reasonable drive times. In such instances, I would keep working until— somehow—I scratched up a gig to keep the tour rolling.

If a tour fell apart, more often than not it was because of something on the band's side, not mine. It could be anything from a vocalist losing his/ her voice, to the truck breaking down, to a band member quitting. Life on the road isn't easy for any band, but from my perspective as an agent, nothing was more frustrating than working my ass off to construct an amazing tour, only to have the drummer quit two weeks in.

Yeah, if someone quit, it was usually the drummer.

* * *

At NTA, we quickly built a roster that included Sussman Lawrence, Fairchild, Zig Zag, Dare Force, Jesse Brady, The Newz, Airkraft, Lipstick, Don't Ask, and Excalibur. While those bands are unknown to most people today, they were staples in the Twin Cities music scene during the early 1980s.

The first two bands I personally managed were Don't Ask, a new wave group that won the 1985 Minnesota Music Award for "Best New Band," and Excalibur, a rock band out of Arkansas.

The members of Excalibur remain friends of mine to this very day. They never made it big, but they had big hearts. After I signed them, they moved north to the Twin Cities and rented a house. There, I worked with them to upgrade their appearance and show before sending them on the road. Years later, Excalibur's leader, Gary Harpole, confessed to me that the band and road crew all traveled together in a truck with a twenty-foot-long box (the size of a common U-Haul moving truck). That meant three people rode in the cab while everyone else was locked in the back box with the PA and the instruments. Imagine what that would be like for a moment. This was before cell phones were practical for road bands, so there was no way people could communicate with the driver if they got sick, claustrophobic, or had to go to the bathroom. Even worse, if the truck got into an accident, no one inside that pitch-dark box would have had any warning to brace themselves or avoid flying equipment. Now that you have that picture in your head, imagine doing it on a hot day, traveling from Knoxville, Tennessee, to Macon, Georgia.

No wonder the drummer quit!

Sometimes I joke about being a decade too early discovering talent out of Arkansas. Lisa Harpole was Excalibur's lead vocalist, but I had her use the name Lisa Lee professionally, because I worried it might hurt the band's popularity if people knew that the hot chick frontwoman was married to the bass player. Ten years later, Arkansas' biggest rock band, Evanescence, splashed onto the scene, fronted by the dynamic Amy Lee.

I loved Lisa but managed the wrong Lee!

Even though the record companies didn't appreciate Excalibur as much as I did, other bands in NTA's stable were starting to make noise. Mark's New York City connections helped with that. To work with both Sussman Lawrence and Fairchild, he brought in recording engineer Glen Kolotkin (who had worked with Carlos Santana and Jimi Hendrix and was the engineer/associate producer for Joan Jett's smash album *I Love Rock 'n' Roll*), and producer Ritchie Cordell (who was the co-producer for Jett's *I Love Rock 'n' Roll* as well as a producer for the Ramones and Tommy James and The Shondells). Mark also successfully pitched an old friend, Danny Goldberg, (a legendary record company executive, who would later become Nirvana's manager) to sign Fairchild to his new label, Gold Mountain/A&M Records.

* * *

While NTA was becoming one of the hottest talent management agencies in the Midwest, my relationship with Deb was heating up too. A memorable date early in our relationship was to see Bruce Springsteen and the E Street Band at the St. Paul Civic Center. Springsteen had chosen the Twin Cities to kick off his *Born in the U.S.A.* tour. I attended the first of three sold-out shows with Jeff Sutherland, the lead singer of the band Lipstick, and brought Deb to the third show. I went with Jeff first, because Deb and I hadn't yet met when tickets went on sale for the first two concerts. Later, when Springsteen added a third show, I snapped up tickets to go with the new woman in my life. Need I say that Springsteen was awesome?

That Deb enjoyed Springsteen's music as much as I did was a major check mark on the compatibility list I kept in my head. She didn't have to like Springsteen, but having similar musical tastes was a definite plus for our relationship. Beyond that, I loved that she possessed an irresistible combination of contrasting qualities. She grew up on a farm as the daughter of two teachers, and she graduated from Concordia College with a major in theater. Altogether, she was smart enough to converse on almost any subject; she was tough enough to do the heavy lifting on a farm, and she was attractive enough to rock high heels and a little black dress.

As a single woman supporting a small child, Deb worked in the parking department at the University of Minnesota and supplemented her income by making backdrops for bands. Despite her obligations, our time together was seldom limited. It helped that her brother, Cal, and his fiancée, Denise, shared her apartment and were happy to babysit while we went to dinner, concerts, plays, and comedy clubs.

Our relationship seemed to be progressing just fine, until I took her to a party celebrating Fairchild's first nationally released album. It was a catered event, attended by the press, music business executives, the band, friends, and other musicians. We even had a cake inscribed with the words "The Empire Begins!"

I had two reasons to be excited that night. Mark, Kurt, and I had worked incredibly hard, and now the first national release from one of our bands was a reality. Just as important was that I had a girlfriend to be proud of, and I was eager to show her off.

During the short time I had known Deb, she was seldom at a loss for words. So when I drove her home after the party and she was silent, I knew something was up.

"What's wrong?" I asked.

"Nothing," she replied.

"Are you sure?"

"I don't want to talk about it now."

"Oh shit. What did I do?"

She took a deep breath—the kind that commonly precedes bad news. I tightened my grip on the steering wheel.

"You need to stop touching me so much," she finally said.

"Touching you? I wasn't even aware I was doing it."

Joe Biden wasn't a household name back then, but if he were, Deb might have accused me of doing a "Biden." Instead, she simply said, "Your hands were all over me."

"I'm sorry," I said.

My mind draws a blank from that moment until after I dropped Deb at her apartment and began the long drive home. Though we were too new as a couple to talk marriage, it had certainly crossed my mind. Somewhere on that drive, I said to myself, "Well, you fucked that one up, asshole! Cross her off the marriage list. It's over."

Yes, I really do talk to myself like that.

Then, to my great amazement, we went out on another date and another and another.

Apparently, we weren't breaking up after all!

Years later, Deb and I discussed what happened and she said, "I wasn't gonna break up with you. I had just escaped a bad marriage and was freaking out because I was falling in love with you."

I still don't fully understand why falling in love with me would cause her to respond the way she did to my Biden, but I've happily chalked it up to "Women work in mysterious ways."

* * *

Even though Fairchild's album did moderately well, and their single "All About Love" garnered quite a bit of airplay, the band never hit it big. That was sad, because not only were they talented, but they were also a great bunch of guys. Never did we have to worry about ego problems or a call from the road that their drummer had abruptly quit or that they had destroyed a hotel room.

Aside from what happened to Fairchild, one of the biggest crimes in all of music history was that we were never able to sign Sussman Lawrence to a national recording deal. The band had a show that was every bit as good as Prince's and songs that put hits from the Replacements to shame. At their peak, no band from the Minneapolis Sound era was better. I realize that music is largely subjective, but when the music industry passed on Sussman Lawrence, they fucked up big time.

Sometimes a band's fate can change on even the smallest things. I remember being in the studio when Sussman Lawrence was working with Glen Kolotkin and Ritchie Cordell, recording the song "Torture Me" as a finished product single to shop to the record companies. Cordell took a break to listen to some of the band's other songs, and when one of my favorites, "I Would Die For You," blasted over the speakers, he quickly dismissed it by saying, "I don't think kids today will buy those lyrics."

Perhaps Cordell was right, but I thought the song was a hit. Later, when Prince's *Purple Rain* album came out, and his song, "I Would Die 4 U," reached number eight on Billboard's Hot 100 chart, I was more convinced than ever that Sussman Lawrence's song with similar lyrics had suffered a premature death.

I still haven't told you about National Talent Associates' most successful act. It's a fun story that I'm saving for later, because telling it now would place it too far out of sequence. The next chapter will bridge the gap.

CHAPTER 9

This Is a Solemn Occasion!

Deb and I had known each other just four months when we took a trip to the Essen family cabin on Stone Lake. This was the same cabin that had been in my family since before I was born, and, fortunately, Lenny had long since ceased driving up and down the road with his DDT fogger. Once my mother divorced my father, she became the sole owner of the cabin and allowed any family member to use it upon reserving it ahead of time.

I've always loved the cabin, and not much had changed from my childhood visits. It was still surrounded by thick pine and birch forest, and the only real difference for me was the drive was longer than the half-hour it used to take to get there from Two Harbors. From Minneapolis to Duluth was one hundred fifty miles, and upon arriving there, I had a choice of driving forty-five miles to the northeast over dirt roads or taking a longer route, passing through Two Harbors, that was paved for all but the final two miles.

This time I took the long way, and as we were turning left onto the dirt road by Hellman's Store, Deb laughed and said, "Oh, my God. We could have walked right by each other and not known it!"

That was because between Deb's junior and senior years in high school she had worked as a counselor at Camp House, which was two miles away if we had turned right instead of left. In other words, Hellman's Store was dead center between Stone Lake and the camp. And since it was the only place of its kind within a half-hour drive, everyone in the area frequented the store, whether it was to get gas, pick up a forgotten grocery item, order a hamburger, play pool, or join the regulars who sat at the bar every day.

Deb's laughter turned into an expression of horror when the dates aligned in her head. "If you had gone to the camp in junior high, I would have been your counselor!"

We arrived on a cold Memorial Day weekend, which was pretty much standard weather for late May in northern Minnesota. The first thing I had to do was get everything running in the cabin. That included turning on the water pump, coaxing the furnace to start, building a fire, and breathing a sigh of relief when nothing blocking the chimney sent smoke pouring back at me.

Outside, the brown and yellow cabin sat close to the lake. In fact, it was so close that if it ever burned down, modern setback regulations would prevent anyone from rebuilding it in the same spot. Inside, the cabin had a large combined living room/dining room, a bedroom on each side, and a kitchen. All the walls were knotty pine, and throw rugs covered the tiled floors. Overall, it was typical of northern Minnesota cabins, and it oozed coziness.

The long drive from Minneapolis meant we had arrived mid-afternoon, and once the cabin was ready for habitation it was almost time for dinner. We enjoyed some wine and a leisurely meal before moving to the couch and cuddling up in front of the fire. Even with the fire roaring, the cabin still felt chilly. I pulled Deb closer and kissed her. We looked into each other's eyes without saying a word. I parted my lips as if to say something, then kissed her again. Thoughts whirled through my brain, as the silence grew awkward.

Finally Deb blurted, "Well, are you going to ask me?"

I smiled and said, "Ask you what?"

She playfully punched me.

"Ow! Will you marry me?"

"Yes!"

If this were a novel, here's where I would write the big sex scene, using lots of descriptive words, like *glistening, throbbing,* and *heaving.* Since this is a memoir, I refuse to write a sex scene with me in it. You'll just have to accept the fact that it was awesome—or at least equivalent to what you'd read in a good romance novel. So instead, we're going to leave the newly engaged couple on the couch and move on from the cabin. We'll come back in a little under four months for the wedding.

* * *

Now that Deb and I were engaged, we had many arrangements to make. When I called my parents to give them the news, they seemed happy for us. My father, of course, wanted to know if Deb had given her life to the Lord, and my mother, I suspected, was a wee bit disappointed that I wasn't going to marry Linda. Even so, those calls went as well as I could have expected.

Later we drove to Willmar, Minnesota, so we could share the news with Deb's parents. Even though I had met Milt and Meredith before, I didn't know them well. My first impression of them had been that they were stern people, and so far that impression remained unchanged. That they both dressed conservatively and had the sturdy builds of those who had spent much of their lives working on a farm only reinforced that image.

After a bit of small talk, we all moved to the kitchen and sat at the table, with Deb plopping down on my lap.

"Mom, Dad," she exclaimed. "We're getting married!"

Silence.

As her parents stared with steely frowns, I did the only thing I could think of. I shifted in my chair to hide behind my fiancée.

"Say something!" Deb shouted.

"That's very nice," Meredith said in a slow monotone. "We are happy for you."

"Yes," Milt said in a similar voice. "We are happy for you."

More silence.

In defense of Milt and Meredith, Deb was less than two years out of a marriage with an abusive husband, and they were naturally concerned that she was getting married again too soon. We stayed long enough for a quiet dinner.

When it was time to head back to the Twin Cities, Milt walked me outside, shook my hand, and said, "I will be proud to have you as my son-in-law."

Armed with the tepid approval from all our parents, we moved on to planning our wedding. Since this would be Deb's second wedding, she didn't want anything big, and I was fine with that. We soon settled on getting married at the cabin, and to satisfy both my father and my sentimentality for the pastor who often quoted "Paul" in his services, we asked Rev. John Reppe to officiate the ceremony.

* * *

As a quick aside, I should point out that practically since the beginning of our relationship, Deb and I have entertained ourselves by assigning amusing nicknames to both people and pets. Naturally, we called Pastor Reppe, "Pastor Whoopee." Not to his face, of course, but we did so everywhere else. In that entertaining spirit, I'm going to call the reverend by his nickname from now on. That will add more fun to the story, don't you think?

* * *

I had assumed that Pastor Whoopee would simply agree to perform the ceremony, go through the motions, cash his check, and that would be it. Instead, the conservative Lutheran Missouri Synod preacher insisted we come to his church for premarital counseling.

That counseling didn't go well.

After I introduced Deb to Pastor Whoopee, the reverend led us into his office. He began by asking a few questions about how my father was doing before diving into his counseling. He covered a few items, which I quickly forgot. Then he asked, "Do you want to use traditional marriage vows?"

"I won't promise to obey!" Deb said.

Whoopee's eyes flickered from Deb to me. "Okay," he said slowly. "We can take that out or, if you want, you can write your own vows."

"We'll write our own," she said.

"I want to see what you come up with. Please bring them with you the next time we meet."

Whoopee continued with questions that made us feel more like we were in an interrogation than a counseling session. My only desire was to tell the reverend what he wanted to hear and get our session over with. Also, I could tell by Deb's clipped answers that if the session didn't end soon, Whoopee was going to experience the wrath of a disobedient woman.

"Have either of you been married before?" he asked.

"I was married for a short time," Deb replied.

"The Bible doesn't approve of divorce," he said. "I can't perform the ceremony if you initiated the divorce."

"My ex-husband threw me up against a wall and tried to strangle me!" Deb shouted. "And you're worried about whether or not the Bible approved of our divorce?"

"The Gospel of Luke states that anyone who marries a divorced woman commits adultery. The Gospel of Matthew allows for an exception if there was infidelity in the marriage, however. Was your husband unfaithful to you?"

"What do you think!" She glared at Whoopee before squeezing my hand and whispering in my ear, "I have to get out of here." She stormed out of the office.

I sat, looking at Whoopee for a moment, before going after my fiancée. In retrospect, I should have crossed the reverend off the list at that moment, but at twenty-two, all I wanted was to find some way to work things out.

To my relief, that was exactly what happened. After everyone took a break, and we returned to the session, Whoopee managed to mellow out his interrogation, and Deb managed to refrain from ripping his face off.

It was a win-win for everyone!

* * *

Other than deciding whom to invite, and where at the cabin to hold the ceremony, the rest of our wedding planning went smoothly. Planning our reception was a little more complicated, and it required my skills as a talent agent. Fairchild's nationally released album was out, and their first single, "All About Love," was getting airplay. I verified schedules, made a few phone calls, and booked a Fairchild concert at Lakeview Castle, with Minnesota Music Award-winners Don't Ask as their opening act.

Yes, both of my wedding bands were better than yours.

Our biggest complication was the dinner for those we invited to the ceremony. While the entire Northland was welcome to the concert downstairs, Lakeview Castle only had a small cordoned-off area upstairs for a private dinner. That meant we were limited to a maximum of thirty-five diners. Cutting our guest list to so few people was painful. In the end, all we could invite were our immediate families and their spouses, a few of our closest friends and their spouses, and the bands Fairchild and Don't Ask.

Although we didn't realize it until it was too late, our limited guest list didn't sit well with the wives of some of the band members. Since both bands worked regularly, it hadn't occurred to us that the women would make the three-hour drive from the Twin Cities for the show. To this day, I feel bad about what happened. A more mature version of me would have figured out a way to accommodate the wives. But on that day, I was too nervous to do much critical thinking.

The reason I mention our guest list predicament is that it caused a delay to the start of our wedding. The plans were for Fairchild to sing an acoustic version of "All About Love" after Deb and I exchanged our rings. When a member of the band failed to show up (apparently staying back at Lakeview Castle with his upset wife), that version of the song, with harmonizing vocals, had to be scrapped in favor of a solo version, with lead vocalist Tom Riopelle and his guitar.

Our ceremony could have been right out of a romantic comedy. On the lakeshore, in front of the cabin, is a round washing-machine-sized rock that our family has kept painted white for as long as I can remember. It was the ideal spot to set up the service. Pastor Whoopee could stand atop the rock, facing away from the lake, while the rest of us faced the water.

We all took our positions, but Whoopee decided he would be more stable standing just in front of the rock. That was fine, except the place he chose to stand was in the middle of a large anthill.

My best man, Mark Alan, had me by twenty-three years. His sense of humor, however, hadn't grown up since high school. He thought blowing his nose at trumpet-level decibels in public places was hilarious—especially if that public place was a fancy restaurant. With that in mind, two weeks before our wedding, Mark showed Deb and me a special handkerchief he bought just for the occasion. As the days grew closer, he'd pull out that handkerchief and wave it around—all while sporting a big smile. He wouldn't really do it, would he?

Sure he would.

I still have a cassette tape of our wedding, and it sounds something like this:

Pastor Whoopee: "Thank you all for coming here today as we celebrate—"

Mark (blows his nose): *"Bbbwaaaaaaaaa! Bbbwaa! Bbwa!"*

Deb and me (looking at the ground and biting our tongues): Audible laughter.

Pastor Whoopee: "This is a solemn occasion!"

Wedding photographer (falls into lake): *Splash!*

Deb and me: More laughter.

As I type this and think back to that day, I have the urge to call Pastor Whoopee (now in his nineties) and let him know that despite what he might have thought thirty-six years ago, Deb's and my marriage has turned out to be a happy one. And while there are many words I could use to describe our marriage, *solemn* is not one of them. One of my ongoing goals in life is to make Deb laugh at least once a day.

After Tom Riopelle closed the ceremony with "All About Love," Mark's final duty as best man was to sign as a witness on our wedding certificate. He pulled out a pen he brought just for the occasion and signed in the smallest script he could write. Then we all headed to Lakeview Castle for the reception dinner and concert.

What happened after that was just your basic rock concert/wedding dance, featuring Don't Ask and Gold Mountain/A&M recording artists Fairchild. Other than lots of dancing and lots of attention from the bands, the details of that night remain a blur.

I do believe, however, it was awesome.

CHAPTER 10

The Big Hit and the Big Goodbye

Mark Alan was a man of extremes. At his best, he was a charming, happy-go-lucky mentor. At his worst, he was a vindictive person you didn't want to cross.

Shortly before my wedding, he kicked Kurt out of our company, refused to return his investment, and punctuated it with a scathing letter to Kurt's father that revealed some personal information. The details of Mark's reasoning are not ethical for me to discuss here. Let me just say that Kurt didn't deserve what happened to him, and that to this day I regret not fighting for him. My only excuse is that I was still a kid with a lot to learn.

Mark's wife, Loretta (everyone called her "Nutsy"), took Kurt's place. Although she too would eventually part ways with Mark, I liked the spunky blond-haired New Yorker, and her presence in the office helped NTA continue to thrive—at least for a while.

Also departing around that time was Sussman Lawrence. Once Mark realized that he wasn't going to be able to get the band a recording deal, he convinced himself that they were going to demand a release from their contract. Rather than face the indignity of that happening, he decided to drop them first. The move left me heartbroken, but it wasn't my decision.

After that, we got our big break and signed André Cymone. You may not recognize the name, but he and Prince grew up together and even played in the same band. André had released two albums on Columbia

Records before he signed with us. Then with NTA behind him for his third, *AC,* he enjoyed his biggest hit, "The Dance Electric." While everyone in the office worked hard to support André, the majority of the credit for the song reaching number three on the R&B charts goes to Prince, for writing it, and to André, for his outstanding performance.

My cut of the royalties from that album and hit song covered the down payment for Deb's and my first house. So while I never met Prince, he had a significant impact on my life.

Regarding André Cymone, I never got to know him well, but he was always friendly to me, and when his car was in the shop, I played his chauffeur for a day. Hey, good managers do *everything* for their clients.

My most vivid memory of André is from when I booked a homecoming show for him at the Carlton Celebrity Room. Of all the places to see entertainment in Minnesota, the Carlton Celebrity Room was my favorite. The large, elegant room was set up like a Las Vegas dinner theater. I had previously seen Bob Newhart and James Brown perform there, and had even been on stage myself during the Minnesota Music Awards when I accepted the "Best New Band" award on behalf of Don't Ask, who were performing out of town at the time. The demolition of the Carlton Celebrity Room in 1987 was a sad loss for the entertainment industry, and today the Mall of America sits atop that hallowed ground.

For that homecoming show, Fairchild opened for André, which really wasn't a good match. But since it was an NTA-booked concert, we wanted our next biggest act to get the exposure. Overall, the event was a tremendous success, with a packed house, and André Cymone putting on a Prince-worthy performance.

That night, unfortunately, taught me that I should never invite my mother to a rock concert. When I was growing up, she was always the cool mom my friends admired, so I thought she'd do just fine. Deb's parents also joined us, though I was unsure of how they would react to the music. We all dressed up for the big night and sat at a table I reserved for us in a prime location. As the concert progressed, I snuck glances around the table and was pleased that everyone seemed to be enjoying the show.

My mother, however, has never been much of a drinker, and in the excitement of the evening she had more than the single drink she was capable of handling. That seemed harmless until the end of the show, when she and my in-laws were to head to our house, and Deb and I were to head to André's post-concert party. Rather than go along with that plan, my mother stood and pleaded to come with us. I was twenty-three at the time, which meant my mother was fifty-eight.

Now, as I type this, I'm the same age that she was, and it doesn't seem that old. Still, I swear fifty-eight was a hell of a lot older back then. There was no way I was bringing my mother to *the* coolest party in the Twin Cities that night.

"You don't want me to come with you, because you think I'm old," she whined.

"This isn't the kind of party you bring your mother to," I said.

"Marcie," Deb said. "This is Marty's special night. Please don't ruin it."

"You think I'm old too!"

Deb stepped to within an inch of my mother and the two went at it! Not physically, of course, but it was a shouting match for the ages. No one wins an argument with Deb (yeah, she kicks my ass too), and after multiple sharply worded volleys my mother gave up and trudged out the door with my in-laws, who had no desire to attend the party.

At this point, you're probably anticipating a candid review of the party to beat all parties. In addition to André Cymone, anyone who was part of the Minneapolis Sound could have been there, including Prince, Morris Day, Sheila E, Wendy & Lisa, Jimmy Jam & Terry Lewis, The Time, and Apollonia 6. I'm sure some of them were there, but the party was so crowded, I had difficulty picking out individuals. Also, I felt almost as out of place as my mother would have been. As much as the management team likes to feel a part of the musician team, there are times when the two do not mix. This was one of those times. Deb and I hung around for about twenty minutes and left.

After that one successful album, André Cymone and National Talent Associates parted ways. This time the situation was much more complicated than just another Mark Alan-related departure. André and Columbia Records disagreed on the direction to take for the next album and both refused to budge. Ultimately, André would go nearly thirty years before releasing another solo album. He turned to producing instead, and for a while was one of the hottest producers in the country, co-writing and producing a string of hits for Grammy Award winner Jody Watley.

* * *

Shortly after NTA parted ways with André, Gold Mountain/A&M Records decided not to put out another Fairchild album. Since our roster needed replenishing, in early 1987 we picked up the 1986 *Star Search* Grand Champion, Peggi Blu. She was due to release the album *Blu Blowin'* on Capital Records later that year. We also added a few regional rock acts. Through all of that, I concluded that Mark's and my financial arrangement was no longer fair. He was still making 50 percent of the profits while paying his wife the 25 percent that used to go to Kurt.

Even though I had just turned twenty-five, I was now as valuable to NTA as Mark was. He still did most of the management for the big name acts, but the day-to-day money coming into the company was from my booking bands into nightclubs across the country.

I approached Mark with a request to adjust our percentages. I didn't ask for an equal share—just a bump up to 33 percent. He refused to budge an inch. Knowing him as well as I did, I knew I either had to continue forever with our original deal or leave. And if I left, there could be hell to pay.

CHAPTER 11

On My Own

I didn't decide to leave immediately, but when I did, money wasn't the only reason. Mark was a chain-smoker, and working with him in a smoky office day after day wasn't healthy (in-office smoking was still legal at the time). He also had a temper, which he took out on both Loretta and me. Although I never witnessed him being physically violent, he was a big man, and once, when I stood up to him, he threatened to throw me through the office window. I had no doubt he was both serious and capable of doing it.

Several times early in the history of NTA, Mark had told both Kurt and me that if we ever wanted to leave, he'd give us our investment back and we could take any bands that wanted to go with us. Kurt never got his money back, and since he hadn't stayed in the music business, there was never an issue of his taking talent. Since I planned to stay in the music business, and Mark and I had yet to have a true falling out, I hoped to get my investment back and bring a band or two with me.

That said, the realist in me knew the chances were good that my departure would not go smoothly. I couldn't afford to lose it all and then go months without income as I built a new agency, so the only way to make sure I came out okay was to be sneaky. To do that, I doubled up on my duties—working hard for NTA's current roster while surreptitiously building a roster for my new agency.

Unfortunately, I couldn't talk to prospective clients on my office phone, because Mark would hear my conversations. My only option was to excuse myself to go to the bathroom and duck into the community conference room down the hall. In there, the building's management had a phone set up that allowed for long distance calling via phone cards.

When the time arrived for me to leave, I only asked one NTA band to come with me—a regional cover band called Mystic. They were never going to become a national act, but I had discovered and developed them, and most importantly, they loved being on the road and would provide me with some steady initial income. Along with Mystic, I signed two bands with strong original material that were eager to tour while I shopped their music to the national record companies: Private Eyes, from Tulsa, Oklahoma, and In Color, from Denver, Colorado.

I gave Mark my two-week notice, and as expected, he requested that I leave right away. Then I asked for my investment back, and he promised to send it once Peggi Blu's royalty checks started coming in. We shook hands, I said goodbye to Loretta, and walked out the door.

Sure, Mark was never going to give me my money back; sure, he was going to be pissed when he found out that I took Mystic from NTA and retaliate by stealing In Color from me; sure, we were going to exchange multiple fuck you letters and threaten to sue each other; but all things considered, I have to say, our parting was remarkably amicable.

I officially opened Twin City Talent (TCT) on May 1, 1987, with offices in the Northeast Minneapolis home Deb and I had recently purchased. Even though I hadn't yet decided to leave NTA when we first looked at the seventy-five-year-old two-story house, I knew that sometime down the road leaving was inevitable. When the realtor showed me the two adjoining rooms that would be perfect for my offices, I had no doubt which house to buy.

Now no longer limited by what I could accomplish in secrecy, I was able to build up TCT quickly. Other than Mystic and Private Eyes, Paul Metsa was my most notable immediate signing. At the time Paul and I started working together, he was already a Twin Cities legend. His music leaned toward folk, and his lyrics were politically liberal. If you were to compare him to anyone, another Minnesota legend, Bob Dylan, would be the obvious choice. But Paul's voice was more powerful and understandable than Dylan's, and even though he sang folk, he could rock it out with the best of them. I booked Paul both as a solo performer and with his band. Normally I don't get excited by the traditional folk singer with a guitar set-up, but with Paul it was different. Without a band behind him, the intensity level of his performances increased. He'd rock the house and be drenched with sweat by the end of the night.

I used to describe Paul as a "lovable putz," but the definition of *putz* that I grew up with in Minnesota is different from the one found in Webster's Dictionary, which defines the word as someone who is stupid or a jerk. Paul was definitely not stupid and generally not a jerk. My revised term for him is that he was a "lovable irresponsible." He would drive me crazy, showing up late for gigs and failing to pay commissions on time. Then, after I'd lecture him, he'd shrug and flash an innocent little smile that made it impossible to stay angry with him.

Other than his mastery of the stage, my most vivid memory of Paul was when he got so far behind on commissions I had no choice but to make him paint my garage. My seventy-five-year-old house had been updated to include aluminum siding, but the garage still had the original wood siding, and it needed to be scraped and repainted. The job would be miserable, and I agreed to forgive Paul's bill in exchange for his doing the work.

Our deal seemed like a good idea at the time. Had I really thought about it, I would have realized that one of the reasons creative people go into entertainment fields is because they aren't suited for manual labor. Sure, that's a stereotype, but it's truer than most, and it applies to a wide spectrum of creative people, including me. That's why I went into radio announcing, talent management, book writing, and college speaking. I've never had a problem working my ass off doing any of those entertainment-field jobs for long hours and without days off, because they don't feel like work. Offer me the same pay—or even more—working half the hours at a job that requires lifting, sawing, or hammering, and I wouldn't take it.

Consequently, Paul did a musician-like job on my garage, forcing me to call him back to redo the work. Then, a year later, the paint started peeling again, and I did what I should have done the first time: I rented a power-washer, completely stripped the garage, and repainted the entire thing myself.

Despite all that, I will always admire Paul's talent and his dedication to noble causes. And though he wasn't a particularly good client, I will always consider him one of my favorite clients.

To this day, Paul remains a Minnesota treasure who frequently lends his music to help others. In fact, the mayor of Minneapolis declared December 23, 2019 "Paul Metsa Day" to honor his forty years as a musician. Paul celebrated the occasion with a performance at the Parkway Theatre to raise money for a food shelf.

* * *

When I look back and compare National Talent Associates to Twin City Talent, my wildest stories are with the latter. One reason for that is that NTA's mainstay acts, Sussman Lawrence, Fairchild, Zig Zag, Dare Force, and Jesse Brady were already mature bands when we signed them, while many of my mainstay acts at TCT were coming up with the next wave. Another reason may be that the vast majority of NTA's acts were from Minnesota, where people are somewhat reserved, and the acts I signed to TCT came from all over North America.

Acts I represented besides Paul Metsa, Private Eyes, and Mystic included Phil Solem (Duluth, Minnesota), William Ellwood (Hamilton, Ontario), Mary Ott (Los Angeles, California), Lapis and Regalia (New York City, New York), The Dolls (Providence, Rhode Island), Scott Moore (Los Angeles, California), Lisa Lee (Jonesboro, Arkansas), Tammy Thomas (Chicago, Illinois), Charmer (Chicago, Illinois), the Mick Furlo Band (Saginaw, Michigan), Toy Jester (Wakefield, Michigan), Rayze (Atlanta, Georgia), One Alternative (Philadelphia, Pennsylvania), David Cullen (Reading, Pennsylvania), Andrew Howard* (Memphis, Tennessee), UN-EZ (Denver, Colorado), Randi Saxon (Minneapolis, Minnesota), Fair Game (Minneapolis, Minnesota), Reel Steel (St. Paul, Minnesota), plus several other short-lived bar bands.

Unless you are an avid music fan of a certain age, the chances are good that most, if not all, of those names are unfamiliar to you. But that doesn't make their stories less compelling. Here are some of my favorites:

Private Eyes had an independent album out that garnered some airplay in the south. Their original music was mainstream rock—not too hard, not too pop. They weren't the type of band that blew me away as being the next INXS or REM, but they were good enough to at least have a shot at getting a record deal, and some of their unrecorded songs were stronger than anything they had on their album. More importantly, they were willing to mix in a high-enough percentage of cover songs to be a successful road band.

As much as I would have loved to handle only all-original performers, like Paul Metsa, I would have quickly gone broke doing so. In the 1980s, cover bands made much more money than up-and-coming original acts—at least until those original acts released successful albums. Therefore, I maintained a diversified roster, with roughly half being original acts that I essentially managed on spec, knowing I'd make my money back if I got them a record deal, and the rest being cover bands that I booked in bars across the country. With only a few exceptions, I managed the original acts and signed the bar bands to agency-only deals.

Since Private Eyes performed both covers and originals, I signed them to a dual agency/management contract. The band's leader, Buck Reeves, was a joy to work with, and I felt he was as much a friend as he was a client. For the band's first tour beyond the South, I booked a series of club engagements that routed them from Tulsa to the Twin Cities, followed by several days of recording studio time in Minneapolis, and then another series of engagements to route them back home.

Private Eyes traveled in a brand new motor home and pulled a trailer behind it with all their gear. Before leaving on the tour, I asked Buck to remind the band to pack warm clothes, since they'd be in the Twin Cities in midwinter.

"How cold will it be?" he asked.

"Anywhere from twenty above zero to twenty below," I replied.

"Twenty below! I've never been anywhere that cold."

Our conversation continued, going over the details of their tour and what songs they were going to record in the studio. Just before hanging up, Buck asked, "Is there a place where I can plug in my motor home at night?"

"Sure. I live on a corner, and the side street is quiet. You can park there and run a cord from my house."

"Thanks. That'll be great."

Once Private Eyes reached the Twin Cities, I brought them over to Logic Studios, owned by Brian Bart of the heavy metal band Dare Force. I knew Brian from working with him at NTA, and his new studio had all the latest equipment.

At the time, the Twin Cities was having a bit of a cold snap. That was something Minnesotans didn't give a second thought about, but the band of Oklahomans found shocking.

After the initial recording session, we headed over to my house, and I ran an extension cord to give the band lights and heat in their motorized band house. Since midnight was approaching, I hung around outside just long enough to make sure everything was working before saying goodnight.

Buck leaned out the door and flashed a thumbs up. "Thanks again," he said.

"If you guys get too cold out there tonight, just knock on my door, and we'll set you up in my living room."

"We've got a good heater. We'll be fine."

"Okay."

He started to shut the door, then hesitated. "What *is* the forecast for tonight?"

"It's not supposed to snow, but the temperature could drop to somewhere between five and ten below zero."

He shivered. "I don't know how anyone can live in a place so cold."

"You get used to it. Really the only time problems arise is if your vehicle doesn't have cold weather tires."

"Cold weather tires?"

"Yeah, everyone here has them. Oh, wait! I should have thought of that earlier. Does your motor home have its original tires?"

"Of course. It's brand new."

"And I suppose you bought it in Oklahoma."

"Yes. . . . What are you getting at?"

"Well, since you almost certainly don't have cold weather tires, you may want to take special precautions to avoid flat spots."

"Flat spots?"

"You know how tires flatten out a bit where they contact the ground?"

"Sure."

"With cold weather tires, you don't have to worry about those flats spots freezing in place, or to the pavement, when the temperature drops below zero."

"My tires could freeze to the street?"

"That only happens rarely. Usually you just get a flat spot that will rattle your teeth as you drive down the road. *Bump! Bump! Bump!"*

Buck's eyes grew wide.

"It's too bad your motor home won't fit in my garage." I paused to stroke my chin. "If you really want to be safe, set an alarm, and move your vehicle a little bit every hour or so."

"Will that work?"

"It couldn't hurt."

For anyone reading this, who has never experienced below-zero weather, everything I told Buck was total bullshit. Should you ever find yourself in a similar situation, don't fall for it. All you will do is create laughter inside your tormentor's house the first time he and his wife hear you start and move your vehicle.

I ended up representing Private Eyes for a little over two years before everything fell apart. The record companies didn't feel their sound was original enough to warrant a deal, and with Buck being the one constant, the band went through multiple member changes. Keeping them on the road became a frustrating endeavor. And though I didn't witness any fights personally, reports got back to me that they were frequent among the musicians, including one brawl that happened on stage.

After Private Eyes disbanded, I lost track of Buck until we reconnected in 2011 on Facebook. We never discussed politics back in the 1980s, but when we started communicating again, my Facebook page reflected my liberal values. Since Buck and I were on opposing political sides, we had a few online disagreements, but nothing serious. Then, all of a sudden, he disappeared.

Later, a former Private Eyes band member emailed me to say that Buck had shot himself. To this day, I don't know whether his death was an accident or a suicide or even if the information the bandmate gave me was accurate. The newspapers were quiet about the cause of death, and I wasn't about to ask his wife such an impolite question. All I know for sure is that Buck was fifty years old when he died, leaving his wife and two children.

* * *

Rayze was another band I managed from the South. They were big in southern nightclubs, and for the most part those clubs booked them for a week at a time. Rayze will always stick in my mind for two middle-of-the-night phone calls.

Call number one:

Deb shakes me and stammers, "Pho-oh-nn!"

I slip out of bed and grab the receiver on the third ring. "Hell-ohh?"

"Marty! It's David."

"Who?"

"David from Rayze."

"Is something wrong?"

"No. Not at all. I just wanted to let you know that we got our new promo shots back, and they turned out great!"

"Oh. . . . That's nice. You called my home line, and it's three in the morning. Can we talk about this tomorrow, on the business line?"

"Sorry. Did I wake you?"

Call number two:

Deb shakes me and stammers, "Pho-oh-nn! If it's David from Rayze, tell him I'm gonna kill him."

I slip out of bed and grab the phone on the third ring. "Hell-ohh?"

"Marty! It's David."

"It's the middle of the night! Why are you calling me on the home line?"

"I need you to wire me two thousand dollars, right away."

"Two thousand dollars! Why?"

"I need it to get out of jail."

"Jail! What did you do?"

"Our truck broke down several months ago. It was gonna be real expensive to fix, so we rented a U-Haul instead."

"So?"

"Well, we liked the U-Haul a lot, and we never got around to returning it."

"And U-Haul tracked you down?"

"Not exactly. Yesterday, the U-Haul broke down too. After I called to get it repaired, the cops showed up and arrested me."

"Wait a minute. Who did you call for repair?"

"U-Haul."

I chuckled and said, "Let me get this straight. You stole a truck from U-Haul, and when that truck broke down, you called U-Haul to repair it?"

"Yes," he said meekly.

"And now you want me to wire you money to get you out of jail?"

"I really need your help this time. I'll pay you back in two weeks. I promise."

"I don't think so."

"But—"

"You're on your own on this one, David. Goodnight!" I hung up the phone.

* * *

Every agent and manager who has been in the music business for more than a few years has misjudged talent. After all, the business is largely subjective. In my case, I remember getting some demos from the St. Paul band Information Society (InSoc) in the mail, listening to them, and tossing them aside. A few years later, their song "What's on Your Mind (Pure Energy)" would hit number one on the dance charts and number three on *Billboard's* Hot 100 Pop Chart.

Yeah, I blew that one.

And even if I correctly judged the talent, I could be wrong on something else—like a name. Phil Solem was one of my most memorable clients. We both grew up in Duluth and went to Duluth East High School, but since he was six years older than me, we had never crossed paths. Then one day I received a demo tape from him that was simply amazing. Practically every song was a potential hit. I called him up and we had a meeting.

Phil had previously been in a band called Great Buildings with Danny Wilde, and they released one album on CBS Records. He wasn't interested in management at the time, because there was a possibility he'd get back together with Danny Wilde, and he didn't want a long-term contract holding him up. Instead, all he wanted was an agency agreement to book his band, Phil Solem and the Accelerators, around Minnesota. Since his band performed all original music, and Phil wasn't a household name, I knew I wasn't going to make much money off the arrangement. Even so, I wasn't about to pass on so much talent.

A few days after signing with TCT, Phil called me up and said, "I'm changing the name of my band. We're gonna be Phil Solem and the Rembrandts."

I didn't laugh at the new name while Phil was on the phone, but when Deb came home from work that evening, the first thing I said to her was, "You're not going to believe this! Phil changed the name of his band. Are you ready?"

"Sure," she said.

"They're gonna be Phil Solem and the Rembrandts!"

She crinkled her nose and said, "The Rembrandts? What a stupid name!"

"I know," I said with a laugh. "The Accelerators was so much better."

I only worked with Phil for a short time before he called to deliver the sad news. "Marty, it's Phil. I need you to release me from our agreement. I'm moving to Los Angeles to form a new band with Danny Wilde."

I gave Phil his release and didn't think much about it until their new band was all over the radio. Their biggest hits were "Just the Way It Is, Baby" (Number 14 on *Billboard's* Hot 100 chart) and "I'll Be There for You" (the theme to the sitcom *Friends,* which hit number 1 on Billboard's Adult Contemporary chart).

The name of the band? The Rembrandts!

Oh, and several of the songs on the demo tapes Phil gave me made it onto The Rembrandts' albums. Personally, I like the grittier versions from Phil's demos better than the slicker versions on the albums. But what do I know?

CHAPTER 12

Christ Had Nothing on My Son

Life in my twenties was one long series of adjustments. In addition to learning to live in a big city, working as a partner in a talent agency, and running my own talent agency, I also had to adjust to life with an instant family. Ever since I could remember, I had been adamant about not having children. Then Deb came into my life with her two-year-old son, Sean. Babies terrified me, but what was I supposed to do, reject her because she came as a package deal?

Suddenly I was doing scary things, like changing shitty diapers, wiping runny noses, and reading bedtime stories. While none of it came naturally for me, and I never could do baby talk, I think I did okay. Deb must have given me a passing grade too, because we weren't married long before she asked me to adopt Sean.

Deb's first husband was technically the father, but in addition to Deb not wanting anything to do with the man, he showed little interest in being in Sean's life, and had gotten far behind on his child support payments. The deal was easy to make. He would give Sean up for adoption in return for forgiveness of the money he owed.

After that, it was just a simple court hearing, and I was a father! The biggest surprise of that court hearing came several weeks after it concluded. Sean's new birth certificate arrived in the mail, with my name replacing Deb's first husband. I did the math: Sean was born in 1982, when I was still avoiding hell by stopping at third base.

The Bible claims that Jesus was born of the Virgin Mary, but he has nothing on Sean, who has an actual birth certificate proving he was born of the Virgin Marty!

Sean would be our only child. We tried to have another, and even went as far as artificial insemination to do it. Though there was nothing physically wrong with either of us, and we could have continued by trying more advanced medical procedures that might have worked, the process was emotionally exhausting, and we ultimately decided we were happy with just one child. I followed up with an appointment to get a vasectomy and that was the end of it.

And if you are wondering if we've ever regretted giving up, that's something the two of us have discussed multiple times over the years. The answer is no.

* * *

During the early years of our marriage, I wasn't the only one switching jobs. First Deb left the University of Minnesota to take a position as a project manager for a parking security systems company. A year later, at a salary review meeting, she learned that her position came with a pay ceiling—at least for a woman. Even though the company's owner praised the work she did, he refused to give her a raise that would pay her equivalent to the male employees. His reason? He knew she was trying to get pregnant!

When Deb was in college, she stage-managed her school's theater, and before her first marriage, she worked on a movie crew. Since she enjoyed that kind of behind the scenes work, she switched careers again, when the opportunity arose for her to become an independent wardrobe stylist for television commercials.

All of those changes contributed to our believing that the phrase "seven-year itch" exists for a reason: it's true. In fact, the entire first seven years of our marriage were easily our roughest. That's not to say that we didn't have numerous wonderful moments during those early years—we did. Mostly we were still getting used to each other—a process exacerbated by the fact that we got engaged at four months and married at eight months.

Adding to our difficulties was that we were now both working in the entertainment business, which is notoriously hard on marriages. We both had trust issues to work through: hers stemming from her first marriage, and mine stemming from being married to an attractive woman.

While Deb's warmth, smarts, and feistiness ultimately won me over, her appearance was what initially caught my attention. Therefore, I wasn't surprised when her wedding ring failed to discourage men from making passes at her. In fact, sometimes I even got a kick out of it, because I was proud of being her husband, and she was so adept at quickly disposing of those men.

My feelings about people making passes at her changed when a woman she worked with sent her flowers and bought her gifts. Deb informed me that the gifts were simply thank-yous for the hard work she had done and insisted that she had no interest in switching to the other team. Though Deb hadn't given me any reason to mistrust her, I didn't trust the other woman. After all, I thought, "A man sending my wife flowers and gifts would have been inappropriate. Why would a woman doing the same thing be any different?" Whether I was right or wrong, the whole situation made me feel insecure. At least if it was a guy sending the flowers, I could have told him to knock it off and made his life miserable if he persisted.

On the opposite side, I tried to put Deb's trust issues at ease and fucked that up in the most klutzy way possible. A woman I had run into a few times while out scouting bands, learned who I was, and invited me to see a band she was friendly with. When I arrived at the club a week later for the show, the woman joined me at my table, dressed to the nines. We had a pleasant conversation between sets, and when the show ended, she asked, "Do you want to walk me to my car?"

I craned back my neck in surprise. Never in my life had I seen a more beautiful woman—at least in person. She had perfect blond hair, the cutest little nose, and expressive bedroom eyes. Then she smiled, leaving no doubt what she meant by "walk me to my car."

I paid my bar tab, and with thoughts of temptation swirling in my head, I accompanied the woman to the parking lot. When we arrived at her car, I pushed those thoughts aside and reached out to shake her hand and thank her for the opportunity to scout the band.

Had I been smart, I wouldn't have said a word to Deb about what happened. Instead, when I arrived home, and she asked how my night went, I blurted out something along the lines of, "Well, if you were ever worried about me cheating on you, you can rest assured I'm impervious to temptation. After the show, this gorgeous woman asked me to walk her to her car, and . . ."

Need I say it didn't go over well?

I still had a lot to learn about women. Though I suppose you can say that about any man at any time in his life.

Once the two of us made it past year seven, we more or less figured each other out, and our marriage blossomed. As I type this, sequestered in my writing room during the COVID-19 pandemic, Deb and I have been married thirty-six years and are still crazy about each other 358 days a year.

* * *

After running Twin City Talent for six months on my own, I made use of the second office in my house and hired an intern. Mark Christenson had written me a letter expressing his desire to get into the entertainment business, and stating that Hamline University had approved my agency for an internship, if I would have him.

I jumped at the opportunity, and the two of us quickly became good friends. Mark was a musician, so he had a good ear. He also played football for Hamline, so he was a good athlete.

Soon Mark was booking bands, scouting talent, and providing me with a valuable second opinion on the demo tapes that arrived each day.

This was also a time in my life when I was beginning to rediscover interests beyond the music business. My two biggest dormant loves were politics and baseball, and Mark's athletic ability helped me with the latter. I had played on multiple Little League teams as a child, and when I was in college, a friend and I would go to the UMD Field House and take turns pitching off the indoor mound.

I wasn't sure how good of a player I was, but when I learned about tryouts for an amateur men's baseball league draft, I decided to give it a shot. Mark joined me, and he was kind enough to let me enter us together, which meant that if one of us got drafted, the other came along in a two-for-one deal. Soon we were proud new teammates on the Twin Cities Mud Hens, with Mark being the prized draft choice and me being the tagalong.

The quality of players in the league we joined varied from men who had recently played college baseball to guys in their early forties who were trying to reclaim the dream. In my case, I had to accept the fact that I was a much better Little League player than I was a men's league player. I worked hard to improve by working overtime in the field and spending hours at the batting cages, where I learned to hit 90-mile-per-hour fastballs with ease. Then I'd get into a game, where players were throwing 75 miles per hour, and strike out. Catching fly balls in the outfield was also an adventure.

Only years later, when I visited an optometrist with an advanced piece of equipment, did I learn why no matter how hard I practiced, baseball gave me fits. My eyes provided virtually no depth of field. I could judge a fastball at the batting cage, because the wall directly behind the pitching machine allowed my eyes and brain to work together and create a virtual depth of field. But out on an open baseball diamond, there were no nearby fixed objects to create the virtual depth of field I needed to judge the speed and location of the baseball. I had a disability and didn't even know I had it!

Despite all that, I didn't *totally* suck as a baseball player. In fact, by my second year on the team, I had improved enough that some might have considered me blazingly mediocre. As for the Mud Hens, they were by far the best amateur men's baseball team in the Twin Cities—if the goal of the game was to have fun. We lost every game that first year, yet I'm pretty sure all but the most hardcore jocks on the opposing teams wished they were Mud Hens.

What the Mud Hens lacked in athletic skills we made up for in personality. While other teams would trash talk their opponents, we'd trash talk ourselves. Baseball is a kids' game, and we played it like kids. Even the umpires got into the spirit of things, and I could often see them chuckling behind their masks. Never before was losing so much fun.

Mark was an offensive lineman when he played college football, and his skillset played similarly in baseball. One memory that sticks with me was when he hammered a pitch off the outfield fence, raced around first base, and slid into second.

"Get up!" everyone on the team yelled. "Keep running!"

He shot us a pained look, pushed himself to his feet, raced down the line, and slid into third.

"Get up!" we yelled. "Come home!"

He pushed back up, gasped for breath, and lumbered halfway down the line before falling and crawling the rest of the way to home plate!

We would have subjected him to less razzing had he struck out.

CHAPTER 13

God Blows It

My sister, Diana, suffered from lupus, an autoimmune disease where a person's immune system can't properly distinguish between its own cells and harmful antigens. Essentially the immune system attacks healthy cells, which can lead to organs shutting down. It's not necessarily a fatal disease, but it can be. Lupus primarily strikes women during their childbearing years, and although there is some disagreement on this, it's likely that pregnancy can even bring on the disease.

Diana developed lupus symptoms in 1985, shortly after giving birth to her son, Tom. Initially, her symptoms weren't life-threatening, and sometimes they even went away. Then in mid-May 1989, my mother called to inform me that my sister was in a Denver hospital and that I should come right away. I booked the next morning's flight out of the Twin Cities and met my mother at the hospital.

She looked at me with bloodshot eyes and said, "Before you go in to see Diana, you need to prepare yourself. She's alert but hooked up to all sorts of machines. She also has a tube down her throat, so she won't be able to talk."

I stepped into the room, chanting silently to myself, "Don't cry. Don't cry. Don't cry."

At the time, my sister was thirty-four, which was seven years older than I was. Other than when she used to pick on me when I was a child, we were very close. During our adult lives, I had only known her as a vibrant woman who was protective of me and loved to laugh. Now all we could do was hold hands. I talked to her for a while, and she responded by blinking. Telling me more than her blinks, however, was the frustration behind her eyes. There had to be a better way to communicate.

Diana was unable to write because she couldn't sit up and had an IV attached to her right hand. Also, no one in our family owned a laptop computer back then. My brother suggested an Etch A Sketch, which my sister's husband, Craig, picked up the next time he went home. Diana was able to manipulate the Etch A Sketch a little better than a pen, though I doubt the toy did much to limit her frustration.

That night I slept in a small auxiliary waiting room, down the hall from my sister. Ultimately, I ended up sleeping there most nights that week. Some nights were quiet, and I could turn off the lights and doze for several hours. Other nights were busy, and every time I'd fall asleep, another group of people would walk in and turn on the lights and the television. The few times I left the hospital, someone else from my family remained there to consult with doctors, alert others, and keep Diana company when she was awake.

My father drove all the way from Florida and was the last to arrive. At first, he wasn't even going to come. It wasn't that he didn't care. He just didn't believe Diana's condition was serious enough to warrant the trip. I screamed at him over the phone until he changed his mind.

His arrival created a new problem. From my point of view, just as there should be no crying in front of my sister, there should be no praying in front of her either. Diana and I hadn't talked religion in many years, but I believed she was as much of a skeptic as I was. More importantly, visible praying would frighten her into thinking her death was imminent.

With that in mind, my brother and I agreed to work together to protect our sister from in-room prayers. Besides, if an all-powerful God existed, he could hear my father's prayers out in the hallway anyway.

Our father's reluctant acceptance of our rule was analogous to a dog that wanted to please but didn't know what he did wrong. My brother and I held firm, knowing that behind Dad's hurt expression was a cat that would slip into a birdcage the moment he was left alone.

Diana's doctor worked tirelessly to make her better and often consulted with doctors in other hospitals for alternatives to try. Though he didn't sugarcoat her condition, he gave us hope that if she could hang on just a little longer, her lupus would go into remission.

Through all of that grief, I enjoyed one light moment. My father and I decided that rather than eat yet another meal in the hospital cafeteria, we would get away for a bit and go to a restaurant. Since I knew Denver better than he did, he handed me the keys to his old Toyota and suggested I drive. The weather was unseasonably hot for May, and when we found a restaurant we could agree on, the only place to park was out front in the sun.

Once inside the cool restaurant, we sat in a booth and placed our order. When our food arrived, my father prayed aloud. Considering the circumstances, I didn't object or make a dash for the bathroom. That seemed to loosen him up a bit, and we managed to avoid talking about Diana or arguing about religion for the entire meal. It was a pleasant change of pace.

When the bill arrived, my father insisted on paying—as he always did—and we stepped back into the sunlight and hurried to the car. I cranked the ignition and the engine wouldn't start.

"Give it a little gas," Dad said.

I pumped the pedal and tried again. The engine refused to catch. I popped the hood, and we both stepped out to have a look.

"Do you know anything about cars?" he asked.

"Not really," I said. Being mechanically inept was something we had in common. I did the guy thing and jiggled the sparkplug wires.

"Then there's only one thing we can do," he said.

"Call for a tow truck?" I asked.

He put his hands on the passenger-side fender and prayed, "Heavenly father, we . . ."

When he finished, I closed the hood, returned to the driver's seat, and turned the key. The engine roared to life!

"We're gonna be rich!" I shouted. "Once Diana is out of the hospital, we'll start a new business together. We'll call it 'Paul's Faith Healing Garage'!"

* * *

Even though I was confident the real reason the car hadn't started was that I had flooded the engine in the heat, a tiny part of me wanted to believe. The potential death of a loved one does that to a person.

As for my father, he was more inspired than ever—if that was possible—and studied his Bible as if it were a book of magic spells. Later, he announced that he had found the perfect scripture to pray on, and that God now *had* to save Diana. It was a done deal!

He was so excited by what he had found that his optimism was infectious. The doctor also brightened everyone's spirits by announcing that Diana's condition had improved a bit.

That was the perfect excuse for me to catch an evening ride to Diana and Craig's house in nearby Louisville. There, for the first time in days, I took a shower and enjoyed a solid night of sleep.

Ah, it was wonderful!

When I returned after a late breakfast, my brother greeted me with a frown. "Dad met a lay minister in the hospital chapel and brought him up to Diana's room. I found them praying over her this morning."

"He brought a complete stranger into her room?"

"Yes."

"Fuck!"

"You should have seen the look on Diana's face. I have no idea how long they were in there. I escorted them out as fast as I could."

I set off in search of my father and found him in the chapel. "You brought a stranger in to see Diana? What's wrong with you!"

He half-smiled. "That lay minister was so full of the Holy Spirit. I just knew he could help." He paused, choked up with emotion. "We prayed over Diana and asked her to invite Jesus into her heart. She nodded her acceptance, and now . . ." His voice caught, and tears streamed down his cheeks. "Now I know that if she leaves this world, I will see her again in heaven."

I wanted to scream, "Diana would have done whatever it took to get you two the *fuck* out of her room!" but I couldn't do it. The ordeal they put her through was over, and if Diana's nod gave my father some comfort, who was I to take that away? So instead of screaming, I calmly said, "Okay, Dad," and walked out of the chapel.

* * *

Over the next two days, Diana's condition continued to improve. Was it because of God, or was it because of science?

All I cared was that my sister was going to live!

Okay, I have to admit that listening to my father preach about "God's miracle" for the rest of his life wasn't something I looked forward to—but that was a small price to pay. Perhaps it was time to rekindle my faith anyway.

During all this time, I had been unable to work, and some of my bands had openings in their schedules that needed filling. When the doctor proclaimed that he thought the worst was over and anticipated removing Diana's respirator in a day or two, I took that as my cue to kiss my sister goodbye and jump on the next flight home.

Once back in my office, I did my best to concentrate on my work and checked in regularly with my mother in Denver. I had only been home for three days, when the phone rang: Diana took a turn for the worse and suddenly died.

* * *

If you've lost someone close to you, you know how crushing it can be. For me, agonizing questions accompanied that crush. Why hadn't I stayed in Denver just three more days? At least I could have been with my sister to the end. Where the fuck was God? If someone suggested to me that "God needed her in heaven," they weren't going to like my response. You know who needed her? Her husband and her four-year-old son! And what about my father, following scripture to the letter? Wasn't his dedication supposed to guarantee my sister's recovery?

My biggest complaint about Christianity is that God only gets credit for the wins and never gets blamed for the losses. Early in the COVID-19 outbreak, Donald Trump declared a National Day of Prayer to appease his evangelical Christian following. Had God existed and given a shit, the pandemic would have been over immediately after those prayers, and those evangelicals would have been shouting from the rooftops about "God's miracle." Instead, COVID-19 deaths increased dramatically the very next day and continued to increase as hundreds of thousands of people died. When that happened, where were the Christians calling out God for either ignoring or not having the power to answer their prayers?

Regarding my sister's death, my father also failed to call out God for doing nothing. Instead, he blamed himself for not having enough faith.

I, on the other hand, was done with God. While I doubted he existed, if he did, I was looking forward to Judgement Day—because I had one hell of a judgement for him. No god worth worshipping would create a disease like lupus that could be pregnancy-activated and leave young children—including my nephew Tom—motherless.

Diana Duffin died on May 21, 1989, at the age of thirty-four. Later, when I started writing the *Time Is Irreverent* series of novels, I created a sister based on Diana for my protagonist, Marty Mann. In *Time Is Irreverent 3: Gone for 16 Seconds*, Marty Mann travels back in time to do what I was unable to do: he holds his sister's hand to the very end. Even though that scene was fictitious, writing it was cathartic.

CHAPTER 14

The Top-20 Triple Crown

Throughout my life, I have observed various industry groups complain because some change was going to make their business less profitable. Extraction industries bitch about environmental regulations, insurance companies bitch about Obamacare, religious organizations bitch about separation of church and state—that sort of thing. While industries with good lobbyists are often able to stop whatever is threatening them, or at least get a pile of government money to lessen their pain, I was about to enter a stage in my life where I would be involved in three industries that crashed. But unlike the loud, greedy industries that make the headlines, mine seemed incapable of putting up a newsworthy fight.

The first happened when the National Minimum Drinking Age Act of 1984 required all states to increase their drinking age to twenty-one by October 1986 or lose 10 percent of their federal highway funds. Not all states raised their drinking age at the same time, but when they did it, those raises were often devastating to the musicians who made a living in the clubs. I'm not saying that increasing the drinking age was bad on the grand scale of things, but many live music clubs—especially those in college towns—lost their crowds. While some of the clubs I worked with survived with minimal changes, many others dropped live music, cut their band budgets, or went out of business. In other words, the golden era of the traveling bar band wasn't yet over, but I could see it fading.

Even though that fade began while I was still at NTA, once I was running TCT, it became more obvious to me that the dominos were going to fall from bars to bands to talent agents. Though my bands were still making a living in the clubs, bumping up their pay was becoming more difficult, and I feared it was only a matter of time before they started breaking up as fast as the musician-friendly clubs were shutting down.

Knowing I couldn't continue indefinitely without some national recording acts, I concentrated my efforts on discovering the next big thing.

I've always enjoyed listening to a wide range of musical genres. Rock in its many forms has always been my favorite, but once I hit my twenties, I got into a habit of starting my mornings with something mellower, like New Age or contemporary jazz. Therefore, when an impressive tape arrived in the mail from New Age/contemporary jazz guitarist David Cullen, I decided to offer him a contract. I didn't plan on booking him—at least not extensively. Instead, my goal was to get him a record deal and make him a successful recording artist.

Within a short time, I had a deal for David on Tall Tree Records, a brand new division of TBA Records out of Los Angeles. I worked directly with Don Mupo, the label's president. Don and I hit it off right away. In fact, when he issued the contract he said, "I'd like to add one more artist to the label and release both at the same time. If you'd like to recommend someone, let me know."

"I have just the act for you," I said. "David's wife, Jill Haley, is in an acoustic trio, called One Alternative."

"Get me a tape right away. I'll have a listen."

And just like that, I had two acts with national recording deals.

Soon two became four. I don't know how he found out about me, but one day a letter and CD arrived from Canadian guitarist William Ellwood, asking if I would represent him. William already had a recording deal with Narada/MCA Records, one of the biggest New Age labels in the world. His music fit right in with David Cullen and One Alternative, and he had a new album, *Vista*, which was due out at about the same time as the albums from my other two acts.

Meanwhile, my working relationship with Don Mupo couldn't have been better. Before long, he called me and said, "Marty! I'm so impressed with the job you're doing. I have an amazing pianist on my label who needs a manager. Do you want him?"

"Sure!"

For reasons that will become clear later, I'm not going to share with you the real name of the pianist. Instead, I'll call him Andrew Howard*.

Months later, all four of my New Age/contemporary jazz acts released their albums. Going from no albums to four all at once forced me to work long hours setting up media interviews and calling radio stations and national radio shows for airplay—but I loved it!

When I opened up the March 1990 copy of *JAZZIZ* magazine, I shouted out a "Woo-hoo!" Like *Billboard* magazine, *JAZZIZ* maintains highly respected charts of radio station airplay. On their *Top-20 New Age Chart*, One Alternative was number fourteen, David Cullen was number seventeen, and William Ellwood was number nineteen. I had three acts in the top twenty!

And that was just the month when everything aligned. Ultimately, William Ellwood's album would outsell the others. He received a great write-up in *Billboard* magazine, made the Top-25 on the *Gavin Report Adult Alternative Chart*, and the Top-25 on the *Radio & Records New Adult Contemporary Chart*.

Andrew Howard* also did well, reaching New & Active status in *Radio & Records* and number forty-two on the *New Horizons Chart*.

All in all, in 1990 I was quite likely the top New Age/contemporary jazz manager in the world under the age of thirty. And now, years later, I can confess that, unlike rock 'n' roll, I knew very little about that genre of music. Sure, I knew what I enjoyed listening to early in the morning, but put a good New Age musician beside an excellent New Age musician and I couldn't tell you with confidence which one was better. Fortunately, once I signed an act to a deal, only a small part of my job was judging musicianship.

CHAPTER 15

My First Professional Writing Gig

Despite my success as a New Age/contemporary jazz manager, I still longed to manage a hit rock or pop act. Over the years, I noticed that *Gig Magazine* was popular among the musicians I worked with, and I'd often see copies lying around in dressing rooms or in recording studios. Since I loved writing, I contacted the magazine with some article ideas, based on my experience as a manager.

The editor of the magazine got right back to me with an offer for a series of three successive cover stories. I accepted the offer, and my first article, "Shopping Your Band to the Labels," was published in the February 1990 issue. In my bio for that article, I included my mailing address, thinking I might hear from a few bands. Never did I expect such a huge response! Mail arrived from all over America. Some musicians wrote just to thank me for giving them inspiration. Others sent promo packs and tapes.

I worked my way through the stacks of mail and ended up signing four incredible rock/pop acts: Mary Ott from Los Angeles, Scott Moore from Los Angeles, Lapis and Regalia from New York City, and The Dolls from Providence. And those were just the acts I signed directly off demos. There were others I planned to meet on upcoming trips to New York City and Los Angeles, and around the same time, I re-signed an old friend, Lisa Lee, the former lead singer of Excalibur.

* * *

I traveled to New York City first, and Deb accompanied me. We each experienced the city quite differently. While I was carrying a briefcase full of tapes and promo packs from record company to record company, she was shopping, going to art museums, and attending Broadway matinées. Then, at night, we'd get together and watch bands.

First, we saw Lapis and Regalia perform a private show for us in their apartment. They weren't really a band, instead they were Diane Goldberg on vocals and Gavin Morrison on guitar and computerized instrumentation. It was the best apartment concert ever! If I were to compare Lapis and Regalia to anyone, they would be a cross between Enya and early Sarah McLachlan. Diane's ethereal vocals sent shivers up my spine.

Later, we went in the opposite musical direction to see two heavy metal bands. Both times our taxi drivers got nervous. The first one drove us to a warehouse in a particularly rough part of town and insisted on waiting until we were absolutely sure we were where we were supposed to be. The second one took us out to a seedy club on Long Island. All the while, he kept repeating, "It's a long drive. It's a long drive." He was obviously not pleased about returning to Manhattan without a fare. When I offered to pay him to wait through the set, and take us back afterward, he practically danced in his seat.

While our New York City trip was a fun adventure, it didn't produce the recording contracts I hoped it would, and the heavy metal bands I scouted weren't worth signing either. I did buy a cool pair of shoes, however.

* * *

I followed up Deb's and my New York City trip with two solo trips to Los Angeles. Both times I stayed at the Beverly Garland Hotel in North Hollywood. Don Mupo recommended the hotel, because it was close to his office and reasonably priced.

I had my first Los Angeles meeting while I was still in the airport. New client, Mary Ott, met me with a great big hug as soon as I got off the airplane. Having grown up in northern Minnesota, where most people have Scandinavian roots, and making eye contact is often too personal, her greeting caught me by surprise. If beautiful women greeting me with hugs were how things were done in LA, I was going to love the city!

From the airport, I was off to see Don Mupo at the headquarters for TBA/Tall Tree Records. He was a graying, chubby-cheeked, very Italian man in his sixties. He smiled almost continuously, and his warm personality filled the room. That contrasted with the headquarters, which were simply a cavernous, personality-free office space, filled with boxes of CDs, cheap desks, and a couple of people busy on their phones. Efficiency, not luxury, was obviously the company's decorating theme. Mupo introduced me to his staff before walking me over to a nearby restaurant, where we talked shop and enjoyed a few drinks.

The days that followed were filled with record company appointments—both major labels and large independents. With all the technology we take for granted today, sometimes it's hard to believe that people ever survived without it. When I think back to 1990, and that week in LA, I don't know how I did it. I had appointments all over the greater Los Angeles area, and I made it to every one on time without the aid of a cell phone or a GPS. Now I can't imagine navigating busy LA traffic with just a paper map.

The energy I felt during that trip was exhilarating, and part of that came from cranking KROQ-FM in my rental car. Depeche Mode had just released the song "Personal Jesus," and the radio station was playing it in heavy rotation. To this day, every time I hear that song I think of Los Angeles.

My most memorable moment from that trip happened when I had a meeting with Toni Lynne Cross of the band Wrestless Natives. Her band was from the LA area, but for some reason she was staying at a motel on Sunset Boulevard. When she suggested meeting there, instead of a public place, it seemed a little strange. Once I arrived at the rundown motel, and climbed the outside stairs to the second floor, alarms went off in my head. Then I knocked on the door, and a gorgeous black woman greeted me with a wide smile.

Oh, boy!

Over the years, I've represented numerous non-white performers. To me, race is irrelevant, and I only bring it up in my books if it's a necessary element to the story I'm about to tell. In this instance, Toni's race is quite relevant.

She stepped onto the landing and swept out her hand. "I know a place where we can talk. Follow me."

She led me down the stairs to a two-foot wide, three-foot-high brick wall that separated the motel's tiny parking lot from the sidewalk and the street. There we sat for the next two hours, having the most delightful conversation. I don't remember enough of that conversation to share any of it with you, but I do remember the continual interruptions by men passing by—all directed at me:

"How much?"

"What's the cost?"

"Oh, baby! How much?"

"Whaddya want for the pretty lady?"

Apparently, when a black woman sits with a white man on a Sunset Boulevard wall, she's a prostitute and he's a pimp! Toni was a good sport, and we both laughed off all the offers.

I don't recall why I didn't sign her band. Perhaps they broke up before I had a chance to do so, or perhaps I didn't have room on my roster at the time. I still have the independently released CD she gave me, and I listened to it while typing this section. The Wrestless Natives were a hell of a good band.

* * *

That first LA trip provided lots of encouragement. It didn't produce any record company offers, however. With that in mind, I returned to Los Angeles in January 1991 with a new strategy. This time I was going to host showcases for Mary Ott and Scott Moore at At My Place in Santa Monica and sent invitations to every record company I could think of.

Scott Moore had recently won the grand prize in the "My Own Smash Hit" contest, which was sponsored by the nationally syndicated *Smash Hits* TV show and hosted by Pirate Radio's Scott Shannon. Scott Moore's prize was having his winning song, "Do You Want It," produced by Gene Simmons of Kiss.

Scott's music reminded me a little of George Michael's music, only with a harder edge and a funkier bottom. I wasn't sure how his style would match up with Gene Simmons, but their studio collaboration created a track that sounded like a "smash hit" to me.

Mary Ott, on the other hand, had a background in opera, and mixed rock, pop, blues, country, and even gospel into her music. I honestly can't think of anyone to compare her to other than to say she'd fit perfectly on a radio station that played Tori Amos, Shawn Colvin, and Suzanne Vega.

We were all optimistic for a huge night. I bought an ad in *Music Connection* magazine to promote the show, and both acts did their part to fill the place. As the music started, I looked around for record company executives. Such people didn't exactly wear nametags or red MAGA (Make A&R Great Again) baseball caps, but they had to be there.

Didn't they?

Mary Ott and Scott Moore nailed their shows, and the crowd adored them. All that was left was to go backstage and field all the million dollar offers.

Okay, where the fuck were they?

I asked Scott, "Have you seen anyone from a record company?"

"No. Not yet."

I cradled my face in my hands before looking at Mary, "Has anyone approached you?"

"Just my usual crowd," she said.

I shook my head in disgust. "I'm so sorry, guys. I had all sorts of confirmations. The record companies promised they'd come."

"I'm from a record company!" a man said, as he stepped through the dressing room door.

He handed me his business card with the glorious EMI Records logo on it.

Fuck yes!

The man spoke enthusiastically for the next few minutes about how much he liked Scott Moore and that he was going to play the demos for his boss. While he couldn't promise a deal, he was going to fight for one, and I would be hearing from him soon.

I'd give you the name of the man from EMI Records, but two weeks later, I got my answer: he was fired.

Fuck no!

I tried to rekindle things with a new contact at EMI but got nowhere.

* * *

Soon after, it was time for the Minnesota Music Awards again. Because most of my acts were from out of state, I didn't have anyone up for an award. That was okay. I had bigger things in mind. Record company executives traditionally flocked to the Twin Cities for the awards and stayed a few days afterward to scout talent. While logistically, it would have been closer for The Dolls to travel from Providence to New York City or for the New York record companies to travel to Providence, I decided to take advantage of being on my home turf.

Since my very first days working as a talent agent, Gary Stark was on my call list. He owned both Starks and Mr. Nib's nightclubs, and later, after Mr. Nib's burned down, he rebuilt it as the Mirage Nightclub. He and I had a love/hate relationship. Okay, it was mostly hate. In the early days, I booked Fairchild, Jesse Brady, Zig Zag, and Dare Force into his clubs. Gary paid the best money in the Twin Cities, so I needed him. My bands were the best match for his clientele, so he needed me too. The problem with Gary was that he could be a moody son of a bitch. If I said something wrong, or if I talked him into booking a band that was "too new wave," he'd be mad at me for weeks. He hung up on me more times than I can count, and that doesn't include all the times he screamed at me. No club owner, anywhere, was more intimidating to deal with than he was.

I mention Gary, because on one of the few days he loved me, I talked him into booking The Dolls at the Mirage Nightclub for a showcase coinciding with the Minnesota Music Awards. The Dolls were a theatrical, over-the-top rock band, with soaring vocal harmonies and emotional, hook-filled lyrics. Imagine Queen with Rob Thomas of Matchbox Twenty on lead vocals.

The Dolls brought the house down that night, and even Gary admitted they were damn good. The record companies, on the other hand, brought me more disappointment. The one record company executive who showed any interest, handed me her card and asked for more material.

* * *

In the end, I managed to acquire serious record company interest for Scott Moore, Mary Ott, The Dolls, and Lapis and Regalia. Or should I say, "acquire serious heartbreak"? Of that interest, three record company A&R representatives got fired before the deals were finalized, one record company went out of business, and another company was acquired in a merger and went in a different musical direction.

To this day, my greatest disappointment from my talent management career is that none of my big-four original acts received the recording deals they deserved. I still have all of their music in digital files and occasionally blast the tracks through my house just to prove to myself that I was right about them. Even after all these years, their music sounds captivating and fresh.

Then I put on something by Lisa Lee, who didn't get a single offer, and I shake my head. *How could anyone pass on her amazing voice?*

All I can say is that if you're one of the millions of people who think the 1990s were contemporary music's weakest decade—don't blame me! I had the acts to improve the decade dramatically. If only the record companies had listened.

CHAPTER 16

Time to Get a Straight Job

Aside from feeling bitter about failing to sign any of my rock/pop acts to national recording deals, two other incidents soured me on the music industry. One happened during the first year of Twin City Talent, and the other convinced me to shut the doors for good.

Even though I'm a huge supporter of women's rights, I have to say that the Me Too movement occasionally makes me feel uncomfortable. When a woman accuses a man of sexual harassment, I agree that the chances are good she's telling the truth, and she should be heard. There are times, however, when unscrupulous women make accusations solely for personal gain. I was a victim of one of those accusations.

I had signed a local woman, who used the stage name Shelley Woolf, to a management contract. She was in her early twenties, good-looking, and had a demo with several potential hits on it. I wrote up a pitch letter and put together a bunch of promo packets for the record companies. I was just about to mail them out when the phone rang.

"Hello, Twin City Talent."

"Marty, it's Shelley."

"Hi Shelley. What's up?"

"I need you to release me from my contract."

"Why? Everything is ready to send out to the record companies."

"An older, more experienced manager wants to sign me."

"Just because he's older, doesn't mean he's better. You haven't even given me a chance."

"I've made up my mind."

"You signed a contract and—"

She hung up.

Later that day, the phone rang again.

"Hello, Twin City Talent."

"Marty, it's Shelley."

"Hi."

"I want out of my contract because you couldn't keep your hands off me."

"What? I've never touched you!"

"You were all over me! And if you don't release me from my contract, I'm going to call the police. I'm also going to tell your wife!"

I wasn't worried about the police. I hadn't laid a hand on the woman or even looked at her lecherously. I was, however, terrified she'd concoct a wild story to tell Deb. At the time, our marriage was young, and the two of us were still learning to trust each other.

Shelley had won. I immediately released her from her contract and never heard from her again.

Or did she win?

Years later, I searched the internet for her and found nothing under either her stage name or her real name. One thing is for sure: she never made it in the music business.

Around the time Al Franken resigned from the U.S. Senate, I told Deb what happened. I hadn't held out all those years because I was worried. The incident just didn't seem worth bringing up until that moment. My wife smiled and nodded her understanding: sometimes the man is innocent.

* * *

By mid-1991, I was growing worried about Twin City Talent's future. Aside from not getting my original rock/pop acts signed to national recording deals, music clubs were shutting their doors, cutting their budgets, or switching to DJs at such an accelerated rate that it was nearly impossible to keep my cover bands working steadily.

I still had all my national New Age/contemporary jazz acts, but they were much better at making my résumé look spiffy than making my bank account look hefty.

The phone rang.

"Hello, Twin City Talent."

"Marty, it's Andrew Howard*."

"Hey Andrew! How's it going?"

"Well, it could be going a lot better, and that's why I'm calling. I've outgrown Tall Tree Records. I want you to book me a showcase in Los Angeles, and invite all the record companies out."

"We can't do that now."

"Why not?"

"You still owe Don Mupo one more album. I'll put together a showcase for you after that."

"My last album should have had ten times the sales. I'm done wasting my talent on Tall Tree."

"But—"

"You work for me!" he shouted. "Book me a showcase or say goodbye!"

With great reluctance, I did what Andrew demanded. In retrospect, I should have at least insisted on a New York City show instead of an LA show. As a small protest, I refused to fly out for the showcase, claiming that I knew who was attending and could talk to any interested parties on the telephone afterwards.

The first record company phone call came the morning after the showcase.

"Hello, Twin City Talent."

"Marty, it's Don Mupo."

"Hi Don! How are you?"

"Not good. I heard that Andrew Howard* was doing an LA show, so I went out to see him. As I was listening, I looked around and saw a half-dozen other record company reps that I know. Why would you do this to me? I thought we were friends!"

"We *are* friends! I reminded Andrew that he owed you another album, but he insisted that I book the showcase. If I didn't do it, he was going to rip up his contract with me."

"That's not what he said when I talked with him after the show. He claimed *you* insisted on the showcase, and that *you* didn't want to honor the commitment for another album."

"That's not true!"

"I really liked you, Marty. But this is unforgiveable. I'm cancelling everyone's contract—David Cullen's, One Alternative's, and Andrew Howard's*. They're all gone!"

He slammed down the phone.

I sat in silence for several minutes, unable to move. I didn't blame Don for what he did. Had the situation been reversed, I might have done the same thing. In retrospect, it's easy to say I should have refused Andrew's demand, but as his manager, I was obligated to work in his best interests, and I couldn't deny he would have been better off on a larger label.

That evening, I discussed my music industry frustrations with Deb. She was supportive in whatever direction I wanted to go from there, and that direction was clear. I had had it with bar bands breaking up or calling from jail. I had had it with having tours destroyed because yet another nightclub shut its doors. I had had it with record company executives with tin for eardrums. And I had had it with unethical and egotistical musicians. It was time to say goodbye to the music business and get a straight job.

* * *

I was a twenty-nine-year-old man who had known nothing but the music business since I was thirteen. I had never even applied for a job before! This was new territory for me, and it was a wee bit scary. My first thought was to go back into radio. Being a DJ was too unstable and didn't pay enough, but advertising sales was a viable option. I opened up a newspaper and spotted exactly what I was looking for: a Minneapolis radio station had an opening for a sales representative. Although it wasn't one of the big stations, the position would give me the opportunity to build a reputation in sales, and once that happened I could go anywhere.

I mailed over my résumé and got called in for an interview a few days later.

It didn't go well.

In radio sales hierarchy, new agents start at the bottom, with either no accounts or poor accounts, and climb their way through the ranks by working harder and smarter than everyone else. The sales manager position is the ultimate goal, because (at least at the radio stations where I had worked) that person gets the national accounts, the political accounts that come in just by answering the phone, and a small percentage of what the other agents sell.

Therefore, I didn't want to be stuck at a radio station where the sales manager position was unobtainable.

Upon my arrival, the general manager gave me a quick tour of the radio station before leading me into his office. "Your résumé looks good," he said. "I see you have a lot of sales experience."

"Thank you. I haven't done radio sales for a while, but when I was at KQDS in Duluth, I split my time between college and sales and still managed to outsell some of the full-time agents."

"If we hire you, how soon can you start?"

"I can start next week. But first I need to know: if I outsell the rest of your staff, will you make me your sales manager?"

"We're not looking for a sales manager."

"I know you aren't now. Still, I'm only interested in working at a radio station where advancement is possible. So I just want to know. If I do what I think I can do, and I blow away the rest of your staff, can I earn the sales manager position?"

He bristled at my question and shouted, "*I'm* the one doing the interviewing here, not you!"

"That answers my question. Thank you very much."

Apparently, I wasn't going back into radio sales.

* * *

I returned home and scoured the want ads. No other radio stations were hiring, but there were a few ads promising be-your-own-boss opportunities that sounded good. After all, I already had years of experience bossing myself around. I mailed my résumé to one and soon had an interview.

When I showed up, a man escorted me into a room with roughly thirty other applicants. He waited a few minutes for others to arrive before standing in the front of the room, introducing himself, and giving a speech on the wonderful opportunity ahead of us.

I raised my hand.

He looked at me and said, "Please hold your questions until the end," and continued with his speech.

I raised my hand again and waved it back and forth until he couldn't ignore me.

"Yes?"

"Am I in the right place? I had an interview at ten."

"This is your interview. We are interviewing all of you at once." He went back into his pitch.

I listened a while longer before standing up, spreading my arms, and loudly announcing, "I hope everyone here knows this *isn't* an interview. It's a multi-level marketing scheme!" I walked out the door, with several others following behind me.

A few days later, I went to another interview and the same thing happened. The only difference was that I didn't stick around for the multi-level marketing speech to begin. As soon as I saw a room full of people, all taking their seats at the same time, I departed the premises.

The problem was that the kind of straight job I was most suited for would likely involve some form of sales, and I was naturally attracted to opportunities that would let me work independently. The key was to sift through the ads, discard the multi-level marketing and pyramid schemes, and find the legitimate sales openings.

Eventually I found what I was looking for: "Regional sales manager wanted for telecommunications company. Exclusive territory."

The company offering the position was Western Group Communications out of Dallas, Texas. I spoke with their president, Phil, multiple times, and after he offered me the exclusive territory, I flew to Dallas for training.

I was entering the business of selling Telesphere long-distance service on payphones. If my becoming a sales manager in the payphone business made you think about my earlier rant about industries that crashed without a newsworthy fight, you get a gold star! But back in 1991, no one dreamed that cell phones would send payphones into extinction. In fact, in 1991, payphone long-distance service was a brand new business.

Even though payphones had been around for more than one hundred years, the long-distance service on them had been a monopoly that the FCC only recently deregulated. In my Midwestern territory, the vast majority of the public payphones had AT&T long-distance service on them. Now, because of deregulation, the person or business that owned the property where the payphone sat could select the long-distance carrier. My job was to put together a sales staff and send my agents out to bars, malls, grocery stores, gas stations, and anywhere else they could find payphones.

The pitch was simple: "You have AT&T on your public payphone and earn little or no money when someone makes an operator-assisted long-distance call on it. If you replace AT&T with Telesphere, you will get a dollar commission on each of those calls."

At first glance, it seemed like the easiest sale ever. Why wouldn't a site owner want a little extra money for providing the space for the payphone? In reality, the sale was more difficult than it looked. Back then, AT&T was synonymous with "Ma Bell," and people were loyal to that company. In fact, telephone deregulation, in general, turned many people off. With payphones in particular, site owners worried about poor service, customer complaints, and high prices.

I too worried about the price Telesphere charged its customers. Any caller could find out the rate by asking the operator before making the call, but people seldom did that and wouldn't see the charges until they appeared on their credit card bill. Conversely, one could argue that Telesphere provided a service for the callers, jobs for their operators, jobs for sales agents, and so forth. Shouldn't callers expect to pay more for the convenience of using a payphone? For me, it was a moral dilemma that had no definitively correct answer. As Phil at Western Group Communications assured me, "At least Telesphere isn't the most expensive company out there."

Before long, I put together a sales staff located in Minnesota and the surrounding states. But just as I was on commission only, so were the people I hired. I went through dozens of agents and was unsuccessful at finding even one who had the patience or the sales ability to stick with the job long enough to make a living. Eventually I changed tactics, bought a payphone location list, and hired an appointment-setter, Stuart. With me as the sole sales representative, Stuart would pick a small town within two hours' driving distance of the Twin Cities and start calling. Once he set the appointments, I'd swoop in and convert most of that town's payphones in a matter of days.

Just as the money started flowing in, Phil called to tell me that

Telesphere had gone out of business. I thought I was going to lose everything and be back to square one all over again. Fortunately, a second call brought good news. Oncor Communications had acquired Telesphere's assets, and other than a short delay in commissions, business would continue as usual.

* * *

Even though I worked an exclusive territory for Western Group Communications, I was still an independent contractor. Nearly losing everything when Telesphere closed its doors convinced me to diversify. I started a new company, Essen Communications Group, and added residential and business long-distance services to my repertoire. Now I had three markets to sell to and direct agreements with multiple long-distance carriers.

I had worked in radio and talent management for love. This was different. For the first time in my life, I was working solely for money. Even so, I couldn't complain. Selling telephone service while working out of my home office was still a hell of a lot better than a desk job somewhere in downtown Minneapolis. Soon I was making more money than I'd ever made before.

* * *

My telecommunications business also gave me more flexibility to take time off. After all, I no longer had to fret over the possibility of a band being stuck on the road with open dates. Through a friend of a friend, Deb and I rented a cabin in far western Montana, near the hamlet of Sula. Ever since my childhood days of searching for frogs, catching snakes, and that invigorating black widow spider incident, nature and wildlife have been major loves of mine.

In Minnesota, my usual animal sightings included deer and well . . . pretty much just deer. Sure, there were moose, wolves, black bears, raccoons, skunks, badgers, and other animals, but the woods in most places were too thick for easy viewing, leaving a chance sighting on a road the most likely option.

Montana, with its mountains, plains, valleys, and meadows, is much more wildlife-viewing friendly. During our stay at the rental cabin, we saw white-tailed deer, mule deer, elk, moose, bighorn sheep, prong-horns, black bears, rattlesnakes, and a long list of smaller animals. It was wildlife heaven!

We enjoyed Montana so much that we rented the same cabin the following year and had just as much fun. As we were driving home after that second vacation, I said to Deb, "We should move to Montana."

My suggestion wasn't serious. I was only attempting to liven up the conversation on the long drive home.

"I agree!" she replied.

"Really?"

"Why not? We both love Montana, and you can sell long-distance service from anywhere."

Who could argue with that?

CHAPTER 17

Goodbye Beloved Minnesota

Deb and I didn't move to Montana immediately. We had to find a realtor, return to Montana to look for land, buy the land, drill a well, buy an adjoining piece of land, design our house, hire a builder, and the list went on.

All of our parents thought we were crazy. Who moves to Montana on a whim?

What I couldn't tell Deb's parents was that I actually put more thought into the move than I let on. Leaving my beloved Minnesota wasn't easy, and when I made a mental list of reasons to stay or go, one of my incentives for wanting to move was to get away from them. At the time, I felt like an asshole for feeling that way. After all, Deb's folks were kind people.

Only recently have I come to terms with the fact that I'm essentially an introvert. I'm perfectly happy going days—even weeks—seeing only my wife. I also enjoy the company of people one-on-one, couple's dinners, and group experiences, such as concerts or baseball games. It's the extended get-togethers, where I can't escape or send people home without being rude, that make me uncomfortable. Also, unlike friends, who have similar interests, you can't pick your family. That means family get-together conversations are practically required to be on a superficial level. Small talk for hours on end bores the shit out of me. I would rather discuss politics, religion, or any other controversial subject.

Even though recognizing and accepting my introverted tendencies is new, such feelings go way back. My mother came from a large family, and when I was a child, she used to drag me to family get-togethers in Goodland, an hour away from Duluth. I dreaded those days, and my mother would always make me feel like there was something wrong with me for not wanting to get to know my extended family. Similarly, Deb's parents lived two hours away from us, and once we bought our Minneapolis house, they got into the habit of visiting too frequently and staying too long. Soon I dreaded their visits as much as I dreaded the Goodland trips my mother forced on me. Montana would take me away from all that.

* * *

Before we move on to Montana, I'd like to share with you a few final Minnesota-related stories:

The Twin Cities was the perfect place for me to spend my early adult years. I'm unaware of any other metropolitan area with so many lakes and parks, and when you add in all the theaters, museums, restaurants, live music clubs, concerts, and sporting events, boredom there was practically impossible.

Deb's and my house was in a quiet neighborhood, on a hill in Northeast Minneapolis. Even though downtown was five miles away, we were high enough that we could see the upper half of the tall buildings there.

I'll never forget when the Minnesota Twins won the 1987 World Series. We didn't have the wherewithal to get tickets to the game, but after the final out, we stood on our tiny front porch, listening and watching as the entire city came alive with cheers and fireworks.

When the Twins reached the World Series again, in 1991, I tried unsuccessfully to buy tickets to one of the games. Then, three hours before game seven, a *ticket scalper*—yes, it's an un-PC term, but that's what people called them back then—I knew called with an offer to sell two obstructed-view tickets for one hundred dollars each.

I set the receiver down to discuss the offer with Deb. It was a short conversation, because we both realized the same thing at the same time: *What the fuck are we discussing this for? We have World Series tickets!*

While fans of other baseball teams might disagree, *Sports Illustrated* said it best when they called the 1991 World Series "the greatest that was ever played." And without a doubt, the greatest game of that greatest World Series was game seven. Deb's and my seats were in the top row, on the first base side, and the only thing obstructed was a tiny corner of right field. They were actually great seats, because we could see all the action at once, and with no one behind us, we didn't have to worry about obstructing anyone else's view. We stood the entire game, screaming our lungs out.

The Twins ultimately prevailed over the Atlanta Braves, 1 to 0 in ten innings. The low score didn't mean a lack of excitement. In just about every inning one team or the other had men on base, only to see the defense get out of the inning with a spectacular play. And the heroics of Twins' pitcher Jack Morris reached legendary status when he famously refused to let manager Tom Kelly pull him out after the ninth inning and went on to pitch the complete game shutout.

Deb's and my World Series story continued ten years later, when we traveled to Florida to visit my father and attend the Twins' spring training. While there, we had a blast watching the practices and the games. We also had a goal: I was going to get my World Series ticket signed by Tom Kelly, and Deb was going to get hers signed by Dan Gladden, the player who scored the winning run.

Getting my ticket signed was easy. I waited by one of the practice field fences and called out to Tom when it appeared as if the players were taking a break. He finished what he was doing and walked over and signed.

Deb's job was trickier, because Dan Gladden had retired and was working as the color commentator for Twins' radio broadcasts. Her plan was to track down Dan when he left the stadium after that night's exhibition game. The initial problem was figuring out what door Dan would exit, since there were several doors to choose from. Luckily, Deb's college roommate, Regina McCombs, worked for KARE-TV in Minneapolis, and she was in Florida covering spring training. Through her, Deb acquired the necessary inside information.

When the game ended, I walked my father to the car, and Deb headed for the door to begin her stakeout. I knew where she was going to wait, so I drove back to the stadium and pulled up in front of the plaza, where the door was.

By then, the crowd had cleared out, and there was no sign of Deb. I waited for a bit before exiting the car and walking the fifty-or-so feet to the door. I pulled on the handle. It was locked. Had Deb given up and walked toward where we had originally parked?

I returned to the car, not quite sure what to do. My father and I rolled down our windows and kept our eyes on the plaza.

The passenger side of the car faced the stadium, so my father was partially blocking my view when he said, "Someone's coming out now."

I leaned forward to see Deb, chatting away with Dan Gladden! I shouldn't have been surprised. She's the kind of person who can be pushing a cart in a supermarket and people will approach her and tell her their life story.

They stopped beside the car, and Dan leaned down to greet my father through the window. I stepped out and walked around to shake his hand. The four of us chatted for a bit, and it soon became obvious that all Deb or I had to do was ask and Dan would join us for a beer.

That would have been incredible, except for one problem. My father was with us, and eventually every conversation involving him and a new acquaintance leads to these eight words: "Have you given your life to Jesus Christ?"

Perhaps Dan would have been fine with that, but even if he was, I believed in the separation of church and baseball and wasn't about to risk such an awkward moment. Deb was thinking the same way, and though we both would have loved to have a beer with the World Series hero, we said our goodbyes after a few more minutes and hopped into the car.

As we drove away, I asked Deb, "How did you get inside?"

"I convinced a security guard to let me in. And when I started down the hall, there was Dan—walking toward me. I introduced myself and we just started talking. He seemed genuinely touched that someone wanted him to sign a World Series ticket after all these years. He even looked at my seat number and tried to figure out where I was sitting. He was such a nice man!"

Those signed World Series tickets, along with the *Sports Illustrated* article, are now framed and displayed in a place of honor in our home.

* * *

My final Minnesota story wasn't in my original plans for this book, but when Deb requested it, I thought, "What the hell. I've been taking requests since my days at WEBC. Why stop now?"

It was a hot summer night in 1990. Since our house didn't have air conditioning, we had all the second floor windows open for air circulation.

Screams woke us in the middle of the night!

"What's that!" I shouted.

Deb sat up and listened to the screaming. "A cat has a bunny!"

"Is Elvis in the house?"

"I didn't let him in. Did you?"

"Shiiit!"

"We have to do something."

All I had on were my briefs and Deb was nude. She grabbed a T-shirt that was long enough to cover her bum, and we raced down the steps and out the side door.

The screaming stopped.

We looked in the back. We looked in the front. We looked on the opposite side. There was no sign of either Elvis or the bunny. Armed with the hope that we had at least given the rabbit a chance to escape, we walked back around to the side door.

"It's locked." I said.

"What?" Deb asked.

"The door is locked."

"Didn't you undo the doorknob?"

"You were behind me. That was your job."

"I didn't shut the door. You did!"

"No I didn't. . . . What do we do now?"

"Wake Sean."

Our eight-year-old son had the second floor bedroom at the front of the house. We walked around and looked up.

"Sean," Deb whispered.

Nothing.

"Sean," I said a little louder.

A car approached, and we ducked behind our pear tree.

The car passed, and we shuffled back under the window.

Deb called out, "Sean!"

"Shhh! Not so loud," I said. "We're gonna wake the neighbors."

I rang the doorbell.

Nothing.

Another car passed, sending us scurrying for cover.

"Sean!" we yelled in unison.

A moment or two passed before our son pressed his face against his screen and looked down at us. "What?"

"Your dad and I locked ourselves outside. Come down and let us in."

"That was really stupid!"

Under normal circumstances, we would have objected to our child calling us "stupid." But what could we say? He had a point.

He descended the stairs, unlocked the door, and climbed back to his room without saying a word.

CHAPTER 18

The Montana Surprise

The land Deb and I bought in Montana is on a forested hill at the edge of the Bitterroot Mountains. Our mailing address lists our town as Victor, an unincorporated community of eight hundred people, but we actually live nine miles away from there. Victor is one of nine small towns in a ninety-five-mile-long area called the Bitterroot Valley (aka Ravalli County). The population of the entire valley is roughly forty thousand people, with the Bitterroot Mountains to the west and the Sapphire Mountains to the east. If you're reaching for a map, look on the far western side of Montana, just south of the city of Missoula.

We purchased our first thirteen acres from Tom Simpson, a man who owned seventy acres on the hill. We also negotiated a first right of refusal on the twelve acres next to it. Buying the second parcel of land wasn't something we wanted to do, at least for a while. And since we had land-locked it, we didn't think anyone would want to buy it. Then, shortly after closing on the first parcel, Tom announced that he had a buyer for the second parcel. I suspected his claim was bullshit, but the possibility of having to allow an access road across our property, and having a neighbor closer than desired, coerced us into the second purchase.

The cost of that second parcel delayed our Montana move by a few years. We adjusted our projected move-in date to the summer of 1996 and worked hard socking away as much money as possible.

During that time, Deb developed a new talent as a house designer. Other than telling her that I wanted a three-office suite with a separate entrance in the daylight basement, the entire design was hers. She also took care of hiring a draftsman to convert her design into structurally sound plans and hiring a builder.

My contributions to the project included hiring a water witch to mark the drilling spot and hiring the well driller after that. Water can be scarce in Montana, and with our land being on a hill, we had no guarantee of finding drinkable water. As a man of science, I don't actually believe that dowsing for water with a divining rod works. Even so, water witches are cheap—about the same as three feet of drilling. Considering how far we might be going down, a little dowsing action seemed worth the chance.

Ultimately, we hit a pocket of good water, with a low but passable flow rate, at roughly one hundred feet. Twelve years later that well would go dry, and we'd have to do it all over again. We passed on the water witch the second time and went down over three hundred feet. Watching the drilling process—at thirty-five dollars a foot—is like gambling. As your money goes down the hole, you have to decide if or when to give up and drill elsewhere. What if we stopped ten feet too soon? Although our second well cost substantially more than the first one, it is better in every way. With a little luck, it will last us for the rest of our lives.

Once the construction of our house began, we kept in contact with our builder so we could coordinate the selling of our Minneapolis home with the move-in date of our new home. In mid-May, our builder estimated he'd be largely finished by mid-July. With that in mind, we put our house on the market, sold it in two weeks, and set a corresponding closing date.

Time moved fast. Soon signing the closing paperwork was just a day away. On that day, Deb squeezed in one final television commercial shoot, and it ran late. When she arrived home after midnight, and stepped into the kitchen, a trickle of water bounced off her head.

"Marty!" she yelled. "Come down here!"

I jumped out of bed, hurried down the stairs, and stepped in a puddle of water. "Ohhh, shit!" I said. I ran into the basement and turned off the water.

A pipe between the first floor and the second floor had burst, and the damage looked substantial. Other than mopping up the floor, there was nothing we could do except toss and turn in bed until morning.

For several tense hours, I was convinced that our closing later that afternoon was going to fall through, and we were going to be stuck with two houses.

Instead, Deb saved the day by contacting a handyman she had met while working on commercials. He rushed over to replace the pipe and repair all the water damage.

In all, everything worked out okay. When we informed the two women buyers of what happened, they were understanding and signed all the paperwork. They did ask for the handyman's phone number, however. And as I learned years later, they kept the man busy with a variety of remodeling projects in the years that followed.

* * *

Three days after our closing, we pulled up to our new house.

"Oh, my God," I said.

"It's not even close to being complete," Deb declared.

"I'm going to kill Mark," I said, referring to our builder.

"Let me talk to him first."

Thus began a frustrating ordeal that would take us into mid-November. To make it through, we put our belongings into storage, set up Sean in a pop-up trailer, and Deb and I rented a small fifth-wheel trailer from Tom Simpson. Our water came directly from a hose, connected to our well, and we set up an open-air shower on the opposite side of Sean's trailer. Those showers were always accompanied by screams of "Holy shit! The water is cold!"

We insisted that our builder install a toilet before doing anything else, so at least we didn't have to shit in the woods. That basement toilet had a curtain for privacy, since the interior walls were not yet in place.

More or less, we ended up on a four-month-long camping trip. Deb and Sean helped the builders during the day, and I set up an office in the fifth-wheel trailer. The worst part of working in the trailer was hitting my head on the ceiling all the time. The edges, where the ceiling angle changed, were especially troublesome. Later, when the weather grew cold, my fingers got so numb that I had difficulty typing on my computer keyboard.

We also learned something very important about Montana: work stops when hunting season starts. Our builder had hired independent contractors for plumbing, electrical, and drywall work. Even though everything was way behind schedule, those contractors disappeared until they shot their elk.

By the end of those four months, Deb wanted to kill me, I wanted to kill Sean, Sean wanted to kill both of us, and we all wanted to kill our builder. Then, on the day we finished moving in, Deb's parents showed up!

Milt and Meredith stayed for what might have been the longest week of my life. Their intentions were good. During that summer, they came out to see the building progress and contributed a lot of work. Now they wanted to see the finished product. Still, how could two people be so clueless as to not understand that after four months of camping we just wanted to experience our new house, sleep in real beds, eat in our own kitchen, and not see another soul for a long time? Had they stayed another day, they too would have been on my kill list.

* * *

By this time, new regulations had caused the payphone long-distance business to nosedive, and what little was left would soon be crushed by cell phones. Fortunately, cell phones were still years away from cooling off business and residential landline long-distance service, and for me, Montana was a warm market.

One of my first business moves was to meet with the Bitterroot Valley Chamber of Commerce to set up a long-distance program with them. In return for endorsing Essen Communications Group, I gave the Chamber a portion of what I made off the long-distance service I sold to their members. The program worked great for both of us, and it was a wonderful way for me to meet business owners up and down the Bitterroot Valley.

Even though I've always been a liberal, I had stopped being a political activist once I left Open School. There were just too many other things to distract me, like girls, rock 'n' roll, marriage, and starting three different businesses. Now that life was seemingly settling down, those activist urges returned. Consequently, the reemerged political me was shocked that the uninvolved me from a few years earlier did absolutely no research ahead of time on the politics of the community I was moving into. What a dumbshit the uninvolved me had been!

Montana is a conservative state, with islands of liberalism in Missoula, Bozeman, Helena, and a few other towns. And of all the conservative regions in Montana, none are more conservative than the Bitterroot Valley. My new home was no stranger to militias, Uzis, and extreme right-wing politics. In fact, if I could have looked into the future, I would have seen that only one resident in nearby Pinesdale (a Mormon polygamist community of 742 people) voted for the Democratic nominee, Al Gore, in the 2000 presidential election.

If you are unfamiliar with the word *Uzi*, it's a type of submachine gun. During one of our first summers in Montana, Deb and I heard what we thought was someone lighting multiple strings of firecrackers. The explosions sounded like they were coming from a little beyond the eastern edge of our property. The noise would continue for several minutes before stopping and returning the next night. Shortly after the explosions stopped for good, we read in the newspaper that the sheriff had arrested a man near us for shooting off his Uzi in an attempt to intimidate a neighbor into moving. The sheriff also found leaking underground fuel tanks and various survivalist items on the man's property.

We have another neighbor to the east of us who has erected a line of Confederate flags along his security gate. I learned that in a most shocking way. I was in the kitchen, washing dishes, when I looked up and saw two men riding across my beautiful wooded property on their ATVs. I raced out the door, scooped up some rocks, and chased the men west to the road. Then I ran back to my garage, jumped into my truck, and followed their tracks on the gravel road. Those tracks led me in a semicircular route along a series of roads and ultimately to a cluster of houses in the woods, not far from the Uzi guy. That's where I encountered the gate, lined with Confederate flags—and the ATV tracks leading to the house behind it.

At that point, I wisely broke off my pursuit and called the sheriff instead. Yeah, I was probably a little crazy, chasing after the men like that, but Deb and I keep our property as natural as possible and have it well marked with no trespassing signs. Also, in Montana's dry climate, land damaged from ATV tires can take years to recover.

Fortunately, the extra twelve-acre piece of land we bought gives us a nice buffer from our questionable neighbors to the east, and since those two incidents, we've never had another Uzi or ATV problem.

All of that brings me back to the Bitterroot Valley Chamber of Commerce. Since I had never belonged to a chamber of commerce before, I had assumed they were an apolitical organization that promoted local businesses. How naïve I was! Both the majority of their members and the issues they supported were far to the right.

Before long, my revived interest in politics began clashing with the Chamber of Commerce. While I was speaking out and writing letters to the editor, advocating for protecting wolves and grizzly bears and for saving local forests from logging, the Chamber was doing the opposite.

Even so, the makeup of the Chamber wasn't entirely far-right business owners. As I was out meeting with members to sign them up for long-distance service, I was learning that a significant minority of them were closet liberals who were too scared to speak out for fear that others would boycott them. Also, I had made quite a splash during my first year or so in the valley, and my snarky newspaper commentaries were becoming popular.

With that in mind, when the Bitterroot Valley Chamber of Commerce announced elections for the board of directors, I decided to run. Maybe with a liberal on the board, some of their far-right stances could be changed or at least moderated. I knew conservatives outnumbered me, but I didn't have to come in first place to get on the board, and many of those conservatives had long-distance service through me and were saving a lot of money. If some of them put politics aside and voted for me, I had a reasonable chance of procuring enough votes to get on the board.

The Chamber's leadership thought I had a chance of winning too, and it terrified them. So instead of letting Chamber members vote for each person, they cheated and changed the rules. For that election, the current board nominated a single slate of candidates—excluding me—and only allowed members to vote up or down on that single slate.

Upon learning that the Bitterroot Valley Chamber of Commerce was going to bar me from the ballot, I brought the story to the valley's two largest newspapers. The Chamber's unscrupulous maneuver became the biggest headline story of the week. The Chamber didn't budge, however, and though I got many pats on the back for my efforts, the story was forgotten with the next news cycle.

At that point, I did the only two things I could do: I canceled my Chamber of Commerce membership and requested that they agree to dissolve our long-distance program. No way was I going to work for liberal causes while simultaneously making money for the Chamber that they could turn around and use for lobbying on the opposite side.

They were thrilled to get rid of me.

CHAPTER 19

If He Can Do It, So Can I

Other than the culture shock of moving from liberal Minneapolis to the conservative Bitterroot Valley, Montana was a hit for the entire family. Even Sean, who had previously declared that our move had "ruined his life," was warming up to his new home state.

Despite our builder being a poor estimator of construction time, he had built us a truly wonderful house. Since he too was a Minnesota transplant, he constructed it to strict Minnesota code rather than to the lax building codes Montana had at the time. It's as solid as a rock and so efficiently insulated that we've never regretted not installing air conditioning. We call our home "the tree house," and from my writing room I can see snowcapped mountains through a natural break in the trees.

Of all the reasons to love Montana, wildlife topped my list. We maintain the twenty-five acres surrounding our house as the Essen Wildlife Refuge, and during hunting season our land is one of the few places in the area animals can go to be safe. We often see deer, moose, elk, black bears, wild turkeys, owls, and eagles, and on special occasions, we see mountain lions, wolves, coyotes, foxes, groundhogs, rubber boas, and pine martens. A couple of peacocks are also long-term residents, though they are most likely escapees from a nearby farm.

In the winters, we go cross-country skiing, and in the summers, we go hiking, backpacking, kayaking, and at least once a year rent a Forest Service cabin. Yeah, for people who enjoy wildlife and the outdoors, Montana is hard to beat.

* * *

During my first two years in Montana, I worked as an independent agent for multiple long-distance carriers, just as I had done in Minnesota. At the beginning of it all, I could sell long-distance service at twenty cents per minute and be competitive. Then rates began dropping—eventually bottoming out in the five-cent-per-minute range. Those plummeting rates required me to stay alert for trends and changes. If a carrier I represented became uncompetitive or unreliable, I would search out and negotiate a deal with a replacement carrier. Having the flexibility to work independently with whatever company I wanted to gave me a big advantage over long-distance sales agents who were employees of single companies.

All of that was possible because of the breakup of the Bell System in 1984. Instead of just AT&T, customers could choose from numerous long-distance carriers. While the public benefited from that deregulation, fierce competition forced many of the newer companies out of business. When that happened to companies I represented, I'd have to drop everything to help my clients move to a different long-distance carrier. In many ways, it was as frustrating as spending days booking the perfect tour for a band, only to have the band break up in the middle of it.

The *Telecommunications Act of 1996* brought more deregulation and a new opportunity: local landline telephone service. One of the disadvantages physically large but sparsely populated states like Montana have is that it's more expensive for companies to offer alternative landline service in them than it is to do the same in more densely populated states. Here the Regional Bell Operating Company (RBOC), US West, still dominated the market, and when I searched for a landline company to represent independently, my best option appeared to be a small firm located just fifteen miles north of me, in the town of Stevensville.

I set up a meeting with the owner, Dave, hoping to put together an agreement that would allow me to sell his company's landline service to my existing Montana long-distance customers. Dave claimed his office wasn't a good place to meet, so he came over to my office instead.

When he arrived, his appearance surprised me. He had unkempt hair and a scraggly beard and wore clothes more fitting for someone working in the woods than working as a telecommunications executive. That was okay. Montana isn't the kind of place where people wear a suit and tie. I was dressed in casual attire myself—just not quite that casual.

We talked for about an hour, and the more we talked, the more I wondered how Dave stayed in business. He had been bright enough to get one of the first landline resale contracts in Montana, but his organizational skills and customer service knowledge appeared to be lacking.

When our meeting concluded, I hurried upstairs to find Deb.

"I'm gonna start offering local phone service," I said, "but not as an agent. I'm going to get my own resale contract, and we'll do our own billing and customer service. I didn't think such a thing would be possible without a huge investment, but Dave said all he did was contact the Montana Public Service Commission, and they put him in touch with the proper person at US West. He was up and running within a month."

"I thought you were meeting with Dave to sell for him."

"That's what I thought too. But I'll be surprised if he's still in business a year from now. If he can do it, I can do it. And I'd rather bet on myself."

Here's a quick explanation of what I did: In September 1998, I converted my sole proprietorship, Essen Communications Group, into an S corporation, Essen Communications Corporation (ECC). Using "Corporation" instead of the usual "inc." at the end of the name was a deliberate but perfectly legal way to make my new company appear bigger than it really was. Then I had the Montana Public Service Commission send me a contract that I could either sign as-is or use as a starting point for negotiations with US West. (I signed the first one without changes and negotiated better terms later on.) This was all possible because it was unrealistic for every landline telephone company to have its own wires, and the *Telecommunications Act of 1996* required all RBOCs to open their networks for other carriers to utilize. Several ways exist for utilizing the phone lines already in the ground, but the simplest way is through resale, and that was the option I chose.

Resale creates a somewhat awkward situation, where the reseller is both a big customer of the RBOC and a competitor at the same time. Essentially ECC rented lines from US West at an 18.1 percent discount. US West handled everything physical on those phone lines, including features, installs, and repairs, and then sent my company one giant bill each month. We would then take that giant bill and turn it into individual bills for our customers. We also handled all customer service and linked our computers with US West's computers for inputting orders, including adding and disconnecting phone lines and features.

Even though US West was required by law to work with us, it was still a sweet deal for them, since they didn't have to send out individual bills, field individual customer service calls, or worry about individual collections. Working with ECC was also a sweet deal for our customers, since we gave them better rates than US West and amazing customer service. In fact, over the years, we even got fan mail from customers who were thrilled by how hard we worked for them and that we never left them on hold, listening to a "your call is very important to us" recording.

I couldn't have offered local phone service without Deb's help. She headed up the billing department, which was a two-pronged job of billing our customers and disputing billing errors from US West. She used Excel spreadsheets for a few months before concluding that we needed a customized billing program. For that, we made use of a customer who was a software developer. Deb worked with that developer for a couple of months to design a billing program that did everything we needed it to do. That program cost us over ten thousand dollars but served our needs for over nineteen years. So what seemed expensive at the time turned out to be a hell of a bargain.

Essen Communications Corporation became every bit as successful as I had hoped it would be. We had entered into the local resale business while it was still relatively new, and for many years we were the largest company of its kind in the state of Montana. I was also correct about Dave. His company soon lost its contract with US West, and I ended up working out a deal with him to acquire all of his customers.

* * *

The biggest headache of running a telephone company in a rural area was finding reliable employees. Deb agreed to work with me until the company got off the ground, but she was also a master handweaver who was eager to start her own weaving kits business. Finding someone to replace her became a priority. Fortunately, computer automation made it possible to do everything with just three people: me to run the company and do sales, a person to take care of billing and order entry, and a person to take care of customer service and order entry.

Unfortunately, teaching the billing program to an employee took several weeks, and teaching the program that interfaced with US West's computers in Denver took a similar amount of time. Learning telecommunications wasn't like learning advanced math, but obviously others found it more difficult than Deb and I did. Additionally, we expected something of our employees that some thought was ridiculous: accuracy.

We deemed it unacceptable to send bills with errors to customers, and we felt the same way about orders. If a customer called to request caller ID, it wasn't acceptable for an employee to enter the code to install call waiting instead and later say, "Oh, well!" when we discovered their error.

The last two miles to our house are on a gravel road, and the final section includes a hairpin turn with a steep climb up a hill. I love the road and take it every morning on my bicycle to get the newspaper. The ride down takes five minutes, but the return is all uphill and takes fifteen minutes. It's great exercise, and I even have studded tires on my bike for winter trips.

In the winter, we call our road "Luge Lane," because sometimes the hill will have just two deep icy tracks. When it's like that, it's possible to take your hands off the steering wheel, and the car will self-steer all the way down, including making the hairpin turn. My bike is a different story. I'm not heavy enough to push the studs into hard ice, and since the studs are only on the bottom of the tires, they don't work well on slippery concave surfaces. After a winter when I had more wipeouts than usual, Deb bought me a T-shirt with "Is my bike okay?" printed in upside down letters.

No matter what the season, animals are a concern too. I'm an early riser, so much of the year my rides take place in the dark. Generally, I only see deer, moose, or grouse, but at certain times of the year, I could easily ride around a blind corner and surprise a bear or a mountain lion. When such animals are in the area, I make up songs and sing them at the top of my lungs wherever the forest borders the road.

What does all of that have to do with telecommunications? When we bought our land and built our house and offices, we did it all without having experienced a Montana winter. We didn't know that the winter temperatures would bounce frequently between twenty-five and forty-five degrees. If snow was on the road, the top layer would melt when it got warm and freeze into an icy coating when it got cold again. We'd hand sand the road, but sometimes it was tough to keep up.

Therefore, we wouldn't even interview a prospective employee who didn't have, at minimum, a front-wheel drive vehicle with studded winter tires. Even applicants with qualifying vehicles would sometimes show up for their interviews looking like they'd seen a ghost, say "No thanks," and head right back down the hill.

Despite our insisting on billing and order entry accuracy, and despite a drive to our office that took some getting used to, there were many reasons for people to want to work for ECC. We paid our employees an above-average wage for the area, we were loyal to those we hired, we tried to make work fun, and no one could ask for a more beautiful setting to work in. We'd even pause work activities for bear, elk, and moose viewing.

Nevertheless, employees came and went. Most frustrating was investing weeks into training an employee only to have that person quit shortly thereafter. Even when we found a dream employee, Gina, who loved the job and did a job we loved, we weren't able to keep her, because her husband abruptly decided that they had to move out of the area. There were tears all around.

We were also shocked that previous telecommunications experience didn't necessarily make an employee any better. We thought we hit a goldmine when we hired a woman who had worked for years at a major telephone company. Then, on the first day of training, she sat staring at her computer screen because she had only worked on mainframe computers and didn't have the slightest idea how to open a PC computer program. Once we got her past that and moved on to more advanced tasks, she'd go out to her car on breaks and come back smelling of alcohol. She quit after several days.

Another memorable employee took advantage of two weeks Deb and I were out of the country to search for a different job. On the day we returned, instead of giving us a report, she proclaimed, "I'm late for my new job," and walked out of the office. Even worse, I still had to pay the woman for her two weeks of company-time abuse.

Some employees didn't even bother to resign. The only way we knew they weren't coming back was when we'd look in their office in the evening and see that they'd quietly removed all their personal belongings.

Eventually we found two women, Nicole and Carlye, out of the Bitterroot Valley, who stayed with us for multiple years, and a gay man, Bryan, out of Missoula, who stayed with us for five years. Having to drive an hour to and from work wasn't easy for Bryan, but he loved both the job and the fact that he didn't have to hide his sexual orientation when he was around Deb and me. The joke—often initiated by him—that he was "coming out of the closet" whenever he exited the office supply closet never got old.

CHAPTER 20

Mud Hens vs. Mud Hens

Montana is a state with no MLB, NFL, NHL, or NBA teams. For Montanans into spectator sports, their main in-state options are to follow college teams or one of the minor league baseball teams. Since I still loved baseball, and wanted to enjoy it as a participant, I searched for an amateur men's baseball league to join. When I learned that that too was lacking in the state, I solved the problem by forming the Bitterroot Baseball League (BBL).

The newspapers, radio stations, and television stations were all happy to get behind my project, and soon I had two teams in Missoula, one team in Hamilton, one team in Stevensville, and my team, representing the smaller towns of Victor and Corvallis. Each team named themselves after a minor league baseball club, and, naturally, I had dibs on the Mud Hens.

When I formed the league, I thought I would be one of the better players. Instead, many of the younger players joined right out of Montana's strong American Legion baseball program, and many of the older players had previously played college baseball. My Victor/Corvallis Mud Hens team was a whole other level better than my Twin Cities Mud Hens team.

In fact, a young lefty pitcher on my team, Brian, threw in the low 90s, and when he was healthy and sober would have held his own in the minor leagues. He was the Mud Hen's closer, and when he wasn't pitching, he manned third base. I got a kick out of playing with Brian.

He was bright, funny, and had a lightning bolt for an arm. According to a player on my team who knew him well, Brian came from a family that had a poor reputation and many wrote him off by sheer association. While I was too new to the area to know if that was true, I couldn't help wondering how far Brian would have gone had he grown up in a different atmosphere and taken better care of his body.

I'll never forget when some of my players were out of town, and I had just nine confirmed for our game, including Brian. When he didn't show up at game time, we had to start shorthanded while Deb hurried over to Brian's trailer to drag him out of bed. When she escorted him onto the field in the third inning, he was so hung-over, he could barely walk. I set him up at third base and prayed no one would hit the ball to him. Then, whenever it was our turn to bat, he'd lie on the bench, moaning and drifting in and out of sleep.

Somehow, through all of that, the Mud Hens still managed to lead the Stevensville River Bandits by a single run in the ninth inning. Unfortunately, the two pitchers I used to get us through the eighth were out of gas. My only options for that final inning were to bring in Brian or someone who had never pitched before.

Brian looked at me through squinted eyes and said, "I can do it."

"Are you sure?"

"It's just three outs. Piece of cake."

What happened next sounds like something out of a baseball movie, but I swear it's true.

First batter: Walked on four straight balls.

Second batter: Walked on four straight balls.

Third batter: Walked on the sixth pitch.

Fourth batter: Reached a full-count before striking out swinging.

Fifth batter: Blown away on three pitches.

Sixth batter: Blown away on three pitches.

Brian shuffled off the mound, shot me an innocent little smile, and fell back asleep on the bench.

* * *

When Deb and I were still in Minnesota, we attended numerous St. Paul Saints baseball games. Mike Veeck and actor/comedian Bill Murray owned the independent minor league team, which became famous for its wild, over-the-top promotions. My Bitterroot Baseball League played the majority of its games in Hamilton, where I had arranged to use the city's beautiful field with its old-fashioned covered grandstand. Though we didn't have the drawing power of the St. Paul Saints, I still arranged goofy promotions, such as free peanuts for everyone if the "bat man" (a player chosen at random) struck out. My son, Sean, did all of the announcing for a little extra spending money.

I bring up the St. Paul Saints, because I wrote Mike Veeck about what I was doing in Montana, and he wrote me back a nice letter of encouragement. Even though I ran the Bitterroot Baseball League for free, a contact like Mike would be a terrible thing to waste.

"Hmm," I said to myself. "Being a sports agent wouldn't be all that much different from being a music agent. Would it?"

I found one of my old agent contracts, modified it to fit baseball, and voilà, I was a sports agent! I signed Brian and the next best pitcher in my league, Roger from the Hamilton Cobras, to a deal that we all agreed to cancel if my plan didn't pan out. Then I wrote Mike Veeck a letter, pitching a tryout for the two players.

Mike quickly wrote me back, saying that he didn't have room on his team, but he had arranged a tryout for my players with another team in the league, the Sioux Falls Canaries. We were in! And by sending us to Sioux Falls, Mike cut a half-day off our drive from Montana.

The following week, we all piled into my Ford Bronco for the thousand-mile drive to Sioux Falls.

"I hurt my arm at work, two days ago," Brian said as he fastened his seatbelt.

"What!" I screamed. "How did you do that?"

"I was lifting some shit in the warehouse. My elbow has been killing me ever since."

"Why didn't you tell me? I could have moved the tryout."

"I thought it would get better."

"We should cancel. If we show up and you can't pitch, Mike Veeck will never trust me again."

"Don't worry, Marty. I can suck it up long enough to make it through the tryout. I promise. They'll never know I'm hurt."

"If you pitch, you can't flinch or show any pain."

"Trust me. I can do it."

So off to Sioux Falls we went. It was on that trip that I realized that behind Brian's "lovable putz" persona was a bright young man. We passed the time playing memory and trivia games, and neither Roger nor I stood a chance against all the obscure information packed away in Brian's brain.

At the tryouts the next day, Roger threw in the mid-eighties and didn't have enough bite on his other pitches to generate any interest. Brian, on the other hand, pitched much better than I expected with his injured arm and threw in the upper-eighties. While I'd seen him throw harder in games, I was impressed that he didn't let on the pain he was feeling. When the tryout was over, the Canaries' manager and pitching coach huddled off to the side and talked.

My heart pounded! They wouldn't be talking like that unless they thought Brian had potential.

Alas, Brian didn't make the team, but apparently he was close. Instead, the pitching coach gave him some things to work on, and the manager gave me the contact information for a team in a lower minor league he thought Brian could make.

I didn't take Brian to another tryout, however, because baseball season ended before he was ready, and the following year he ended up in Nevada, using his electric arm to quarterback a team in a semipro football league.

* * *

Even though I intended the Bitterroot Baseball League solely for fun, my natural inclination to promote both helped and hurt the league. It helped, because I had to get the word out, so we'd have a pool of players to keep team rosters full. It hurt, because players started taking games too seriously (who knew when a pro scout might show up?), and Chester Webster*, the manager of the Hamilton American Legion team, grew jealous of the media coverage I was getting and furious about a speech I made.

One of my most difficult tasks as owner of the baseball league was finding fields to play on. We couldn't play on a softball or a little league field. We needed standard-sized baseball fields, and those were hard to come by in western Montana. Every week it seemed as if some incident arose to threaten our use of a field. The speech I made that angered Chester Webster* didn't help matters.

That incident happened when the mayor of Hamilton, Laurel Frankenfield, called me to request that I speak at a City Council meeting for a proposed baseball field at Hieronymus Park. Knowing how badly the area needed another full-sized field, I was eager to lend my voice to the cause.

I had my entire speech memorized and felt honored that the mayor had requested my presence. When she called the meeting to order, and people lined up to speak, I was near the end of the line. I stood listening and was surprised that roughly half of the people were objecting to the baseball field. Their primary objection was that it would sit right next to the Bitterroot River, where herbicides and fertilizer could leach into the water. When my turn to speak came up, I said this:

"I'm Marty Essen, and I own the Bitterroot Baseball League. Here in the Bitterroot Valley, I'm only aware of two adult-sized baseball fields—one in Hamilton and one in Florence. We desperately need another field, and I came here today to speak in favor of the Hieronymus Park field. That said, after listening to the statements given by those ahead of me, I've changed my mind. Not about the *need* for a field, but about the *location* of the field. The Bitterroot River is one of the valley's most precious resources, and it would be irresponsible to build a baseball field so close to the water that chemical runoff could pollute it. Therefore, I strongly encourage you to reject the field—at least at that location. The river is more important than baseball!"

Much of the audience burst into applause.

The other people? Not so much. In fact, when the meeting adjourned, many of them were waiting for me outside, forcing me to walk a gauntlet as they pelted me with insults.

I didn't realize the impact of my speech until a few weeks afterward. The Mud Hens had a game in Missoula, and when it was over, I decided to drive south to Hamilton to catch the last few innings of the BBL game there.

After that game ended and everyone departed, I quickly checked the dugouts to make sure no one left any trash in them, turned off the field lights, and headed for the exit. I was just about out of the stadium when Chester approached and shoved me against the side of the grandstand.

The American Legion team manager was a crotchety man in his mid-to-late-fifties, and his breath smelled strongly of alcohol.

"What's wrong, Chester?" I asked.

"You knocked my team out of the newspaper headlines, and now you stopped the Hieronymus Park baseball field!"

"I did what?"

He shoved me harder. "You heard what I said! Everything was going smoothly until you opened your big mouth." He pushed me again. "Either you retract your statement or every one of your games here is going to be rained out."

"Rained out?"

"I'll make sure the sprinklers flood the field on game days!"

At that moment, I realized I was in a no-win situation, similar to when Mark Alan asked me to pudding-wrestle two women back in my KQDS days. I could either let Chester continue to assault me, or I could push back and risk escalating the confrontation to the point where I'd have no choice other than to kick the shit out of a man who was at least twenty years older than me. Considering how horrible such a fight would look, and the possibility that he might claim I was the aggressor, I selected the first option and let him pound me in the chest some more. When he concluded I wasn't going to fight back, he shot me a contemptuous look and walked away.

I reported the incident the next day. As far as I know, other than the fields staying dry before our games and Chester leaving me alone, nothing else came of it.

* * *

Chester wasn't the only person showing me his dark side. I was beginning to see the dark side of some BBL players too. I had two cops on my team, and they couldn't have been more opposite. When I wrote up the league rules at the beginning of the season, I added a requirement that every player who shows up must play at least half the game. Naturally, the better players played the entire game and the less talented players played half that. Since I doubled as the Mud Hens' manager, I applied the same rule to myself and never played a full game, unless only nine players showed up.

Of the two cops, Paul was one of the nicest guys on the team and an above average player. The other cop, Jeff, was harder to get to know and an even more blazingly mediocre player than I was. Consequently, he and I split most games in right field. Jeff really wanted to play catcher, but I had two good catchers ahead of him, and he was a disaster at the position in practices. Then one evening the phone rang, and it was Jeff, sounding like I'd never heard him sound before. He was probably drunk, though I can't say for sure. I can't even recite the phone call for you because of the bizarre way he rambled on. All I could think was, "This is the weirdest, most inappropriate phone call I've ever received." Though he didn't directly threaten to harm me if I didn't play him at catcher, he certainly made me feel threatened.

At a practice around that same time, my number one catcher, Randy, had a tantrum when I wanted to keep the catcher's glove (which I owned) with the team equipment, in case he missed a practice or a game. When I refused to give in, he tossed all the catcher's gear onto the field and temporarily quit the team.

And then there was James. He played for the Hamilton Cobras and was one of the more talented players on his team. The problem with him was that if something went wrong, like an umpire calling him out on a questionable strike, he'd have a tantrum and quit. I'll never forget one particular game, when my team played against his team. He had a tantrum and quit; changed his mind and came back the next inning; and had another tantrum and quit. Later, when he did it for a third time, I had to put my BBL owner's hat on and say, "Sorry James. You can come back for the next game, but I've just instituted a new rule: three quits and you're out!"

* * *

On the bright side, my buddies from the Twin Cities Mud Hens were coming to Montana for a weekend tournament. Only about half the team could make it, so I had to recruit some players to become temporary Mud Hens.

The boys from the Twin Cities arrived a day early, and I set up a joint practice between the two Mud Hens teams. Of the players who made the trip, Joel Burns was likely the best. The sinewy, easy-going blond normally played shortstop, but he was also a pitcher with a funky side-armed delivery. We were roughly a half-hour into the practice when Joel wanted to get a feel for the speed of the Montana pitchers and took an at-bat against Bucky, one of my better players. Everyone was having a great time—until a pitch got away from Bucky and nailed Joel in the eye!

Yes, there was blood.

Bucky pulled off his own shirt, wrapped it around Joel's head, and we raced to the hospital!

Joel was conscious, so as some teammates walked him into the nearly empty emergency room waiting area, I hurried to the front desk. "We need a doctor right away!" I said. "My friend got hit in the eye with a baseball."

"Please give me the patient's name and have a seat," said the receptionist. "Someone will be with him shortly."

Ten minutes passed.

I stepped up to the desk. "Excuse me! My friend is bleeding and needs a doctor."

The woman looked up from whatever she was reading and frowned. "A doctor will see him when one becomes available. Please sit down."

Five minutes passed.

I returned to the desk. "Why is this taking so long? You don't exactly appear to be busy."

"We are aware of the situation, sir. Please sit down."

Another five minutes passed.

I stomped up to the receptionist and screamed, "This delay could cost my friend his eye! If you don't get a doctor right now," I pointed, "I'm gonna go back there and find one myself!"

The receptionist stepped into the back and returned a minute later. "Mr. Burns? A doctor will see you now."

Joel followed the receptionist through the double doors.

The rest of us sat quietly in the lobby and waited. The only words came from my shortstop, TJ, who whispered, "Hey, Marty. If I ever get hurt and have to go to the hospital, will you come with me?"

An hour or so later, Joel walked out with a bandage under his eye. Although both eyes were open, his face was swollen, and he was going to have one hell of a shiner.

He held out the bloody T-shirt to Bucky and said, "Here's your shirt back."

"Ahhh . . . No thanks," he replied. "You can keep it."

"Is your eye okay?" I asked.

"Yeah. I got six stitches, just below my eye. The doctor said my sight is fine."

"Oh, thank God!" I said, "Because the only thing that really matters to any of us is . . . can you play tomorrow?"

"It all depends on how much the swelling goes down."

Joel did play the next day. In fact, he pitched. His funky delivery fooled everyone on my team, shutting down the first eight batters in order—with strikeout after strikeout. When I stepped into the box, as the ninth batter, Joel and I smiled at each other. I may have been a blazingly mediocre player, with no natural depth-of-field eyesight, but I had played on the same team with Joel for multiple seasons. I knew exactly what pitch was coming and hammered a double to centerfield!

From there, the game stayed close until Joel tired and moved to shortstop. Then the Victor/Corvallis Mud Hens broke the game open, defeating the Twin Cities Mud Hens 15 to 4. After that game, I switched teams and played with my Minnesota friends. My presence didn't help, but we had lots of fun, losing every game in the tournament.

* * *

For the second year of the Bitterroot Baseball League, I came up with a high-profile promotion to start the season. The University of Montana plays in the NCAA Division 1 for football and basketball. For baseball, they play at the no-scholarship club level. Even so, they had some good players and still wore the venerated Montana Grizzlies jerseys. How would the players from my league, who ranged in age from 19 to 43, stack up against them?

To find out, I arranged a BBL All-stars vs. the Montana Grizzlies game. For that contest, I didn't play or manage. Instead, I was the color commentator for the public television broadcast. I interviewed players before the game and had a blast being on the air again. The Montana Grizzlies prevailed, but the score was close all the way to the end.

From that high point, the second year went straight into the dumpster. The dark side I saw in a few of the guys the previous year spread like a virus, as players started taking themselves and the game too seriously. Every week I had to scramble to find umpires, because the players were treating them so poorly. Even paying the umpires more money did little good. They were miserable—and so was I.

The worst incidents happened in games I wasn't involved in. When a report came back to me that a player screamed at and then threw his bat at an umpire after he struck out, I called that player and kicked him out of the league. He responded by promising to come over to my house to beat me bloody with his bat.

My most reliable umpire, Ian Root, had become my good friend. He took abuse in game after game and kept coming back. When he told me that a catcher on one of the teams had conspired with his pitcher to accidentally-on-purpose miss multiple fastballs to pummel him in the shoulders and chest, I realized that the contingent of poor sportsmen in the league had grown too large for me to control.

Whether played by 13-year-olds or 43-year-olds, baseball is a game, and it's supposed to be fun. While I still believed a majority of the BBL players understood that, I had little doubt that sooner or later the rot of poor sportsmanship was going to cause a serious injury to either a player or an umpire. I didn't want to be responsible for that and had better things to volunteer my time for. Halfway through that second season, I turned the league over to the manager of the Stevensville River Bandits and walked away.

CHAPTER 21

Belligerent Cops

Part of being a liberal in an ultraconservative region of Montana is that if you speak out enough eventually the death threats will come. During my early years in Montana, the reintroduction of wolves was one of the biggest controversies in the state. People on the right were frequently writing into the newspapers, saying things like "The wolves are going to kill our children!"

I wrote a number of science-based letters to the editor and guest columns in favor of the reintroduction and protection of wolves, and after a particularly effective column, my phone rang.

"Hello."

"Is this Marty Essen?"

"Yes it is. Who's calling?"

"You need to shut up!"

"Shut up about what?"

"Don't get smart with me. You know what I'm talking about!"

"I do?"

"Wolves! You get one warning. I don't ever want to see anything from you about wolves in the newspapers again!"

"Or what?"

"You should be shot!"

"Do you think you can intimidate me, motherfucker? Go fuck yourself, asshole. I'll write whatever I fucking want!" I slammed down the receiver.

The right-wing man wasn't too bright. I looked at my caller ID, wrote down his name and phone number, and dialed 911 to report the death threat.

My phone rang a half-hour later. I looked at my caller ID and answered.

"Hello."

"Is this Mr. Essen?"

"Yes, this is Marty."

"This is Deputy Smith*, from the Ravalli County Sheriff's office, responding to the complaint you called in about a death threat."

"Oh, good! Thanks for calling me back."

"I gave Mr. White* a call to get his side of the story. He says you swore at him."

"So! He threatened my life."

"Swearing over public telephone lines is a crime. I also know Mr. White*. He's just a good ol' boy, and I don't think he's serious about shooting you. I tell ya what. I'm going to give you two choices. You can drop your complaint, or, if you insist on pursuing the matter, I will arrest both of you—Mr. White* for his alleged threat, and you for swearing over the phone."

"I don't believe this!" I paused and took a deep breath. "Well, I guess you give me no choice. I drop my complaint."

"I think that's wise, Mr. Essen. Goodbye."

* * *

Deb also had her life threatened, but in a more indirect way. She ran as a Democrat for the Montana House of Representatives in 2004 and for the Montana State Senate in 2006. She didn't have a chance of winning in Ravalli County, but that didn't stop her from making waves.

Later, after Barack Obama became president, Dave Hurtt, from the Bitterroot Valley town of Florence, put an outhouse on a trailer, attached a sign proclaiming it the "Obama Presidential Library," and shot it full of bullet holes. He then parked it outside the state Republican convention, drove it up and down the valley, and entered it in parades.

Inside the outhouse was a bullet-ridden plaque with the names of major Democrats. Near the top-left—inches from a bullet hole—were the names Van Jones, Maxine Waters, and Al Sharpton written at odd angles surrounding the name Deb Essen.

Dave Hurtt declared the outhouse a product of his sense of humor, the Montana Republican Party disavowed the outhouse after people complained, and law enforcement ignored the outhouse altogether. Hurtt's project did make national news, however, and you can still find stories about it on the internet by searching "Dave Hurtt Obama Outhouse." Near the top of those search results, you'll see a *Billings Gazette* article featuring an interview with Deb about the outhouse, and a *Crooks and Liars* article featuring a video that clearly shows the bullet-ridden plaque.

* * *

Over the years, my interactions with law enforcement have been half positive and half negative. I will get to a positive story before the end of this chapter, but first I'm going to share with you two more stories that are negative. Both are from Montana:

Earlier, I mentioned that I go on a bicycle ride each morning. Those rides follow two private dirt roads. Six houses share the road I live on, and several times that number share the road it connects to. In both cases, the residents who use the roads pitch in to share maintenance. Therefore, the amount of trash I find and pick up on my rides always shocks me. Littering is bad enough, but doing so on your own road? That's fucked up!

One morning, on my ride back home, I saw a beer bottle lying at the edge of the Pattersons' property. I picked it up, and since it was wet, I didn't want to throw it into my bike pack. Instead, I pedaled ahead a short distance and dropped it into the garbage can at the end of their long driveway.

Elvira Patterson* stormed out her front door and screamed, "You take that out of my can right now!"

"Hi! I was picking up trash. It was just a beer bottle I found at the edge of your property."

"That can is for *my* garbage only!"

"But—"

"Pull it out, *now!*"

Because of the distance between us, I assumed she couldn't hear me correctly. I stepped off my bike and walked with it partway up her driveway. "I don't think you understand," I said. "It was just an empty beer bottle someone tossed out a car window."

"I don't care!" she screamed. "Take it out!"

"I was doing a good deed! Why are you being such a bitch?"

"I've had quite enough of you, Marty!"

Even though we hadn't met before, I wasn't surprised that she knew who I was. My picture had been in the newspapers a lot, and Deb had mentioned that Elvira slammed the door in her face when she was campaigning for the Montana State Senate.

I wasn't about to lean into a big four-foot-tall garbage can to fish out a beer bottle. Instead, I got back on my bike and pedaled home.

An hour later, I heard a knock. When I opened the door, a young, wide-shouldered sheriff's deputy was standing on my front porch.

"I'm looking for Martin Essen."

"I'm Marty."

"My name is Deputy Hanson*. I'm responding to a complaint from Elvira Patterson*. She claims you threw trash in her garbage can and then swore at her."

"Swore at her?"

He squared his shoulders. "She said you called her a 'bitch.'"

"No I didn't. I asked her *why* she was being a bitch."

"Let's not get into semantics here. You also trespassed on her property."

"I picked up a beer bottle at the edge of her yard."

"You also rode your bike up her driveway. I followed your tire tracks."

I shook my head in disbelief. "I was trying to explain to Mrs. Patterson that I was doing a good deed. She kept screaming at me, so I moved a little closer, hoping she could hear me over her screams."

"That's still trespassing!" he said in a belligerent voice.

"What is it with you? You're talking to me like I'm a criminal!"

"Keep it up, and I will haul you in!"

I pushed out my hands. "Wait a minute! Just listen to me. I was doing a good deed! Every morning I ride my bike to the mailbox and pick up trash on the way back. On today's ride, I spotted a beer bottle on the side of the road—technically on Mrs. Patterson's property. Since it was wet, I tossed it into her garbage can. After that, all I was trying to do was explain to her what happened. She screamed at me, and now you're here interrogating me. Does no good deed go unpunished? Arrest me if you want, but I promise the newspapers will be all over this story."

He retreated a step. "I'm going to speak with Mrs. Patterson again. If I'm not satisfied, I'll be back."

He never returned.

* * *

My next cop confrontation happened when I read a story in the *Ravalli Republic* newspaper about a rattlesnake that showed up in someone's yard in the southern Bitterroot Valley town of Darby. According to the article, the town's long-time marshal, Larry Rose, responded to the call and removed the snake. Rose is one of Montana's bigger-than-life lawmen. He's made national news multiple times, including when he ticketed comedian David Letterman for speeding and when he punched a judge during a city council meeting. He's also made Darby, population 720, infamous for having more surveillance cameras than any other town in Montana. Consequently, locals know never to risk driving through the town at even a mile an hour over the speed limit.

Despite living thirty miles north of Darby, I had met Larry Rose before, and he was certainly aware of my politics. I knew nothing good could come from calling the man. Still, the animal lover in me required that I do it.

I picked up the telephone receiver and chanted to myself, "Don't swear. Don't swear. Don't swear. . . ."

I dialed the number. He answered on the second ring.

"Marshal Rose."

"Hello, Larry. This is Marty Essen."

"Yeah, I know who you are. What can I do for you?"

"I just read the story in the newspaper about the rattlesnake in the woman's yard. I have experience working with snakes and wanted to make sure the snake was okay and offer my help if necessary."

"I took care of it."

"Oh, did you move it to someplace away from people?"

"I skinned it out."

"You what?"

"I skinned it."

"You son of a bitch! Why did you do that?" (*Yeah, so much for my chanting, but it was pure reflex.*)

"It was a rattlesnake."

"And that was enough reason to kill it?"

"Yep."

"What a heartless thing to do! I would have been happy to pick up the snake and move it someplace safe."

"You know what I'm going to do, Marty? I'm going to find ten more rattlesnakes and skin them just for you!"

At that point, I might have unleashed a string of obscenities, but I really can't say.

Because Larry Rose is still the marshal, and I occasionally have to drive through Darby.

* * *

Finally, in the interest of fairness, I'm going to share with you my favorite good cop story. This one comes from 2013, when I was on a college speaking tour. (I'll cover my college speaking later.) I had flown from Cincinnati to Miami for a show at St. Thomas University the next day. When I checked into my hotel and asked where I could buy a bottle of wine, the front desk clerk told me there was a CVS store a mile up the road, on the right.

I returned to my car and had only traveled a block before I spotted a seafood restaurant that looked promising. Since it was already getting late, and I was starving, I pulled in for dinner. I avoid chain restaurants whenever possible, and this local restaurant served me delicious crab cakes, which I washed down with their drink special—a Long Island iced tea.

Once back on the road, I drove a little way and started searching for the CVS. Businesses of all types lined the busy four-lane road, and I slowed down a few times when passing strip malls where the CVS could be located.

Lights flashed in my rearview mirror! I pulled to the right so the police car could pass. Instead, it stayed on my tail. "Oh, shit!" I thought.

I eased forward, turned into a dark parking lot, and stopped. Two police cars pinned me in—spotlights on my face!

When one of the police officers got out of his car, I lowered my window and put my hands on the steering wheel, so he could see them.

"Good evening sir. Can I see your license, registration, and proof of insurance?"

"Sure. This is a rental car, but the other two items are in my back pocket. I'm going to reach for them now."

When he nodded, I pulled out my wallet and handed him my license and insurance card. He looked at them and said, "We pulled you over because you were driving erratically."

"Oh! That's because I was looking for the CVS. The clerk at the Holiday Inn down the street said there was one nearby."

"Sir, have you been drinking?"

"I had one drink with my dinner. Hold on. I'm going to get my receipt." I fished the receipt out of my wallet and handed it to the officer. "See, it says right there—one drink."

He handed the receipt and insurance card back to me but held onto my license. "Stay here, while I run this."

As the officer ran my license, thoughts raced through my head: "How many shots of alcohol are in a Long Island ice tea? Could I be legally drunk? What if he detains me and I can't make my gig tomorrow? What if I have to fly all the way back from Montana for a court date? This could be expensive. I'm fucked!"

The officer returned and said, "Step out of the car, please."

I did as he requested.

"I want you to walk a few steps forward, in a straight line."

I did so, and though I felt like I walked straight, I also felt like the Long Island ice tea had chosen that very moment to kick me in the head.

"Stand still," he said. "I'm going to shine a light into your eyes."

"Oh, fuck!" I thought. "Maybe I didn't walk so straight after all. I can really feel that ice tea."

The officer looked at me with a confused expression. He called the officer over from the other car, and he also looked into my eyes. They stepped back and spoke quietly to one another.

When they turned back to me, the first officer said, "We're going to give you a breathalyzer."

While the second officer retrieved the breathalyzer from his car, the first officer said, "Don't worry. If you don't pass, I'm not gonna arrest you. I'll just call a cab to take you back to your hotel."

"Thank you," I said.

The second officer returned, and I did the blowy thing into the tube. He looked at the readout and showed it to the first officer. They both laughed.

The first officer flashed me a smile and said, "I was a little worried when I looked into your eyes, but you weren't even close! Have a good night, sir."

"Good night, sir," the second officer said.

"The same to both of you," I said.

The first officer took a step before leaning back. "The CVS is just up the road, on your right. You can't miss it."

As the two police cars pulled out of the parking lot, I speculated about the eye test. Despite my minor depth of field problem, my eyes look perfectly normal. The only thing I could think of was that my unusual contact lens set-up had fooled the officers. I had worn contact lenses since the early 1990s, but as I grew older, I started having difficulty seeing up-close with both of them in and switched to wearing just one contact lens. I wear the contact in my left eye, for distance, and go naked in the right, for reading. It took me a few days to feel comfortable using my eyes independently that way, but now I joke that I have chameleon eyes.

No matter what triggered their caution, those two men in blue were among the most polite police officers I'd ever met. They weren't there to intimidate me or to raise their arrest count. Instead, they were simply doing their job of protecting others from a possible drunk driver. That I can respect.

CHAPTER 22

I Don't Play Well With Others

Post Bitterroot Baseball League, I interacted with Montanans in different ways. My newspaper guest columns and letters to the editor continued to shake things up. In fact, as I learned later from *Ravalli Republic* editor, Wayne Adair, local Republicans had tried to get me banned from that newspaper's editorial page, and he had to fight for me. On the other side, the chairwoman of the Ravalli County Democratic Central Committee (RCDCC) admired my opinion pieces and invited me to attend one of their meetings.

I took her up on the offer, and ended up being elected to the board of directors at that first meeting. The timing was such that the election for the chair position was two meetings after that, and the chairwoman was retiring. Someone nominated me, and the next thing I knew I was elected as chairman of the RCDCC. During my 2000–2002 term, Ian Root, my umpire friend from the Bitterroot Baseball League, served as my secretary/treasurer, and together we pushed the local party as far to the left as we could.

The best part of being involved with the Democrats was all the politicians I got to know. Montana is a small-population state, but for some reason its politicians gain an extraordinary amount of national attention.

Brian Schweitzer is one of those nationally famous politicians. I first worked with him when he was an unknown running for the U.S. Senate—inviting him to speak at my initial RCDCC dinner and setting up an interview for him with the *Ravalli Republic.* If you're unfamil-iar with Brian, he eventually became Montana's two-term governor (2005–2013), and his over-the-top personality (he used to veto bills with a branding iron) garnered him a prime speaking spot at the 2008 Demo-cratic National Convention and appearances all over national television.

My favorite Brian Schweitzer story took place in 2009. Deb was then the vice-chairwoman of the RCDCC, and she worked through former Democratic congressman Pat Williams to get a signed copy of Hillary Rodham Clinton's book, *It Takes a Village,* for a fundraiser.

Schweitzer attended that fundraiser specifically to help auction off items. He knew me not only from my term as the RCDCC chairman, but also from when I presented him with a copy of my first book, *Cool Creatures, Hot Planet: Exploring the Seven Continents,* at a different fund-raiser. He also knew Deb and campaigned for her when she ran for the Montana State Senate.

With that in mind, Schweitzer was gleefully determined to make sure I bought Hillary Clinton's book. Here's how that auction went, minus much of the auctioneer chant, which the governor had perfected:

Governor Schweitzer: "For our final item tonight, we have a signed copy of *It Takes a Village* from former first lady, U.S. senator, and current secretary of state Hillary Clinton." He paused to look at me. "Marty. Would you like to start the bidding at fifty dollars?"

Me: "Here!"

Governor Schweitzer: "Do I hear one hundred dollars?"

Another bidder: "Here!"

Governor Schweitzer turns back to me: "Marty. Do I hear one-fifty?"

Me, a little more reluctantly: "Here."

Governor Schweitzer: "Do I hear two hundred? Two hundred! Two Hundred! Anybody? Two hundred?"

Another bidder: "Here!"

Governor Schweitzer: "Marty! Marty! Marty! Do I hear two-fifty? Two-fifty! Two-fifty!"

Deb and I look at each other. She grins and shrugs.

I turn back to the stage and call out, "Here!"

Sure, as an author, I collect autographed books, with a signed Kurt Vonnegut being one of my more prized possessions. Therefore, I was interested in the Clinton book, and was initially willing to bid up to two hundred dollars. But how could I say "no" to the Governor of Montana in a room full of people?

Once we passed three hundred dollars, Deb echoed my thoughts by whispering to me, "It's only money."

From that point on, all limits were off. I sheepishly raised my hand and said, "Here," every time the governor called out my name.

When the bidding got down to just me and one other bidder, that person soon realized that no matter what he bid, I was going to beat it. He sadistically continued for a few more rounds just to make more money for the Democrats.

I don't remember exactly what I paid for the book. All I remember was that it hurt a lot. At least the money went for a good cause. Looking back at it now, I prize the story of how I acquired the book even more than I do the book itself.

* * *

Two other notable Democrats I worked with were Max Baucus and Steve Bullock. Senator Baucus was one of the architects behind the Affordable Care Act (Obamacare) and later was the U.S. ambassador to China. He spoke at every RCDCC dinner I hosted.

Steve Bullock succeeded Brian Schweitzer as Montana's governor and later became a candidate for president of the United States. Back in 2000, he sat facing me, six feet away, as I attempted to give a comedy speech to open up an RCDCC dinner. That was before I became an accomplished public speaker, and I was as nervous as hell. I still remember Bullock looking me in the eyes to give me encouragement as I totally blew my routine.

* * *

Jon Tester burst onto the national scene when he became a U.S. senator in 2007. Not only is he on numerous important Senate committees, but he's also a frequent guest on programs, including *Real Time with Bill Maher* and *The Rachel Maddow Show*. Tester, like Schweitzer and Baucus, amazes me by his ability to remember names and faces. In 2006, when Deb was running for the Montana State Senate and he was running for the U.S. Senate, the two participated in a few campaign events together. Years later, Tester can still pick Deb out of a crowd to give her a great big hug.

I don't know Senator Tester as well as Deb does, but I will always be thankful for the time he went to bat for me. The FCC had fined Essen Communications Corporation twenty thousand dollars. It was the most ridiculous fine imaginable! The FCC had set up a new filing requirement for a Customer Proprietary Network Information form, but did a poor job of announcing the requirement and didn't even supply the actual form. Instead, the commission required telecommunications companies to make up their own forms. Besides my company, a large number of small to medium-sized companies—who couldn't afford on-staff attorneys to keep track of everything the FCC did—were hit with similar fines for failing to file the form they knew nothing about. Shortly after Tester wrote a letter to the FCC on my company's behalf, the commission issued a mea culpa and dropped not only my fine but the fines they levied on others as well.

* * *

Although I initially enjoyed chairing the RCDCC, I eventually grew tired of the hassle. In general, Montana Democrats are a moderately conservative bunch. This is especially true in Ravalli County. A memorable argument among the board of directors happened when we planned our booth for the Ravalli County Fair. Every year, the Democrats held a raffle to attract people to their booth, and this time several on the board wanted that raffle item to be a rifle. Ian and I were vehemently opposed to giving away a gun on both moral and liability grounds. The fight grew nasty, and when we prevailed by a single vote, the person who had proposed the gun raffle berated us and resigned from the board. When my two-year term expired, I decided not to run again.

Shortly thereafter, a friend talked me into joining Footloose Montana, a group dedicated to passing a statewide animal trapping ban. Even though I was enthusiastic about the cause, I joined only after making it clear that I was doing so as a worker bee, and that I had no interest in leading the group.

Eighteen months later, I resigned as the president of Footloose Montana. Like the meetings I led for the RCDCC, those I led for Footloose sometimes grew contentious but mostly grew tedious. For me, the best way to learn not to like someone is to work on a committee with that person.

At that point, I realized that when it came to political issues I was passionate about, I didn't play well with others. I hated committees, and they were a major reason why I would never run for any political office. I work much better alone. And what could be more solitary than using my skills as a writer to advocate for social and environmental change?

CHAPTER 23

You Can't Have Too Many Careers

On January 20, 2001, George W. Bush's Inauguration Day, Deb and I left the country on our first real vacation in eight years. Sure, some could argue that living in Montana is a nonstop vacation, but from the moment we decided to move there, we had to work our asses off. First, we needed to make enough money to afford to build our dream house; then we had to establish ourselves in our new state.

Not everything was work, of course. Beginning with our second year in Montana, we took multiple long weekends in the summer to rent Forest Service cabins or go hiking. Even when we didn't take a Friday off, we'd occasionally cut out of work early, toss our inflatable kayaks into the truck, and float the Bitterroot River.

Still, there's nothing quite like an entire week off without the phone or the internet. For that, we headed to the tiny Central American country of Belize. My attraction to Belize originated back in Minneapolis, when a neighbor who was a photographer showed me stunning images he had captured while visiting the country. I also had a lifelong interest in tropical wildlife—especially snakes—since I had two boa constrictors as a child.

Deb and I had a delightful time in Belize, splitting our vacation between the Turneffe Islands, thirty miles off the coast, and the moist tropical forest on the far western side. We didn't see any snakes, but butterflies, birds, and iguanas were plentiful.

Upon returning to the United States, we found ourselves eager for international travel that was even more exotic and soon planned a trip deep into the Amazon Rainforest of Peru.

Before departing for the Amazon, however, we had an anniversary to celebrate. I had formed Essen Communications Corporation (originally Essen Communications Group) in mid-1991, and one of the keys to successful marketing is to never let a promotion opportunity pass you by. I alerted the media: "ECC is ten years old!"

At the time, I had no idea that I was about to experience my biggest life-changing event since Deb walked into National Talent Associates in 1984. This time it was Rod Daniels, of the *Ravalli Republic*, who walked into my office.

Rod had stopped by to interview me for a front-page story he was writing about my company. His story turned out wonderful, focusing on how ECC had rapidly become one of the most successful independent local phone companies in Montana. But more important than his story was how we said goodbye after the interview.

I walked him to the door, shook his hand, and said, "I'll see ya later. Deb and I are heading to the Amazon Rainforest next week."

Rod's eyes grew wide, and he said, "Really? You should write a story about it for my newspaper."

If it weren't for that short exchange, you almost certainly wouldn't be reading this book. When I returned from the Amazon, I wrote a feature story about our adventures that ran in both the *Ravalli Republic* and the *Missoulian* newspapers. In the weeks that followed, whenever I was out in public, people would recognize me from my author photo and tell me how much they enjoyed what I wrote. Local schools also called to request that I come to talk about my adventures.

* * *

A trip to Australia followed, and just as I had done previously, I wrote another feature newspaper article. When that article received a similar positive response, I started thinking, "What if Deb and I traveled to all seven continents, and I wrote a book about it?" I did some research and learned that at that moment fewer than one hundred thousand people in the history of the world had ever stepped onto Antarctica. That meant that far fewer than one hundred thousand had traveled to all seven continents. Next, I looked for books written by people who had traveled to all the continents. When I found a couple of those, I narrowed the subject to travel to every continent in search of rare and interesting wildlife. There was nothing. I had my topic!

Deb and I kept going, ultimately traveling to all seven continents and Central America over a three-and-a-half-year period. The stories and photos from our travels not only became my first book, *Cool Creatures, Hot Planet: Exploring the Seven Continents,* but they also became my live college show, *Around the World in 90 Minutes.* The book sold out its initial printing and won six national awards. The college show did even better. As I type this, I have performed *Around the World in 90 Minutes* at hundreds of colleges in forty-five states. Since the colleges pay me good money for the shows, and the students love them, I see no reason to stop—unless for some reason I become physically unable to perform them. In keeping with my desire for positive change, both projects use adventure travel as a way to advocate for protecting the environment and endangered species.

I will return to the subject of writing the book and developing and performing the show later, but in an effort to cover events in a somewhat linear fashion, I'm going to spend the next five chapters discussing our travels.

CHAPTER 24

Lizards Think I'm Ugly

As I sat in front of my computer, trying to come up with a way to write about what happened during Deb's and my epic seven-continents adventure that was different from what I wrote in *Cool Creatures, Hot Planet: Exploring the Seven Continents,* it occurred to me that it's impossible for me to plagiarize myself. After all, I wrote the words, and I own the copyright. Therefore, to give you a taste of our adventures, I'm going to borrow bits and pieces from that book and add some new observations along the way. *Cool Creatures, Hot Planet* came in at 178,362 words, which is roughly twice the length of the book you have in your hands now. If you want the complete story, *Cool Creatures, Hot Planet* is still available in e-book and paperback formats.

With that in mind, I'm going to begin with the first part of the Amazon chapter from that book, because even years later, it still serves as a good introduction:

After we arrived home from Belize, I was still feeling discouraged about my failure to find a snake. I felt as if I were a modern day Saint Patrick who had rid the entire country of snakes. Wait a minute . . . that was it. I was Saint Martin of Belize! Soon statues of me would be going up all over the country, parades would be held in my honor, a day would be named after me, Belikin would brew a special beer. . . .

I reveled in my new sainthood for a while before realizing that being a living saint would be a lot of work. First, my followers would want me to bless everything; then they'd want more miracles. Who wants to live under that sort of pressure? I'd rather find a boa constrictor or a fer-de-lance anyway. And you know, as soon as I went somewhere and found a snake, I'd be promptly "decanonized."

Of all the places in the world to look for snakes, I couldn't think of anywhere I'd have a better chance for success than the Amazon River and rainforest region of Peru. I just needed to convince my wife to go with me.

Deb and I had been married for seventeen years, yet as international travel partners we were newlyweds. Even though I knew her outgoing personality well, I wouldn't fully appreciate her bravery until further into our travels. Therefore, after joining her on the couch in our living room, I broached the subject tentatively, half expecting her to declare that such a trip would give her the creeps. To my surprise she replied, "I'll go with you to Peru, if you promise to go with me to Australia after that."

I asked for one trip and received two instead. Did I marry a great woman, or what? Perhaps she was the saint, not me. We were headed for Peru, a country with far too many snakes for either of us to rid in a single visit.

While the decision to travel to the Amazon happened quickly, it was actually the culmination of a dream hatched back in grade school when I wanted to become a herpetologist. In my mind, such a journey was like a religious pilgrimage to a holy site—a virtual requirement for anyone who loves herpetofauna. Although my career plans changed when I grew older, my Amazon dream would now become a reality.

From sixteenth-century Spanish explorer Francisco de Orellana's claims of a female warrior race to tales of poisonous snakes, man-eating piranhas, huge spiders, tropical diseases, and headhunters, no place on Earth surpasses the Amazon for mystery and perceived danger. When I informed family and friends of our travel plans, most thought we were insane. My mother burst into tears, and my attorney insisted we immediately draw up our wills. While the adult in me was touched by their concern, my evil inner child couldn't help blurting out, "And my goal is to photograph a fer-de-lance, up close!"

* * *

I won't quote any further from my Amazon chapter, but I will say that I did get to photograph a fer-de-lance up close. Although it's not the most venomous snake in the Western Hemisphere, many consider it to be the hemisphere's deadliest snake. That's because their markings make them difficult to spot on the forest floor, and when people step on them, the snakes have little choice but to bite. The fer-de-lance I photographed was small and never even opened its mouth.

A bullet ant—famous for being the insect with the most painful sting in the world—made up for the fer-de-lance's lack of aggression by nailing me in the calf. For twenty-four hours afterward, my calf felt like it was going to explode from all the pressure that built up from the venom injected by the sting. Then the pain went away, leaving me with a big red welt that lasted for about a month.

In addition to looking for rare and interesting wildlife on all seven continents, the other theme of Deb's and my travels was to go to out-of-the-way places, where tourists seldom go. For instance, in Australia we rented a cabin from two wildlife rehabilitators in the tiny Outback town of Chillagoe. There we were able to feed a baby wallaroo and a juvenile wallaby and hold a frogmouth bird. Later we headed up the Queensland coast to Cape Tribulation, where we visited a rehabilitation center for bats and got to feed and hold a black flying fox. We also enjoyed multiple hikes in the rainforest and found a wide variety of snakes, lizards, and frogs.

My wife and I have many common interests, but one thing she does that I don't do is scuba dive. Consequently, my favorite Australian adventure took place while she was away, scuba diving the Great Barrier Reef. Here's what happened:

I had decided to hike up every river within a ten-mile stretch of Queensland coast. Since all the rivers dropped down from the mountains, I only hiked partway up each one. Whenever a climb grew too steep, or some obstruction prevented me from going farther, I would retreat to a dirt road near the coast and proceed to the next river.

I reached Emmagen Creek late that afternoon. The twenty-five-foot-wide river was the largest in the area, and bordering it was a broad, hard dirt bank that gave way to thick rainforest. Before heading upriver, I hiked to the mouth to check for crocodiles. When none were in sight, I reversed course and strolled along the riverbank. I hadn't gone far when I heard something large rustling across the leaf litter. It was heading toward me. A crocodile? The last place I wanted to be was between a croc and the river!

I froze and listened. Whatever it was, it was just inside the forest, low to the ground, and about fifty feet ahead of me. I could hear what sounded like a tail sweeping and see ferns moving, ever so slightly. Then I caught a glimpse of its tapered snout. It wasn't a croc. But what was it?

When the five-foot-long animal stepped into the open, I could see dark-gray beady scales, cream-colored spots, and raptor-like claws. Folds in her thick skin gave her an armored dinosaur-like appearance. Now I recognized her. She was a lace monitor—a lizard closely related to the Komodo dragon.

Though I knew what she was, I knew nothing about her natural history or temperament. If I startled her, would she fight or flee? I got down on my hands and knees, so as not to appear threatening, and snapped some photos.

I expected her to turn away at any moment, but instead she continued toward me. Her movements were slow, and she stopped often to search for food in holes and hollow logs. I decided to mimic her movements and crawl toward her.

As the gap closed between us, our eyes met several times. Soon we were less than twenty feet apart. I was excited and a bit nervous. Never before had a wild animal reacted to me in such a way. At ten feet, I stopped crawling to let the monitor decide how close we'd get. I was too big for her to consider me prey. She wasn't confusing me for another monitor, was she? If so, did she think of me as competition or a prospective mate? I quickly purged the last possibility from my mind. That a large lizard might consider me attractive wasn't exactly an ego boost.

When only a few feet separated us, the monitor paused and flicked out her tongue as if she were saying, "You are the ugliest lizard I've ever seen!"

She turned and headed in the opposite direction.

Our encounter could have ended there, but when would I ever get the chance to be a giant lizard again? I decided to follow. For the next fifteen minutes or so, the monitor let me share her world as she continued searching for food.

Every once in a while I'd whistle to get her attention, and she'd look over her shoulder and flick out her tongue, as if saying, "Nah. . . . You're still ugly!"

She had an aura of intelligence that I'd never sensed in a lizard before. In fact, if I were able to follow her long enough, I could have watched her do something truly amazing: manipulate another species into protecting her eggs.

She'd accomplish this by ripping open a termite mound with her claws and then depositing her eggs in the hole. When the termites repaired the damage, they'd seal her eggs inside, creating the perfect incubator. Later—and this part is speculative—she'd return to extract her hatchlings.

Some people may call the monitor's maternal behavior "instinct," but if humans could do something comparable—perhaps convince another species to provide free, reliable daycare for our children during the terrible twos stage—we'd think we were pretty smart.

Eventually the monitor had enough of me and jumped into the river.

At that point, I decided, "Nah. . . . I don't want to be a giant lizard anymore!" and that was the end of our relationship.

* * *

Three years later, in 2005, Australian scientist Bryan Fry announced a new discovery—lace monitors are venomous! They aren't deadly to humans, but that such a big and common species had escaped venomous status for so long was truly surprising.

CHAPTER 25

The Ends of the World

For our North America adventure, we took our dogs, Kate and Annie, on a road trip to Inuvik, Northwest Territories. That drive to the top of Canada and back was longer than a drive from Los Angeles to New York City and back. I still get warm feelings of contentment when I reminisce about that trip and all the once-in-a-lifetime experiences we enjoyed. Included among those experiences were hiking with the Porcupine caribou migration and a late-night visit from wolves that howled around our tent. Our most memorable adventure occurred on a remote dirt road, in the Yukon Territory. Here's what happened:

We continued west and once again had the road to ourselves. I was enjoying the fall colors on a long straightaway when I noticed an animal standing in the middle of the road. "Is that a dog?" I asked.

"How could a dog get out here?" Deb said.

"Maybe someone dumped it."

"No, I think it's a bear."

I slowed the truck as we neared. The animal dashed into the woods.

"It's a wolf!" we yelled in unison.

What threw us off was that this wolf didn't have the familiar salt-and-pepper fur with a hint of brown. Instead, it was black.

Wolves are one of my favorite animals. They're highly intelligent, mysteriously secretive, and greatly misunderstood. When we were leaving Montana, I mentioned to Deb that seeing wolves up close during the day and hearing them howl near our tent at night were among the experiences I most desired on our trip. She wholeheartedly concurred.

I pulled the truck even with where the wolf had entered the woods, hoping to catch another glimpse.

Nothing.

The forest on both sides of the road was thick. The wolf could have been watching us from ten feet away, and we wouldn't have seen it. My heart sank. While I had technically achieved my desired wolf sighting, I had envisioned the experience lasting longer.

Since wolves travel in packs, I eased the truck forward while watching the road in my rearview mirror. "There's another wolf!" I shouted.

"Where?" Deb asked.

"She crossed right behind us—a gray one."

"Ah, I missed her!"

"If there are two, there should be more. I'm gonna drive down the road a bit and park."

I proceeded about a hundred feet and U-turned to face where the wolves had been. "Where's my camera?" I asked.

"Right here," Deb said, handing it to me.

"Damn! Wrong lens." I sifted through my daypack until finding my largest zoom lens. When not in a hurry, I can switch lenses instantly. Now, I fumbled about, nearly breaking my camera in the process.

Finally successful, I turned to my wife and asked, "Are you coming?"

"No, I'll wait for you here."

"Okay, keep the dogs from barking if you can."

I opened the door as quietly as possible.

Ding! Ding! Ding! Ding!

I snatched the keys from the ignition and stuffed them into my pocket.

Between the ignition alarm and the time lost changing lenses, my klutziness had likely cost me the opportunity to see another wolf. Still, on the slim chance the pack wasn't already halfway to the Arctic Circle, I carefully shut the door and tiptoed down the center of the road.

With each step, I scanned the forest for movement and listened for a crackle or a snap. Stillness and silence prevailed. I knew wolf attacks on people were grossly blown out of proportion, but at 130 feet from the truck I began to wonder, "Should I feel uneasy?"

Oooooooooooooo. A wolf howled! I spun toward the sound but saw only a wall of trees. Wherever the wolf was, it was close, very close.

Ooooooooooooo. The second howl came from the opposite direction. I spun again and gazed into the shadowy forest.

Ooooooooooooo. Ooooooooooooo. Ooooooooooooo. The rest of the pack joined in.

I was surrounded!

When I turned to face Deb, sunlight glared back at me from the windshield. While I couldn't see either my wife or the wolves, I knew they could see me just fine. Whether I should feel uneasy was no longer a question. I felt exhilarated!

Ooooooooooooo. I cupped my hand to my left ear and leaned toward the howl.

Ooooooooooooo. I cupped my hand to my right ear and leaned again.

Suddenly I was the conductor of an all-wolf opera, leaning with each successive howl. Left! Right! Together! At least six wolves sang solos, and when they sang as a chorus, their howls blended into an eerie song.

Thoughts whisked through my head as I conducted: Right! "This is so cool!" Forward! "I can't believe how loud they are." Left! "Why hasn't Deb come out to join me?" Together!—

The truck door popped open and Deb yelled, "Behind you!"

I pivoted just in time to see the black wolf dart down the road, away from me, and cut left toward the forest. I lifted my camera to locate him in the viewfinder.

Nothing.

I lowered my camera and spotted him again. Instead of disappearing into the woods, he had changed his course and was running along the inner edge of the trees—toward me!

I raised my camera. He was at 120 feet and closing fast! Each time I glimpsed him in the viewfinder a tree promptly obstructed my shot. I chanced a look to the side. He was headed toward an opening. I'd have the perfect shot! My finger tensed on the shutter button. . . .

He was gone!

Though I'd lost the photo opportunity, it was a minor disappointment compared to the thrill of being so close to the pack. I jogged back to the truck to share the experience with Deb.

"Couldn't you see me?" she asked as I climbed into the cab.

"No, all I could see was sunshine reflecting off the windshield."

"The wolf was standing *directly* behind you! I kept waving to get your attention. I knew if I opened the door I'd frighten him, and I couldn't roll down the windows because the truck was off and you had the keys."

"How close was he?"

"Oh, he was close—about fifteen feet."

"Wow! How long was he there?"

"At least twenty seconds. He stood with his tail held low, staring at you curiously."

Now my feelings were truly mixed. Although I had just enjoyed a once-in-a-lifetime experience, I had not only failed to get a wolf on film, but I had also missed out on a possible extended close-range encounter. What would the wolf have done if I had slowly turned around before Deb's shout frightened him? He wasn't being aggressive.

In less than fifteen minutes, I had seen either two or three wolves, depending on whether I had seen two individual black wolves or the same one twice. Though the howling had ceased, and the chances of seeing another wolf were slim, I felt like an addict. Just one more hit of *Canis lupus* and I'd have my fix.

Since the last howl came from behind the truck, I slipped back out of the cab and walked in that direction. Fifty feet later, I stopped and waited. The forest was silent. Eventually I gave up and turned to walk back toward—another wolf!

The gray and white beauty was crossing the road near where I had been conducting the opera of howls. I snapped a quick photo before she vanished. Because of distance and camera shake, I knew my shot would be blurry, but at least I had something.

Now, if I could just get a *close up* wolf photo, I'd have my fix. . . .

* * *

Antarctica was supposed to be our final adventure. When Deb and I saw magazine advertisements listing Antarctica trips from $8,000 to $15,000 per person, we agreed that before forking over that kind of money we had to survive the other six continents first.

In July 2002, a year before we even expected to begin planning an Antarctica trip, my curiosity led me to do some preliminary internet research. Knowledge, after all, is a good thing. Right?

First, I learned that the best way to get from the United States to Antarctica was to fly to Ushuaia, Tierra del Fuego, Argentina, and sail the rest of the way by ship. Because of Antarctica's extreme weather, most commercial ships restricted their voyages to late November through early March (essentially the Southern Hemisphere's summer).

Next, I wanted to see if we could reach Antarctica for less than the cost of an automobile. Within a few clicks, I found prices lower than in the magazine ads, and from there, I narrowed my search to Polar Cruises, a firm out of Oregon.

Although I intended to do a more thorough search later, I dialed the number for Polar Cruises and reached the owner, Lynn Cross. I expected Lynn to be a typical brochure-quoting travel agent and was surprised to learn she had worked for six years on Antarctica-bound vessels. Not only did she have firsthand answers for all my questions, she also had access to multiple ships ranging in capacity from 49 to 150 passengers. The smaller ships, which would provide more intimate wildlife viewing, piqued my interest.

Near the end of our conversation, I asked, "If I decide to do this, how far should I book in advance?"

"Most people make reservations at least a year ahead," she said. "This coming season is already pretty much booked up."

"Is there anything left on the smaller ships?"

"That depends. Would you want a cabin with two or three berths?"

"I'll be traveling with my wife, so I'd need a double."

"As of two days ago the *Professor Multanovskiy*, a forty-nine-passenger ship, had one double cabin left in February. But I'm not sure if it's still available."

Even though she was telling the truth (she couldn't know for sure because other agencies also booked the ship), she had used the classic "limited availability" sales close.

"Can you check for me?"

"One moment, please." She put me on hold for a few minutes before returning to say, "Yes, it's still available."

"Great. I'll take it."

Just because a close is a classic doesn't mean it's no longer effective.

After giving Lynn my address and credit card number, I hung up, shocked yet excited by what had transpired. I ran upstairs to find my wife.

"Deb! Guess where we're going in February."

"Where?"

"Antarctica! I booked the only cabin left on the ship, and it was a *really* good deal."

"You did what!" Her initial reaction told me I was in trouble. Then she cracked a smile and started laughing.

You're probably wondering, so I'll tell: our voyage on the *Professor Multanovskiy* cost $4,495 per person, plus airfare. Since rooms with private baths ranged from $5,295 to $6,395 per person, we would be "roughing it" on the deck with shared bathrooms. Where we stayed on the ship wasn't a concern for us, however. As Deb pointed out, "We didn't have a problem sharing bathrooms on our Amazon trip. Why would this be any different?"

Our Antarctica trip turned out to be worth every penny. The wildlife was amazing, and the scenery was stunning. People from fourteen different countries also contributed greatly to the experience. In fact, we continue to stay in contact with several of them, and one, Laurel Pfund, became our travel partner. Following Antarctica, Laurel joined us for a second trip to the Amazon Rainforest, and after that, she joined us on a trip to the Arctic, which I featured in my second book, *Endangered Edens: Exploring the Arctic National Wildlife Refuge, Costa Rica, the Everglades, and Puerto Rico*.

Every moment of traveling to and from Antarctica was a moment to treasure. Well, except for the getting seasick part. The animal encounters were particularly special. Even though rules prevented us from approaching any animal closer than fifteen feet, the animals didn't have any rules and could approach us as close as they wanted to—and they did!

Adorable gentoo penguin chicks waddled up to us to pull on our shoelaces, elephant seals roared from their wallows, and fur seals showed off in vigorous sparring matches. Best of all were the humpback whales that played with us when we were in Zodiacs (rubber rafts) along Antarctica's coast. They'd surface two hundred feet away and come right at us, as if they were going to knock us into the water. Then, at the last moment, they'd dive underneath us and surface on the other side with a great big blow! The control they had over their forty-five-foot-long bodies was simply amazing.

CHAPTER 26

The Headhunters' Shortcut

Another theme of our seven continents of adventures was traveling during wartime. Our trip to Belize began on George W. Bush's Inauguration Day; we left for Antarctica on the day after the world's largest anti-war protests; we landed in Malaysia (a Muslim country) on the day after U.S. soldiers tore down Saddam Hussein's statue, and we traveled through France shortly after Republicans in congress renamed French fries "freedom fries" and French toast "freedom toast" in their cafeterias to insult France for not supporting America in the Iraq War. All of that led to many memorable human encounters. Most commonly, however, was that people all over the world treated Deb and me kindly, and they had no problem separating Americans, whom they liked, from George W. Bush, whom they despised.

* * *

For our Asia trip, we spent much of our time in the rainforest of Malaysian Borneo. There we observed orangutans and saw spectacular wildlife found nowhere else. Our biggest adventure happened while backpacking with the Iban tribe. At one time, the Iban were headhunters. Though that activity was in their past, much of their territory was still unexplored by non-native people. In fact, Deb and I had the privilege of being only the third outsiders to backpack their newly opened Red Ape Trail.

On that backpacking trip, our guide, Bayang, had to abandon us deep in the mountainous rainforest after Jonathan, Luang, and Ugan from the Iban tribe tracked us down with news that his father had died. That left us with three Iban we didn't know and Blonsai, who had started out with us but didn't speak English. Our new escorts were armed with machetes and a rifle, making our hand-over to them nerve-racking to say the least.

I was already exhausted from hiking in rivers and trudging up mountains in the heat and humidity, so when our new situation encouraged my mind to veer off into irrational thoughts, it was all too happy to comply: "Were the Iban truly a *reformed* headhunting tribe? Had they ever seen a blond-haired woman before? Surely Deb's head would be a rare and cherished prize!"

Because you are reading this now, you know we survived with our heads attached. That didn't prevent us from having some narrow escapes, however.

The following story takes place after a day and a half of backpacking with Bayang, his departure, and several more hours of backpacking with our new escorts. Jonathan, the leader, was the only Iban who spoke English, and Ugan had mysteriously disappeared:

Finally! We arrived at our destination for the evening. The camp was a crude hunting shelter the Iban had built a few months earlier. Although it didn't have walls, the thatched roof supported by wooden poles would provide a dry place to sleep.

The mystery of what happened to Ugan was solved. While I was imagining him sinisterly hiding in the trees with his finger on the trigger, he was actually hurrying ahead to get an early start on dinner.

Tonight's meal was chicken chunks (chopped into small pieces, bones and all), rainforest plants, and rice. This was a repeat of our earlier meals, which the Iban cooked inside a thick section of bamboo. After eating all we could, that same piece of bamboo would become "jungle-Tupperware." Whoever was in charge of cooking would stuff all the leftovers back inside, plug the ends with leaves, and carry it along to reheat over a fire at the next stop.

The Iban cook their chicken with a pungent curry. At lunchtime, I had been able to handle the seasoning okay, but this time it made me feel nauseated after a few bites. I had to force myself to eat enough to keep up my energy. Deb, on the other hand, thought the chicken tasted just fine.

Despite my lack of appetite, the meal provided an opportunity to have a relaxed conversation with our new guide. When Jonathan filled my cup with hot tea, I asked him, "How did you ever find us so deep in the jungle?"

"We knew when you started hiking and how far you should have traveled. Cut through jungle to where we thought you'd be."

"Did it take you long to find us?"

"No. Found you right away."

"Amazing!"

Then Jonathan had a question for me: "What is itinerary?"

"What do you mean?" I asked.

"Where we supposed to take you?"

His question surprised me. How could our guide not know where we were going? I relayed what Bayang had told me earlier: "We're supposed to hike all day tomorrow and camp by a river. After that we have a half-day hike to a longhouse."

"That is Nanga Sumpa—my longhouse," he said. "I guess your itinerary work, but there is festival at Nanga Sumpa in two days you would enjoy very much. Miss most of festival with your schedule. If we hike longer tomorrow, we reach longhouse by dark."

Although I suspected Jonathan was more interested in the festival for himself than for either Deb or me, reaching the longhouse early did have an appeal. I conferred with my wife before saying, "We're willing to try to make it to your longhouse tomorrow, as long as we have the option of staying one more night in the jungle if we get too tired."

"No problem," he said.

After dinner, Jonathan and the others went to work constructing hammocks. When I learned we were going to sleep in hammocks, I expected the kind that swing on ropes between trees. Instead, these were like stretchers. The Iban assembled them by stringing pre-sewn fabric between two delimbed tree trunks and then resting each trunk end horizontally on a large perpendicular log. To complete the project, they placed Deb's and my hammocks side by side and hung a mosquito net over the top.

The white netting reminded me of a wedding veil. "Look honey," I said, "they've prepared the bridal suite for us!"

When Deb and I turned in for the night, the Iban slept next to us in similar hammocks—minus the mosquito netting. Every hour or so one of them would wake up and break into spontaneous conversation with the others. Laughter followed each exchange. Generations of communal living had made the Iban extraordinarily social people.

I wished for an understanding of their language. Were they talking about us? Then again, perhaps the language barrier was a good thing.

* * *

Deb and I awoke feeling mentally refreshed but physically beat from our various nicks, cuts, and sore muscles. As a consequence of being wet for much of the previous two days, blisters encased my toes, and a rash inflamed my inner thighs. I wrapped my injuries with medical tape, hoping to reduce further damage. Since the tape would rub off too easily if I placed gauze underneath it, I stuck it directly to my wounds, knowing I'd have to deal with the pain of removing the tape later. At least today, the sun was shining. Perhaps I'd have a chance to dry out a little.

Jonathan hadn't told us we were leaving the Red Ape Trail, but figuring it out didn't take too long. After hiking up the steepest mountain yet and surviving a controlled fall down the other side, I asked the obvious question: "We're not on the original trail, are we?"

"This is shortcut," he said sheepishly, "old hunters' trail."

Even though the route was more demanding than the Red Ape Trail—something I wouldn't have thought possible—I did get a certain perverse pleasure from witnessing that even the Iban were having trouble hiking it. When the sure-footed Jonathan took a nasty fall and hit his head on a rock, my pleasure turned to concern. We couldn't lose another guide.

Deb's travel theory, "the worse the road, the better the surprises along the way," also applies to trails. In this case, we could hear an orangutan in the distance moving through the trees.

Rustle, snap, crash! Rustle, snap, crash!

Ugan cupped his hands around his mouth and let loose a series of whoops. I figured he'd never fool such an intelligent animal, but within minutes, the male orangutan was in sight. He was much larger than the females from the previous day and likely weighed 175 pounds. Once he spotted us, and realized we'd tricked him, he started lobbing branch and treetop missiles at us. I wasn't sure if he was angry, frightened, or a little of both, but his fury made him appear Bigfoot size.

The Sasquatch of Borneo was raining weapons of mass destruction upon us!

Fortunately, the trees were close enough together to block any branches thrown horizontally. As long as he didn't climb directly above us, we were safe.

Eventually the orangutan realized we weren't going to harm him, and curiosity took over. He traversed to a big tree, thirty-five feet away from us, and peered down from a low branch. With his hairless forehead, rusty beard, and intelligent eyes, he looked so . . . human.

Many scientists believe orangutans and humans evolved from a common ancestor, and many Iban believe their dead live again as orangutans. As I stood there admiring and photographing the orangutan, I couldn't disagree with either belief.

As the orangutan grew more at ease with us, a strange feeling came over me. I felt as if I were looking back in time and into the eyes of one of my own ancestors. "Great-great-great-great-great-great-great-great-great-grandfather," I thought, "is that you?"

If Deb and I had our way, we would have spent the entire day with the orangutan. Jonathan, however, was determined to reach his longhouse by nightfall. After fifteen minutes, he insisted we move on and started walking off without us. Although we were upset about being pulled away from a once-in-a-lifetime event, we were in no position to argue and hurried to catch up.

As the day progressed, the rainforest's extreme heat and humidity drained off all my energy. I drank water and tea to keep myself hydrated but quickly sweated off whatever liquid I consumed. After lumbering to the top of a steep climb, I physically couldn't go any farther and had to remove my pack and rest. My stomach was in knots, and my head felt as if it were going to burst into flames—I had heat exhaustion.

Though I knew heatstroke was a possibility if I continued, I also knew we were a half hour from a river. If I could make it that far, there'd be plenty of water to cool me down. After a ten-minute break, I told Jonathan I was ready to go.

We began another controlled fall down a mountainside. As we

progressed, we grabbed trees, roots, and vines to slow our descent. Just as I was about to grasp the trunk of an ordinary-looking tree, Jonathan yelled, "Don't touch! Tree poisonous! Your hand burn for weeks!"

I pulled back with an inch to spare.

Before long, I was overheating again. When the ground leveled off, I could hear the faint gurgle of water in the distance. We were almost there. As I plodded forward, I dipped into the river with my mind. It was so cool, so refreshing.

I froze in midstep. A break in the trees revealed my goal. The river was in a deep gorge bordered by walls of slick mud and rock. The descent was steep enough to warrant a rope. Did anyone bring a rope?

Ha! What would the Iban need a rope for?

I flashed back to a cartoon I'd seen depicting the skeleton of a man who had died in the desert a few feet before reaching an oasis. Although I couldn't remember what made the cartoon funny, I felt a certain kinship with the skeleton. I could practically smell the river, yet if I attempted to reach it, I would almost certainly fall onto the rocks below and die just a few feet from the water.

By the time I finished my thought, Luang and Blonsai were already halfway down the wall.

God, I hated the Iban!

Like an obedient servant, I followed. Whether I died on top of the gorge or on the way down really wouldn't matter in the end. My brain went numb, and my legs tensed with anxiety. As I slid down the wall, my hands, my feet, and even my butt cheeks grabbed whatever they could along the way. Somehow, we all made it to the river.

I stripped off my backpack, eased into a shallow pool, and leaned back until my head was underwater. Soon I began to feel better.

"From here, we walk in river," Jonathan said.

"That'll be great," I replied. "It should help keep me cool."

The river averaged twenty feet in width and varied in depth from six inches near the banks to more than six feet in pools and narrow passages. As we proceeded, we encountered some sections where the water squeezed between gorge walls and others where the gorge was wide enough that we could walk on spits of dry rock and pebble. Numerous times, we had precarious portages around deep water, rapids, and waterfalls.

The relief I had felt from lying in the river was temporary. Soon my stomach cramps and burning headache returned. When Jonathan mentioned an old hunting shelter, forty minutes downriver, reaching it became my short-term goal. I slogged along, thinking of nothing but the next step.

By the time we arrived at the shelter, I was feeling as miserable as I'd ever felt in my life. Then the aroma of Ugan's curried chicken chunks wafted in my direction.

I thought my stomach would turn inside out.

Moving away from the cooking area helped—until Jonathan handed me a plateful of the pungent dish. Out of both politeness and the need for energy, I choked down a few bites. Afterward, I excused myself to lie down on a bed of narrow tree trunks stretched between two logs.

Jonathan let me rest for a while before announcing we had to make a decision. If we wanted to reach the longhouse before dark, we needed to leave immediately. Otherwise, we could spend the night where we were and hike out in the morning.

"What's the rest of the hike like?" I asked.

"All downhill," he replied. "The worst is behind us."

From a medical standpoint, I should have elected to stay at the shelter, but I was too stubborn to hold us up. "Let's go for it," I said.

"Are you sure?" Deb asked. "Don't feel pressured. Staying here tonight isn't a problem."

"I'll be okay. Besides, the rash on my thighs is getting worse. I'm gonna have a hard time walking tomorrow."

Twenty minutes later, we were in the midst of our most dangerous portage yet. I was forty feet above a roaring waterfall, clinging to a muddy gorge wall, while trying to find just one solid root to hold on to. When I discovered every exposed root within my reach was rotten, I barked at Jonathan, "Damn it! You said the 'worst was behind us'!"

"I forgot to mention this spot."

"Is this the *last* portage?"

"Easy past here," he said as he jammed his walking stick into the mud to make a handhold. "Don't look down."

I looked down.

God, I hated heights!

I shimmied past the waterfall and cautiously descended to the river.

I waited until Deb caught up and whispered to her, "This feels more like a rescue operation than a guided backpacking trip."

"You're right," she whispered back. "And to think we paid good money to do this."

"Honey, you can't buy moments like this."

The sky rumbled! Soon we could hear rain hitting the trees, getting louder by the second. We had been concentrating so hard on not falling that we had failed to notice the clouds. Moments later, we were drenched in sheets of rain. As the drops pummeled the river, they hissed like a radio tuned to static and turned all the way up.

"Great," I yelled to Deb. "Just when I thought we'd get out of here alive, Mother Nature throws a thunder-and-lightning storm at us!"

My pessimism was premature. I hadn't considered the effect the wonderfully cool rain would have on my body. My temperature began to drop, and I started to regain my energy. After several minutes, I felt better than I had since the beginning of the trip. The rain had saved me.

Of course, it only saved me so I could put up a good fight before it drowned me. Before long, the river resembled a giant centipede—each leg a newly formed tributary pouring into its body.

"We need to move quickly!" Jonathan yelled. "River get very deep."

Though I hadn't thought it possible, our hike had taken on more urgency.

Now that I was feeling better, it was Deb's turn to suffer. She was so exhausted she was shaking. Because Jonathan's new, rapid pace made it difficult for her to keep up, I yo-yoed between the two—reminding Jonathan to slow down and making sure Deb was okay.

"Do you want to rest?" I asked her. "I can tell him to stop."

"No, no, let's get this over with!" she shouted. "I just need to get myself pissed off, and I'll be okay."

The rising water frequently forced us out of the river to avoid rapids, pools, and other hazards, and the perilous gorge walls repeatedly forced us back in. Deb slipped and fell several times on the slick rocks near the water's edge but each time returned to her feet and marched on.

I had just scrambled over some boulders when out of the corner of my eye I saw her go down again. This time she tripped on a submerged rock and fell face-first into the river. I raced back to her, but she was already pushing herself up, cursing in pain. Although for the most part her Teva sandals worked well for river hiking, they provided little protection for the tops of her feet.

"Are you okay?" I yelled.

"I caught my toe on a rock, and it hurts like hell! I think it's broken."

"This is stupid! I'm gonna tell Jonathan we need to stop. If we keep up this pace, someone's going to get seriously hurt—or worse."

"No, let's just go! If we stop now, my foot will balloon up. The cool water will help keep the swelling down."

I knew arguing would be fruitless. She was as stubborn as I was. We were either going to reach the longhouse by nightfall or die trying.

A bit farther downstream, the gorge narrowed and forced us to wade waist deep in rapids. Each step had to be deliberate because we could no longer see our feet. This was one place where the Ibans' open-weave basket-packs had a distinct advantage over Deb's and my nylon backpacks. If we tripped, our backpacks could fill with water and hold us under.

The river rushed around a corner and dropped into an impressive waterfall. We had been wading as far to the right as possible. When we peered over the falls to find a way down, the "safest" route was on the opposite bank. Since the water at mid-river was deep, we'd have to cross at the crest of the falls, where the river had deposited a line of rocks.

We started across, leaning against the current and hoping our feet wouldn't slip out from under us. I glanced back at Deb. She wore a look of grim determination as the water pounded her hipbone and threatened to wash her over the edge.

The rocks grew larger as we approached the bank, and the last one stuck out of the water. Concentrating on keeping my weight upriver, I tried to step onto the boulder in one smooth motion. My momentum sent my feet sliding in opposite directions, and I landed in the splits on top of it. "Luckily," men have evolved with two natural pillows between our legs to break our falls on such occasions. I caught my breath and clambered to my feet.

Once everyone made it across the waterfall, we started down a near-vertical wall of hard, slick mud. Jonathan led the way, followed by me, Deb, Blonsai, Luang, and Ugan. This time we didn't even have a rotten root to grab. Although the wall wasn't as high as some of the others, a fall would have been just as deadly. As we descended, visions of all our narrow escapes flooded my brain—the slips where footing suddenly took hold, the last-second grabs of trees or roots—we could only be lucky for so long. I knew I'd make it down. Deb was the one who worried me. I had gotten her into this mess and was afraid of losing her. She was exhausted and walking on a badly injured toe. If she slipped now, nothing could stop her from crashing onto the rocks below. I couldn't look up because I had to watch my feet. Instead, I listened for the tumble I knew was coming.

"Take your time, Deb."

"I'm okay."

"Don't take any chances. When I get down, Jonathan can climb back up and help you."

"No, really. I'm okay."

And she was okay. When I reached the bottom, she was right behind me. I breathed a sigh of relief. We had survived another portage from hell.

My relief turned into anger. I was tired of risking my life. Jonathan was leading us on an insane route. There had to be an alternative. As we hurried downriver, I shouted to him, "I don't care if we have to slide down every waterfall or swim rapids over our heads, I'm *not* doing another portage like that!"

"No more. Easy past here."

I wanted to snap back that I'd heard that line before, but antagonizing the man responsible for getting our butts to the longhouse didn't seem like a wise idea.

We were running out of time. The river was still rising, and evening was approaching. "How much farther to the longhouse?" I yelled.

"One hour, thirty minutes," he shouted. We puffed along for a few moments before he continued. "I have idea. I send Ugan for longboat. He pick us up at end of river. Save forty minutes."

As rain poured over the brim of my baseball cap and thunder crashed above me, my anger turned into anticipation. We were beyond exhaustion, and although forty minutes was a small amount of time to save, all we needed was a little good news to raise our spirits. Deb had grown so pale she looked like a drowning victim. Once she knew we were near our goal, some color returned to her face.

Yes, we had to tackle more portages, but at least the steepest ones were behind us. We maintained a brisk pace and reached the mouth of the river a few minutes shy of Jonathan's predicted time.

We'd made it!

* * *

Despite my earlier comments about Jonathan and the Iban, all those negative feelings melted away once the longboat was in sight. Soon we were on our way up a wider, quieter river.

Upon reaching Nanga Sumpa, no one showed us where to go. Jonathan, who had told us earlier we'd be staying in his room, left us standing on the dock and went to bail out another longboat.

The dock sat in a narrow inlet, and on each side of the water were stilted buildings. On the near side was a new, uniformly constructed, wooden building. On the far side was an older, larger building—obviously the longhouse—that appeared to have been haphazardly constructed over time with randomly acquired building materials. When Ugan noticed Deb and me abandoned on the dock, he walked over and escorted us into the new building. We would be spending the next two nights in the guest lodge.

Although we were still in the rainforest and far away from electricity, the lodge felt almost luxurious. Our room had an uncovered open-frame window, a curtain door, and a mosquito-net-covered mattress on the floor. The dining room had elaborately carved wooden tables, and the bathrooms had cold-water showers and flush toilets.

I was curious about how the Iban accomplished running water. When I asked about it later, Jonathan informed me that they piped it down from a mountain spring, using the elevation drop to create the water pressure.

After settling in, Deb and I discussed our adventure and both agreed we had never pushed ourselves so hard before.

"It's amazing what you can do when your only alternative is death," I said. "Still, I wouldn't trade these past three days for anything."

"You're right," Deb said. "I'm glad we did it. I really learned something about myself."

"Of course, we only say that now that we've made it safely to Nanga Sumpa," I added.

We both laughed.

Jonathan knocked on our doorframe and peeked around the curtain. "Village headman is here. Please join us for drinks."

We hobbled into the dining room and sat at a large table with the headman, Jonathan, Blonsai, Luang, and Ugan. The headman appeared to be about seventy years old, and he had a shapeless blue tattoo covering his throat. Since Jonathan was still our only English-speaking contact, our greetings were limited to handshakes and smiles.

"Thank you for getting us here, Jonathan," I said. "Although I must say, I wasn't thankful on the trail when you kept telling us the section ahead would be easy. Every time you said the terrain would get better, it got worse."

"I said that so it not seem so hard. Didn't want you to get discouraged."

I considered telling him that being straight with us would have saved a lot of frustration, but I let his comment pass.

"I was impressed with how gracefully all of you moved through the jungle," Deb said. "You carried yourselves so effortlessly."

"We felt so inferior," I added.

"No need to feel inferior," Jonathan replied. "Very few of my people have hiked the trail you did. Too difficult. Less than 5 percent of long-house could do it."

I had a hard time believing Jonathan. The Iban were at home in the rainforest, and many of them had sculpted oversized calf muscles as proof of their frequent strenuous climbs. Even so, his compliment was a nice ego boost.

An hour later, Deb and I excused ourselves to go to bed. As much as we would have enjoyed spending the entire evening drinking tuak (a strong rice wine) with our hosts, we had to get some rest.

"You can sleep in tomorrow," Jonathan said. "Festival postponed. Man who runs it delayed at another longhouse."

Although the festival would have been interesting, we weren't disappointed. A solid eight hours of sleep followed by a day of relaxation would feel wonderful—especially for Deb with her broken toe.

Unfortunately, an undisturbed night of slumber was not to be. One of the resident cats was in heat, and she and her suitors yowled throughout the night. When the cats took a break, crowing roosters, squealing pigs, and the ever-talking Iban filled the silence. At least now, I knew what had driven the tribe to headhunting—they never got any REM sleep.

CHAPTER 27

Drunk Shopping

I wasn't enthusiastic about the European leg of our travels. After all, the continent is famous for its tourist attractions, not its exotic wildlife. We ended up visiting Spain, France, Switzerland, and Andorra, and by the time our travels were complete, my attitude had changed. We had successfully avoided the touristy areas, saw quite a bit of wildlife, and explored old castles and ruins that we had all to ourselves. We even climbed partway up the Matterhorn with a friend we had met on our Antarctica trip—stopping just short of our one-third-of-the-way-up goal when we hit ice.

Instead of choosing an adventure story from Europe, I'm going to share with you three stories that revolve around food and drink: one that didn't go well and two that were delightful. My first story takes place in rural western Spain, on our third day in Europe.

By the time we returned to the Hotel Carvajal, it was already after nine o'clock. The residents of Torrejón el Rubio were out for walks and milling about in the streets—the town was buzzing as much as a tiny town could buzz. Deb and I took advantage of the beautiful evening and strolled to a restaurant a few blocks away. When we stepped inside, the bartender informed us that they didn't serve food on Friday nights. In fact, the only place in town serving dinner was the restaurant at our hotel.

We ambled back to the Hotel Carvajal. Unlike our austere room, the hotel's restaurant was elegant and probably the best in the area. We were early by Spanish standards, and people were just beginning to trickle in. Within the hour, all the tables would be full.

Once the proprietor seated us, a young woman waited on us. Most of the time, Deb and I found communicating with younger people to be easier than communicating with older people. This time the opposite was true, and our waitress soon grew frustrated with us.

After watching Deb place her order with considerable pointing and repeating, I decided to make things easy for our waitress by ordering the five-course dinner special. I had no idea what the meal included but figured Saint Ambrose's wisdom about Rome would adapt quite well to our current situation: "When in Spain, eat as the Spaniards do."

Placed first on our table was the traditional loaf of hard, crusty bread. I hadn't seen any butter since arriving in Spain but couldn't see any harm in requesting some. I looked up *butter* in our Spanish translation book and showed the word to Deb, who was much better at pronouncing non-English words than I was.

The next time our waitress walked by, Deb asked, *"Mantequilla por favor?"*

The woman stopped dead in her tracks, shot us an icy glare, and repeated in a shrill voice, *"Mantequilla!"*

A man sitting with his family at the table next to us halted his conversation and craned his neck to stare at us.

Apparently, we had just insulted the entire country of Spain.

Although the waitress acquiesced to our wishes, she defiantly deposited the butter on our table as if it were a forty-pound sack of flour.

Minutes later, she returned with a bowl of soup and a tray full of sausages. She tilted the tray to show me its contents. Although I was trying to eat like a Spaniard, a news story I had seen in the United States about environmentally destructive hog farms flashed through my brain. I mimed a polite "No thank you."

The waitress scowled at me for a moment, then thrust the bowl of soup in front of my face.

"I think the soup is mine," Deb said.

I knew the waitress couldn't understand, so I took the bowl and handed it to my wife.

The young woman's eyes grew wide. She clenched her teeth and stormed off to the kitchen! A muffled but lively conversation drifted through the doors. The next time she entered the dining room, I noticed her deliberately avoiding eye contact with me.

"I think our waitress fired us," I said.

"No, she just got confused," Deb said.

When the next course arrived, the proprietor served us, and the waitress stayed as far away as possible.

"Oh, my God. You're right!" Deb said with a wry smile. "She did fire us!"

Our meal progressed smoothly until the proprietor served me a plate of fried potatoes. I took a bite. Not bad, but they needed something—ketchup.

I knew I should have eaten the potatoes plain, but as the person paying for the meal, I felt it was my prerogative to season my food how I pleased. When I asked Deb for language assistance, she shot me a frosty glare that even the waitress couldn't beat. This was something I'd have to do myself.

The next time the proprietor checked on us, I requested in English, "Ketchup, please?"

A moment passed before the man figured out what I wanted. Then a look of revulsion flowed over his face. Roughly interpreting his Spanish words, he said, "I'm sorry sir, but we do not serve *caaatch-up* in this restaurant!"

What is it about ketchup that is offensive? Even in the United States, people get upset if you put ketchup on their dishes. It's just an innocent concoction of tomato sauce and spices! No one ever feels insulted if you season with salt or pepper. Ketchup manufacturers need a better public relations firm.

In fairness to the proprietor, cultural differences could have caused me to misinterpret the tone of his voice. Perhaps he wasn't upset with me for insulting his chef and was just disappointed that he didn't have a generous supply of the red delicacy on hand.

Yeah, that must have been it.

Our dinner concluded a little before midnight. Although we were both stuffed, the meal had been draining. Deb's words echoed my thoughts: "Next time I wanna find a place where we can just eat and get out. I'm tired of every meal being an event."

Shortly after we went to bed, my body began to ache. I felt as if I were a punching bag for a heavyweight fighter. My first thought was, "Oh, great, food poisoning," but then I began to cough. Considering how many people I had come in contact with during my world travels—especially on airplanes—I had been amazingly healthy. I was due to get sick. The chills came next. I wrapped myself in an extra blanket, cranked up the heat, and shivered. Poor Deb. Having to put up with my coughing and shivering in the sweltering room made the night as miserable for her as it was for me.

* * *

Even though Spain is small when compared to the United States, it has distinct regions with unique traditions and foods. Our one-day drive from Torrejón el Rubio, in the Extremadura autonomous community of western Spain, to Cangas de Onís, in the Asturias autonomous community of northern Spain, showed off those differences. One tradition both regions had in common, however, was that restaurants opened late by American standards. In Cangas de Onís, Deb and I were ready to eat dinner at five o'clock but couldn't find a single restaurant that opened before eight.

We were sitting in our hotel room when I checked my watch. It was two minutes before eight o'clock. "Okay, let's go for it," I said.

Three minutes later, we were at the doorstep of El Molin Restaurant. After the waitress seated us, we watched townsfolk drift in and out and exchange pleasantries with the man behind the bar. This was obviously where the locals dined.

Our waitress had given us Spanish language menus, but when she noticed us laboring to translate them, she came to our rescue with menus in English. Now, for the first time in Spain, we could order with confidence. Waltzing before my eyes were shellfish and other choices that hadn't been options for our previous meals. My taste buds tap-danced for joy.

Once we finished our excellent meal, the man from behind the bar walked over and introduced himself as Angel, one of the restaurant's owners. He looked about thirty-five years old and had a round face that complemented his receding hairline. Having noticed the invisible "We are Americans" signs on our backs, he wanted to welcome us to Spain and find out what part of the United States we came from.

After several days of conversing only between ourselves, Deb and I relished the opportunity to speak with someone different. Angel spoke excellent English, a skill he had learned while visiting England and traveling as a professional kayaker.

Deb commented to Angel, "Once we got out of Madrid, we fell in love with Spain. It's much different from what we expected."

"We're not like the big cities," he said. "Everyone expects us to be all about *'toro, toro,'* but that's not us."

Throughout the evening, Angel had been serving special drinks to his patrons. He'd hold an unlabeled three-quarter-liter bottle far above his head and pour the golden liquid so it just caught the edge of a tilted glass held below his waist. Each pour was enough for one drink, and each drink was swallowed in a single gulp. After serving a round, he'd leave the bottle on the table or the bar until summoned back for a refill.

"What are you pouring for everyone?" I asked.

"Sidra natural, a traditional Asturias drink made from fermented apples."

Although the two of us had already consumed a bottle of Spanish wine and an after-dinner drink, we couldn't resist a taste. "A glass for each of us, please," I said.

Angel opened a bottle and performed a showy pour. After Deb and I each downed a glass, he ducked behind the bar, brought out an English translation of the book *Asturias,* flipped to the proper page, and handed it to me. "To pour the *culines* (cider glasses) requires great expertise, but all Asturians claim they are experts," it said.

"Is there a reason for the tall pour?" I asked.

"Sidra natural is not a high-quality drink. The pour adds effervescence."

I liked sidra natural. It had a refreshing, semi-sweet, sour apple taste with a bite. Even so, one pour was plenty. We had drunk more than enough alcohol for the night.

As our mostly full bottle sat in front of us, I looked around and noticed that all the other customers had finished their bottles. If we didn't do the same, would it be offensive, like butter or ketchup? We couldn't take the chance. When in Spain . . .

Next came the biggest surprise of the evening. Since I had already paid for our meal, the bill for the sidra natural came separately. How much do you think a bottle of the local special, complete with ten show-pours, would be worth? In some countries you might expect to pay twenty-five, perhaps even fifty euros. But here in Spain, the entire drink and show package cost only two euros ($2.36 U.S.).

I never get sloppy drunk, but I occasionally get happily intoxicated. When Deb and I left El Molin, we were both feeling extremely happy. Since it was almost eleven o'clock, we planned to head directly to our hotel. Then we noticed that most of the stores were still open for business. What could be more fun than inebriated late-night shopping with a nearly empty charge card?

We strolled down the main street and ended up in one of the town's less-tacky gift stores. Shopping primarily for relatives, we picked up various items and soon found ourselves by the stuffed animal shelves.

"What about this for Fiona?" I asked, holding up a large stuffed bull.

"Great idea! She'll love that," Deb said.

"Wait! This one's softer," I said as I rubbed my cheek against the animal's plush fabric.

The bulls were perfectly huggable—understuffed, as if a child had carried them around for years. I decided testing just two bulls wouldn't be enough. With Deb laughing and the store clerk straining her neck to keep an eye on us, I applied the cheek test to every bull on the shelf. "This one's very nice. Oh, this one's even better. I wanna buy one for myself, too. Can I? Can I?"

"They're fifty euros apiece! But I suppose if you *really* want one, you can have one."

Regrettably, I had a flash of maturity. I put down the bull I had selected for myself and carried the gift bull—the softest one in the store—to the counter.

Before long we had a healthy pile of gifts. When the clerk realized we weren't going to break or steal anything, she warmed up to us and began laughing. As she rang us up, I added more items to the pile. "Wait! I didn't buy anything for myself. How 'bout a CD, so we have something to listen to in the car? Better yet, how 'bout two?"

We carried our gifts back to the hotel, laughing all the way.

* * *

My final food and drink story takes place after Deb and I spent a day exploring Parc Naturel Régional de Camargue, a 210,040-acre park on the Mediterranean coast of France.

Rather than return to the tollway, we decided to take the alternate route. We thought the old two-lane highway would provide quick access to restaurants, but soon regretted our decision. The dark and lonely road led us through miles of nothingness.

This was a dangerous, possibly lethal, situation. When Deb is hungry she's like a female black widow spider, and that would um . . . make me her mate.

"On the left!" she screamed. "There's a restaurant!"

When I glanced to where Deb was pointing, my eyes were drawn to the multiple rows of semitrailer trucks in the parking lot. I was looking forward to a meal of traditional French food, not truck stop food.

"Are you sure you want to eat *there?* Let's drive a little farther."

"I need to eat, *now!*"

I dutifully swerved into the lot and parked the car.

We entered the restaurant dressed in our mud-smeared shorts, casual shirts, and invisible "We are Americans" signs. I scanned the crowded main room. About fifty men were inside. Some were standing at the bar, and the rest were sitting at tables.

"You're the only woman in here," I said.

"You're right," she replied. "Oh, wait. The bartender is a woman."

"She doesn't count."

Imagine stepping into a restaurant filled with burly truckers. Members of the Republican Party in your home country have recently insulted the truckers' nation, heritage, and even their manhood with degrading comments and jokes. Now you feel their eyes upon you, as if you were the one to blame for the insults. You look for an open table and catch your breath when you realize the closest one is on the far side of the room. You cross to it, as if walking a gauntlet. Intimidation floats in the air. Then you notice a small detail that changes everything. The truckers, many with tattoos covering their muscular arms, aren't drinking hefty mugs of beer—they're sipping dainty glasses of wine.

I know I'm playing with stereotypes here. Certainly not every trucker is a beefy redneck looking to start a fight. But picture Arnold Schwarzenegger playing The Terminator with a glass of red wine in his hand. It just wouldn't work.

As things turned out, the restaurant's customers and employees were unconcerned about Republicans renaming French fries and French toast and other political taunts. Instead, they went out of their way to make us feel comfortable.

Most memorable was our waiter. I knew about three French words. Deb, on the other hand, had taken French in high school and was just rusty at speaking it. Once our waiter figured that out, he spoke to me in English while patiently encouraging Deb to converse in French. As Deb commented later, "My impromptu French lesson was just delightful!"

As for the food, Deb ordered from the menu, and I opted for the buffet. Midway through our meal, she subtly pointed to the large snails the truckers next to us were eating and said, "I'm surprised you didn't try the escargot."

"Oh, I overlooked them. I'll be back."

When I returned to the table, I smiled, pulled an escargot from its shell, popped it into my mouth, and washed it down with a splash of wine. "Mmmm—truck stop food!"

CHAPTER 28

The Death Seat

Our seven continents of adventures concluded in Zimbabwe, Africa. At the time, Robert Mugabe was ranked among the world's worst dictators, but his country still had a reputation for outstanding wildlife. I had saved Zimbabwe for last, hoping to give my book a big finish—and boy did the trip come through.

I hired Skip Horner as our coordinating guide. The slightly graying but svelte man lived just a few miles away from me, and he was famous for being the first person to guide clients to the top of the highest peak on each of the seven continents. Skip then hired Brian Worsley (a man who claimed to be distantly related to Frank Worsley of Ernest Shackleton's Imperial Trans-Antarctic Expedition but looked more like he was related to Teddy Roosevelt) to be our local guide. Also on our trip were four Americans that I recruited: Susan and Joe (a couple in their early fifties), and Jill and Sam (a couple in their early thirties).

Our Zimbabwe adventure included a fifty-three mile hike across Mana Pools National Park over five days, a return via a three-day canoe trip down the Zambezi River, and a ninety-minute bush plane flight to Victoria Falls that wrapped it all up. Along the way, we observed a black rhinoceros, a black mamba, a leopard, lions, zebras, warthogs, elephants, chacma baboons, waterbucks, impalas, Cape buffalo, African painted dogs, Nile crocodiles, and numerous other species. I also got to live my dream of catching and releasing a huge African rock python.

Deb's and my biggest and most famous adventure took place on the first day of our canoe trip down the Zambezi River. Here's what happened:

Before getting on the river, we all gathered around for instructions on our three-day canoe trip. Humphrey Gumpo, a specialized canoe guide, would be joining us for this portion of our expedition. The twenty-five-year-old native Zimbabwean had stopped by our camp a few days earlier, so we were already familiar with his instantly likeable, happy-go-lucky personality. He could be serious when necessary but often told elaborate stories that sounded convincing—until he flashed a wide grin.

As Humphrey warned us about hazards on the river, his seriousness was unquestionable: "There are four dangers you need to be prepared for, but they're not in the order you'd expect. The greatest danger is the sun, because you can quickly become sunburned or dehydrated. Be sure to put on lots of cream and drink plenty of liquids.

"Snags, such as submerged trees, are the second greatest danger. Brian and I will point out snags as we see them. Give them a wide berth. But if you can't steer out of the way, hit them straight on. The water current is moderately fast, and if you drift into a snag off-center, your canoe could capsize. If you do get caught, lean into the current until we arrive to assist you.

"The other two dangers are crocodiles and hippos. The main thing with crocodiles is to avoid dangling your feet or hands in the water—like bait. We will have close encounters with hippos. The important thing to know is that hippos always move to deep water. Most of the time, we'll be canoeing in shallow water. If hippos block our way, we'll stop to give them time to move. The one place we don't want to be is between a hippo and deep water. We also need to be careful near high riverbanks, as we can't always see what's on top. If we startle a grazing hippo, it will plunge into the river unaware that we're below it in our canoes."

Jill and Susan gasped.

"Finally," Humphrey continued, "a hippo could surface under your canoe. This is very rare, but if it happens you'll feel a little bump, and the hippo will sink back down until you pass over it."

When Jill and Susan gasped again, Brian did his best to calm their fears: "I've been doing this for eighteen years, and I've never had a client in the water. Once we start paddling, your nerves will settle down, and you'll be surprised how safe and easy the canoeing is. Just relax and enjoy the scenery."

While on the Zambezi River, we would paddle approximately forty miles, pass fifteen hundred hippos, and float over hundreds—possibly thousands—of crocodiles. I wasn't as nervous about the dangers ahead as Jill and Susan were, but I was definitely on edge. Though I was technically just another member of the expedition, with no leadership duties, if it wasn't for me, none of us would be here. Therefore, I felt obligated to put on a stoic front.

Since Jill seemed to be the most nervous of all, as we walked the half-mile trail to the canoe launching area, I said to her, "Deb and I have canoeing experience. We can canoe ahead of you, or if you prefer, between you and the hippos. Just let me know how we can help."

"Thank you," she said. "I'll keep that in mind."

One by one we pushed off from shore onto a narrow channel of flat water. Humphrey and Brian led our convoy of five canoes, followed by Deb and me, Susan and Joe, Jill and Sam, and Skip.

I hadn't canoed since Belize and was looking forward to using the initial unchallenging section of river to hone my strokes. On the Zambezi, however, even the most placid water can become challenging in a hurry. We were only ten minutes into our journey when we encountered our first hippo. My paddling refresher course would have to wait.

A young bull was in shallow water, caught between us and a herd of hippos with a dominant male. When he stood his ground and roared at us, we paddled to the riverbank and held on to the long grass. He continued roaring as he considered his options. He obviously preferred to deal with us rather than the dominant male downriver but eventually chose a third option and climbed onto the opposite bank. As we floated by, he opened his mouth in a classic "yawn" of aggression.

Yes, his big tusks were intimidating.

Slipping past the young bull was one thing. Now we had to face down the dominant male and six other hippos who were blocking our entrance to the main river channel. As we floated toward thirty-five thousand pounds of snorting attitude, I wondered how we'd reach camp before nightfall. Surely, these hippos weren't going anywhere.

Then, in what seemed like a miracle, the hippos did what they were supposed to do—they submerged. Canoeing past an underwater herd of hippos for the first time was the ultimate exercise in trust. Although Brian and Humphrey had floated the river numerous times, could anyone really predict how a hippo would react? I gripped my paddle as if it were a rope in a game of tug of war.

The tension I felt paled in comparison to how Joe and Susan felt. The typically jovial couple had virtually no canoeing experience, and I could hear them bickering behind me. No matter what Joe did, Susan retorted it was wrong, and vice versa. They reminded me of the first time Deb and I canoed together, except their pitch was much more fevered.

The current in the main channel was faster than I expected. We moved along at a good clip with a minimum of paddling.

"There's a snag to the right!" Humphrey shouted.

"I see it!" Deb yelled.

As we drifted past the snag, I turned from my position in the stern, pointed at the low-floating tree trunk, and shouted to Joe and Susan, "Watch out for the snag! It's right there!"

All they needed to do was steer two feet to the left, but instead they veered just enough to hit the trunk off-center. I cringed as I watched their canoe turn sideways.

"Aaahhh!" Susan screamed.

"Brian! Humphrey!" Deb yelled. "Joe and Susan are caught on the snag!"

Joe shouted to Susan, "Lean into the current!" but she was too terrified to react. Their canoe listed precariously downstream.

We had all seen huge crocodiles along the riverbanks, and now in Susan's mind even bigger crocs were waiting to rip her to shreds the moment she splashed into the water. "Oh my God! Oh my God! We're gonna tip over! Oh my God! Oh my God! We're gonna tip over! Oh my God! . . ." she chanted.

"You're gonna be okay!" Humphrey yelled. "Just lean into the current!"

"Oh my God! Oh my God! We're gonna tip over! . . ." she continued.

Brian and Humphrey paddled upstream of the frightened couple's canoe and attempted to dislodge it. The heavy current held it in place.

"Aaahhh!" Susan screamed, as the canoe rocked.

Humphrey jumped into the dark, four-foot-deep water and pushed on the bow. It wouldn't budge. He repositioned himself and wiggled the stern. The canoe slipped free!

Two tense situations in a short amount of time had raised everyone's anxiety level. Moments after we continued on our way, Susan, still panic-stricken, pointed at a ripple in the water and screamed, "There's a hippo right there! He's swimming straight toward us! Aaahhh!"

"It's just the current, Susan!" Joe yelled. *"Calm down!"*

A bit farther downstream, the river widened to a quarter mile across and the current slowed. Per Humphrey's instructions, we changed the order of our single-file paddling. Joe and Susan moved up to second in line, Jill and Sam took over the third spot, Deb and I lingered in the fourth position, and Skip brought up the rear.

As the sun dropped in the sky, an idyllic calm came over the river, and a gentle breeze kept us comfortable. Best of all, the hippos were spread out and moving to deep water without much fuss. I could feel the tension melt off my shoulders. Others in our group seemed to relax as well. The adventure part of our canoe trip was surely behind us, and from now on sunburn would be our greatest worry.

A smile creased my face as I thought about what the next few days would be like: my feet would be enjoying a well-deserved break, the wildlife sightings would be spectacular, and the hippos would be serenading us along the way.

Ah, life on the river would be sweet.

The depth of the Zambezi wasn't always proportional to the distance from its banks. Sometimes we canoed inches from land and were unable to touch bottom with our paddles; other times we'd nearly run aground at midstream. Actually seeing bottom was rare, however, as the water's visibility was little more than a foot.

Deb and I were canoeing next to a low, flat riverbank when we felt a sharp bump. Perhaps we'd hit a rock. We were too close to land for it to be a—

Grrraaarrr!

Something huge chomped through the middle of our canoe and thrust us into the air!

At first, I thought it was a crocodile. Then I saw the hippo's giant mouth!

As we continued skyward, my eyes shifted to Deb, who was rising higher than I was. At peak height, our canoe rolled shoreward, dumping us like a front-end loader would. I hit the ground first, followed by

Deb—who landed on her side with an eerie thud!

The hippo dropped the canoe and vanished into the river.

Fearing the worst, I scrambled to my feet, calling to my wife, "Deb, are you okay? Deb, are you—"

She jumped up and we both wheeled toward the river, ready to spring out of the way if the hippo came at us again.

"Yes, I think so," she said while scanning the water. "I'm gonna have some bruises, but nothing feels broken. How 'bout you?"

"I wrenched my back, but I'll be fine."

The hippo had dumped us on a shallow bed of mud. Though we looked like pigs after a good wallow, we couldn't have landed in a better spot. Adding to our good fortune was that despite the ferociousness of the attack, it was over before we fully realized what had happened.

Once we were sure the hippo wouldn't return, we hugged, whispered "I love you" to each other, and burst into laughter.

"We were attacked by a *fucking* hippo!" I chortled.

"I know," Deb said between giggles, "and we're just filthy!"

"I can't believe you got up after that fall."

"Mud is wonderful stuff!"

"A *fucking* hippo attacked us!"

As we stood by the river, giggling, Skip came running. "Are you guys okay? Is anyone hurt?"

"We're gonna be a little sore," Deb said, "but other than that we're *great!*"

When Skip realized we were laughing, not crying, he grinned and said, "I saw the entire attack! The hippo lifted your canoe six feet into the air. It was *so-ooo* cool!"

When the hippo struck, the rest of our group was ten canoe lengths downriver. After pulling ashore, they ran back to us.

"Deb, Marty, are either of you injured?" Brian asked.

"No, we're fine," I said. "Look at what the hippo did to our canoe!"

We had been paddling a heavy-duty, wooden-keeled, fiberglass Canadian canoe. The hippo's upper teeth had snapped the gunwale, and its lower teeth had smashed through the bottom of the canoe, ripped out a sixteen-inch-long section of keel, and pierced my dry bag and daypack. The canoe was beyond repair, but we could mend the dry bag and daypack once we reached camp.

"Eighteen bloody years, and this has *never* happened before!" Brian lamented.

"Sorry to break your winning streak," Deb said.

The attack troubled Brian so much that he immediately conferred with Humphrey to figure out what they, as guides, had done wrong. Jill, Sam, Joe, and Susan were also troubled and obviously debating internally whether to continue on the canoe trip. As for Deb and me, we were still giggling away.

"I can't believe you two are laughing about this," Jill said. "If the hippo had attacked Sam and me, we'd be totally freaked out."

"The only way I can explain it, Jill, is that Deb and I have just lived through something very few people have ever experienced. I feel like we've been given a gift."

"All I can say is that it happened to the right couple," Joe said. "If it had happened to Susan and me, we'd be done. As it is, we may still be done."

"Yes, we're very fortunate the hippo chose your canoe," Skip added. "You two have handled the situation perfectly."

"What are we gonna do with our canoe?" I asked.

"Leave it here for now," Brian said. "Tomorrow we'll send someone with a boat to pick it up."

For the next several minutes, Susan, Joe, Jill, and Sam debated what they were going to do. They wanted to hike out, but the sun would be setting soon, and hiking through the African bush at night could be even more dangerous than continuing on to camp via canoe. Once they agreed to continue, we pushed onto the river arranged quite differently from how we had started. Humphrey paddled alone, Jill and Sam maintained their original partnership, Joe and Susan shared a canoe with Brian, and Deb and I shared a canoe with Skip.

As we began paddling, I noticed Susan and Jill shaking with fear. I also noticed that Deb and Susan were sitting in the middle seats of their respective canoes. With a big smile and in a voice just a little too loud, I couldn't help announcing, "Hey Deb. You're sitting in the *death* seat!"

Skip shushed me, and rightfully so. While the hippo attack had confirmed the other couples' worst fears, it had done the opposite for me. I was so high on adrenaline—I was slaphappy.

Later that evening, once we made it to camp and were sitting around a campfire, my adrenaline wore off, and I was just as nervous as everyone else.

We had two more days of facing the hippos.

* * *

Epilogue: Once *Cool Creatures, Hot Planet: Exploring the Seven Continents* was published, Deb and I chuckled each time reviewers chose to use the same words to describe us: "Adventurer Marty Essen and his intrepid wife, Deb." After the third or fourth time it happened, I felt compelled to buy Deb a custom-printed T-shirt with her new moniker: "Intrepid Wife."

CHAPTER 29

A Surprising New Friend

There is a big difference between dreaming about writing a book and actually following through with it. Like so many other people, I had dreamed of writing a book since high school. In fact, in the 1990s, after writing for *Gig Magazine* and having numerous political commentaries published in the newspapers, I gave it my first shot. I wanted to write a time-travel novel, where the protagonist went back to the time of Jesus Christ, interacted with biblical characters, and upon returning to present time learned that he had replaced Christ in the Bible.

I worked on that novel for several days before giving up. At that stage in my life, I didn't have the chops to write good dialogue. Some twenty years later, I returned to that idea with increased confidence and ability and wrote the *Time Is Irreverent* series of novels. To date, I've written three novels in that series and will likely write more after finishing this book.

In late 2002, well before *Time Is Irreverent*, I started writing *Cool Creatures, Hot Planet: Exploring the Seven Continents*, believing that a nonfiction adventure-travel book would be easier to write than a dialogue-driven novel. After all, the dialogue only needed to be sporadic, and I already knew the plot.

I wrote the first three chapters of the book, Belize from scratch, and the Amazon and Australia chapters by expanding on the newspaper stories I had already written. At that point, my experience as a talent agent kicked in. I planned to shop the first three chapters to the publishing companies, just as I had previously shopped sample songs from bands I managed to the record companies. The industry was different, but the process was similar.

Then I remembered that I was skipping a key step. In the music business, record company executives frequently claimed they could recognize hit songs from demos, recorded with only vocals and an acoustic guitar. Although I suppose they occasionally did that, record company executives flatter themselves. The best way to get a recording deal is to have the artist record finished-product songs in a studio, with an accomplished producer, before sending them out. If that worked for music, wouldn't the same work for writing? And in the writing business, the closest comparison to a producer is an editor.

I searched for a top-notch independent editor and selected Laurie Rosin, the editor of thirty-eight national best sellers. I sent my partial manuscript to her, confident that she'd return it with a note saying something like, "I wish I could help you, but other than some minor punctuation changes, there's nothing I can do to improve your nearly perfect writing."

Instead, Laurie returned my manuscript marked up like a wall of graffiti, and accompanied it with pages of improvement suggestions. I stared at what she sent me, unable to move until my bladder required it. Did I really suck that much as a writer?

I allowed myself to mourn for a day before getting back to work. The first thing I had to do was buy myself a copy of the *Chicago Manual of Style, Fifteenth Edition*, which is a thick, ugly, orange book of writing rules. To this day, that book sits next to me—all marked up with handwritten comments, stars, and sticky notes. While that manual would help me with mechanical issues, according to Laurie, my biggest problem was not including enough detail in my storytelling. That made sense. All my previous writing had been for newspapers and magazines that required me to work within strict word-count limitations. Books generally don't have such limitations.

For instance, in a newspaper story I might write, "I stepped into the rainforest," and let the readers fill in the details. In a book, I needed to create for my readers a mental image of that rainforest. What did it look like? What did it smell like? What did it sound like? What did it feel like? That sort of thing. The process was difficult for me, because I'm not naturally the kind of person who needs every single detail.

Laurie had other lessons for me, but sharing them all with you here really would be too much detail. Instead, I'll just say that for me she was more like a professor teaching a master class in writing than an editor—and that's a compliment.

I ripped apart my first three chapters, rewrote them using what I had learned, and returned them to Laurie. She gave me a gold star for being her most-improved student!

* * *

Since each trip in *Cool Creatures, Hot Planet* made up a chapter, after those first three chapters, I wrote as much as I could between adventures. The uncertainties that came with writing a book in close to real-time included worrying about the possibility of a boring trip and not knowing how the story would end. The biggest surprise was how political Deb's and my travels were becoming. That meant my book was going to be much more than just a travelogue with fun and hair-raising adventures. It was also going to be a commentary on endangered species, protecting the environment, George W. Bush, and how people in other countries viewed Americans and the Iraq war.

With that in mind, I set a goal to do my part to prevent the reelection of George W. Bush. If I were to accomplish that, my book would have to be published before the November 2, 2004 election. Consequently, I wrote sixteen hours a day and stayed alert by swallowing caffeine pills with my coffee.

In my favor was that during that time, Essen Communications Corporation was enjoying its most reliable employees ever, and I only had to give the company minimal attention each day. Deb also pitched in, reading chapters aloud to me, while I followed along, looking for missing words, clunky sentences, and other errors.

* * *

Pro tip: Should you ever write a book, don't put a loved one through the chore of reading it aloud to you. Instead, use the Microsoft Word text-to-speech feature. That little gem—which I discovered while writing my second book—is hidden deep inside Word's feature list. If you can't find it, search the internet for instructions.

* * *

All of that help wasn't enough, however. One night I got a headache that was so bad, I thought my head was going to explode. Marcus Daly Memorial Hospital in Hamilton was twenty minutes away. That hospital has improved over the years to become an outstanding small-town facility, but back then it wasn't uncommon for locals to call it "Carcass Daily Memorial Hospital." With that in mind, my wife and I decided that for exploding head syndrome it was worth the extra time to race north to one of the two excellent hospitals in Missoula. So that's what we did. Well, actually Deb did the racing. I sat in the passenger seat, clutching my head.

By the time we reached the hospital, I felt a touch better. Therefore I did the guy thing and said, "I think I'm gonna be okay. Let's turn around."

"The *hell* we are!" Deb spat.

A nurse took my blood pressure as soon as I entered the emergency room and hurried to find a doctor. I don't remember the exact reading, but my blood pressure was obviously in the danger area for a stroke. And who knows how high it soared before we reached the hospital?

Hitting my publication date goal wasn't worth dying for. Once the doctor got my blood pressure down, I returned home, tossed the caffeine tablets into the garbage, and adopted a more reasonable writing schedule of twelve hours per day. Ultimately, the election flew by, and my book wouldn't hit the stores until January 2007.

* * *

Upon finishing the writing portion of *Cool Creatures, Hot Planet,* I put on my agent hat and started shopping the manuscript to the publishing companies. Soon I learned that I had two things working against me: the book was too long and it had color photographs. While length isn't important for an established author, it is for a new one, and adding color photographs to the equation made it virtually impossible to sell. Quite simply, the publishing companies judged the print costs to be too high to take the risk. Sure, cutting the manuscript by 70,000 words and dropping the photos would have solved my problem, but I wasn't going to sell out and ruin all my hard work.

Damn you, Laurie Rosin! If I hadn't followed her advice about adding all the sensory details, the book would have been just about the correct length.

I'm kidding.

While Laurie most definitely contributed to the length, I have never regretted her guidance.

Fortunately, I had a Plan B. I had owned two talent agencies and still owned a telephone company. Why not own a publishing company too? I formed Encante Press, LLC (named after the mythical city of gold under the Amazon River, where the shape-shifting pink dolphins live) and got to work on a national distribution deal. Soon I had three deals. The primary one was with Midpoint Trade out of New York City, for distribution to bookstores. The secondary ones were with Quality Books and Unique Books, for distribution to libraries. While those were among the most important steps on my new journey, I still had lots to do.

For the cover, I wanted an eye-catching photo and came up with the idea of having a tailless whip-scorpion (a fierce-looking but mostly harmless arachnid) climbing up my face. To get that photo, Deb and I traveled back to the Amazon Rainforest, and this time Laurel Pfund, whom we met on our Antarctica trip, joined us. With Deb as my photographer, I got the photo I desired, and then the three of us hiked, kayaked, and looked for critters for the remainder of our visit.

Next on my list was to send my manuscript out to celebrities for back cover blurbs. For those I hit gold. Here they are:

"An exciting and adventurous read. *Cool Creatures, Hot Planet* by Marty Essen is a roller coaster ride through the natural world that will both entertain and enlighten readers."—Jeff Corwin, *The Jeff Corwin Experience*

"This is a wonderful book—a labor of love—that describes in soul-stirring language what it is like to live with the people, the animals, the birds, the snakes, the insects, the jungles, the treacherous rivers, the gorgeous scenery of seven continents. It is the best travel and exploratory work I have yet encountered. Marty Essen and his wife, Deb, are two highly intelligent, imaginative, and brave people."—Senator George McGovern, 1972 Democratic nominee for president

If you are unfamiliar with *The Jeff Corwin Experience*, it was a show on the Animal Planet Channel, similar to Steve Irwin's *The Crocodile Hunter*. In fact, I liked Jeff's show better than Steve's show, because of his sense of humor and gentler interactions with animals.

The blurb from Jeff was easy to get. I simply worked through his agent to send him the manuscript and had my blurb in less than a month.

Acquiring the blurb from Senator McGovern is a more amusing story. His daughter, Ann, lives in the Bitterroot Valley town of Stevensville, and the senator and his wife had a summer home there too. I called Ann to get her father's phone number. Then I stared at my phone for several minutes, working up the nerve to call the senator.

I took a deep breath, cleared my throat, and dialed the number.

"Hell . . . oo," he answered groggily.

Shit, I woke him up!

"Senator McGovern?"

"Yes."

"My name is Marty Essen. I live in Victor and am the former chair of the Ravalli County Democratic Central Committee. I'm calling you this morning because I have written a book about my wife's and my travels to all seven continents, the people we met in other countries, and their reactions to the Iraq War. It's a very liberal book, and I would be honored if you would write a blurb for the back cover."

He hesitated before saying, "You can send it over, but don't get your hopes up. I'm really busy right now. If I get to it at all, it's going to be several weeks."

He gave me his address, and I hung up feeling that I had somehow blown the phone call. I asked myself, "Should I even bother mailing the manuscript?"

I tossed the package into the mail, expecting nothing to come of it.

Two weeks later, I received McGovern's beautiful blurb, along with a note asking, "Would you and Deb like to get together for dinner?"

Later that week, the three of us met at a Victor restaurant and had a delightful meal. We talked for nearly two hours, interrupted occasionally by admirers wanting to greet the man who in 1972 finished second in the race to become the world's most powerful human. All the while, the conversation between us flowed so naturally that it felt like we had been friends for many years.

As I drove Deb back home, she looked over to me and said, "I think we solved all of the world's problems tonight!"

* * *

Now that I had my blurbs—and a surprising new friend—next on my list was finding a talented person to design the book's cover and interior. I chose Michele DeFilippo of 1106 Design in Arizona for that. I also had to find a book printer, capable of high-quality color photo reproductions. I chose Friesens Corporation out of Canada for that. Other tasks, a bit further down the road, would include shipping boxes of books to my distributors and promoting my book launch.

The entire process was an incredible learning experience.

Months later, I enjoyed the satisfying feeling of holding my first book, knowing how many thousands of hours I put into it and how close it had come to killing me. But as George McGovern wrote in his blurb, it was "a labor of love."

Some authors have big prerelease parties to celebrate a new book. I had a party of three. Senator McGovern came over to our house for dinner, and Deb cooked her special glazed salmon recipe. During our time together, we solved more of the world's problems, watched a little baseball, and exchanged signed copies of our books.

After I handed McGovern *Cool Creatures, Hot Planet*, he handed me *The Essential America: Our Founders and the Liberal Tradition* and *The Third Freedom: Ending Hunger in our Time*. The latter book he signed as follows:

"For Deb and Marty with admiration of their friend, George McGovern, June 13, 2006"

And that wasn't all. Knowing that Deb was running for the Montana State Senate that year, McGovern reached into his wallet, pulled out a crisp one hundred dollar bill, and handed it to her as he said, "I wish you all the luck in the world with your campaign. I hope this helps."

George McGovern died on October 21, 2012, at the age of 90. During one of our conversations in 2006, I commented about how impressively he was holding back the years. He responded by saying, "As a congressman, senator, and ambassador, I've always had the best health care in the world. I *should* be in good shape. I just wish every American could have what I've had. And there's no valid reason they shouldn't."

Imagine how different the world would be today if McGovern, not Richard Nixon, had won the 1972 presidential election.

CHAPTER 30

Blood and Snakes

After publishing *Cool Creatures, Hot Planet*, I entered it in a bunch of contests. The book did well, winning six awards. Of all the awards that cater to independent publishers, the Benjamin Franklin Award is among the most prestigious. When I learned that my book was one of the three finalists in their travel-essay category, Deb and I headed to BookExpo America in New York City to attend the 2007 Benjamin Franklin Award ceremony.

We reached New York City with just enough time to check into our hotel, change into dressy clothes, and walk down the street to the Javits Center. The ceremony was in a large room and dinner was included. I know that dinners are traditionally served before awards, but who could possibly eat without first knowing the results? As I tried to calm my stomach enough to enjoy my meal, I also did my best to temper my expectations. One of the books I was competing against was from a big independent publisher, so my best shot was for second place.

Once the awards began, I concentrated on looking cool and relaxed. That calm exterior fell apart when the emcee announced, "And the winner is . . . *Cool Creatures, Hot Planet: Exploring the Seven Continents* by Marty Essen!"

"Yes!" I shouted.

I hurried up onto the stage and gave a short acceptance speech, which included my thanks to both Jeff Corwin and Senator George McGovern for their help in bringing attention to my book. Hey, I was in New York

City, with countless publishing executives in the room. Who knew what a little name-dropping might get me?

My Benjamin Franklin Award was not some small medal to wear around my neck. It was a thick, rectangular piece of glass mounted on a wood base. It weighed almost four pounds. When the ceremony concluded, people gathered around me to offer congratulations and ask questions. I don't remember the first questions. I only remember that the last one launched me into the story about Deb and me surviving the hippo attack.

Near the end of my story, I spread my arms to make a point—and nailed a woman in the face with my award!

The pretty brunette had been hurrying across the floor behind me at the exact wrong moment. She clutched her eye and began crying as blood seeped under her hand.

I tried to steady the woman but gave way to Deb, whose maternal abilities made her better equipped to help. Once the woman stopped crying, Deb convinced her to pull her hand back.

I didn't show it, but I was panicking inside. Just as terrifying as the possibility that the accident had put out the woman's eye was the possibility that she could sue me for every penny I had. I tensed as she slowly dropped her hand, fully expecting to see a gruesome injury that included her eyeball falling onto the floor.

Deb pulled a clean tissue out of her purse and dabbed away the blood. There, on the upper fleshy part of the woman's cheek, was a tiny cut.

Phew! She was okay!

Even so, facial cuts bleed like hell, and a search for a Band-Aid commenced. Surely a building as large as the Javits Center had first aid kits everywhere. Didn't they? I went one way and Deb went another. Ultimately, it wasn't a first aid kit that provided the bandage. It was a bystander who found one in her purse.

Deb applied the bandage, and the two of us stayed with the woman for a bit to make sure there were no unseen physical complications. Once she smiled and assured us everything was fine, we headed out the door to attend one of the many publishing company parties going on that night.

Unfortunately, I can't tell you a thing about that party (which for all I know featured J. K. Rowling and Steven King standing in a tub of liquid chocolate, serving Jell-O shots) because the whiplash of going from the high of winning a Benjamin Franklin Award to the low of nailing a woman in the face with that award had exhausted me. I just wanted to return to our hotel room and curl up in bed next to my wife. So that's what I did.

* * *

Overall, I was pleased with the job my distributors were doing. The book was selling well, and Midpoint Trade came through for me with a healthy Barnes and Noble order. That order was something many indie publishers only dream about.

Then one day my contact at Midpoint Trade called and asked, "Are you open to changing your book cover?"

"Why?" I asked. "I love that book cover."

"I love it too, but some Barnes and Noble store managers are complaining that it's scaring their customers—especially the women. They see your face with that big spider on it and hurry to the opposite side of the store!"

It's always something!

I didn't change my book cover immediately. No way was I going to waste what was left of the initial print run. I only made the change after all those books sold out, and I needed to set up a second printing. So if you ever come across a copy of *Cool Creatures, Hot Planet*, featuring a tailless whip-scorpion on my eye, buy it! It's now a collector's item.

* * *

Before I move on from *Cool Creatures, Hot Planet*, I'm going to take you back a few months to February 2007, and my first book tour. That tour ultimately inspired me to become a college speaker (something I'm still doing today) and to open my third talent agency, Encante Entertainment, Inc.

One of the highlights of my first Amazon Rainforest trip was a rainbow boa some boys from the Yagua tribe brought to me in exchange for some T-shirts. I kept the snake long enough to hold it and take some pictures before releasing it back into the wild. That encounter encouraged me to search for a domestic rainbow boa breeder once I returned to the United States. (I would never take any animal out of the wild.) Soon I owned two baby rainbow boas. Eve arrived first, and when I worried she'd be lonely, I ordered Adam.

Yeah, like snakes really care about companionship.

Adam's arrival was unforgettable, because Federal Express delivered him in a container the size of a margarine-tub just hours after the 9/11 terrorist attacks stopped all air traffic.

In the years that followed, I brought my snakes to schools in the Bitterroot Valley and Missoula as part of an educational digital slide-show based on my world travels. For my book tour, I decided to do the same thing. Telling stories, showing photos, and bringing out an exotic snake just seemed more entertaining than simply opening up my book and reading.

The biggest obstacle to my idea was figuring out how to keep a nearly seven-foot-long snake warm while driving across Montana, North Dakota, South Dakota, and Minnesota in the dead of winter. Yes, the snakes had grown a lot since their margarine-tub days! Also, do snakes ever get carsick? Of my two snakes, Eve has always been my favorite. She's curious and gentle. Never have I had to worry about her biting anyone—even when a half-dozen excited children are holding her at the same time. Adam is generally calm too, and during those rare times when he feels the need to bite someone, he reserves that privilege exclusively for me.

Consequently, deciding which snake to take with me on this somewhat risky trip was easy. This was going to be a boys' trip. I set up Adam on the front seat in a big marine cooler, which I heated with hot water bottles. As we drove along, every hour or so I'd reach into the cooler and grab the thermometer to make sure Adam was enjoying eighty-five-degree rainforest temperatures. Snakes don't require nearly as much oxygen as mammals do, so my temperature checks served the dual purpose of letting in all the oxygen Adam needed and then some. I had a coffee-cup water heater that I could plug into the cigarette lighter in an emergency, but mostly I reheated the water bottles in microwave ovens wherever we stopped.

On that road trip, Adam officially became the World's Most Famous Rainbow Boa. Okay, he likely became the World's *Only* Famous Rainbow

Boa, and just semi-famous at that, but part of good marketing is making things appear more exceptional than they really are.

Our first stop was at the Barnes and Noble in Billings, Montana. I couldn't do my slideshow there, because the store wasn't set up for that kind of event. Nevertheless, I sold a lot of books, with Adam enticing people to gather around. And when a television station showed up for an interview, Adam joined in too.

We were a good team as we crossed North Dakota, stopping at independent bookstores and radio stations along the way. On the far side of our tour, we had shows and book signings in my dual hometowns of Two Harbors and Duluth. Then we headed to Minneapolis for a show and book signing at Magers & Quinn, continued a little south, and worked our way back home through South Dakota.

Most of our stops weren't eventful enough to write about, but my hometowns didn't disappoint. In Two Harbors, it was "local boy makes good" stuff, with one public and two student shows in the high school auditorium. Then we headed to Duluth for a Barnes and Noble book signing and one public and two student shows in the Little Theatre at Duluth East High School.

At my old high school, I got into trouble with the principal one last time! To get a laugh, I confessed to the entire senior class about hitting golf balls off the stage when I was their age. I even pointed to the ding on the brass railing. Yeah, I didn't think about the possibility of encouraging a copycat golfer. I offered my apologies to the principal later, but she still gave me the dreaded evil eye.

* * *

Adam firmly established his fame when we did our Duluth radio and TV interviews. First, we were on the WDIO-TV *Good Morning Northland* show. My interview with the anchorwoman went swimmingly, and she was even brave enough to pet Adam. At the end of our conversation, both she and the anchorman asked me to stick around for another segment before turning to banter with the weatherman as they transitioned into his segment.

As the three chatted, I got pulled right back into the shot when the weatherman confessed that he was terrified of snakes and wanted to make sure he was safe standing in front of his green screen. I assured him that Adam was harmless, and I would never push a snake on anyone who was fearful.

When the weatherman launched into his forecast, I assumed that was the end of it. The anchorman thought differently, however, and snuck up behind him with a snake-like piece of rubber tubing. The weatherman screamed and ran off the set!

He returned moments later to finish his forecast. Though I don't advocate using snakes—real or fake—to scare people, hearing a grown man scream on live TV was outstanding entertainment.

As soon as I got off the air at WDIO-TV, I raced down the hill to KQDS-FM, for a morning show interview with Jason Manning. While I enjoyed being back on the air at my old radio station, it didn't feel much like a homecoming. The studios were in a different building, the entire staff had changed, and the format had switched from cool-and-adventurous rock to straightforward classic rock. In reality, the call letters were all that remained.

Once that interview was over, I called KDAL-AM. I normally set up interviews far in advance, but Rhonda Grussendorf of the *Help Me Rhonda* show had been on vacation. She picked up the phone and said, "The program director told me you were going to call. I'd love to have you on my show! Where are you now?"

"I'm at KQDS, down by the bridge."

"I can fit you in after the commercial break in fifteen minutes. If you hurry, you'll just make it."

"I'm on my way!"

I raced back up the hill, cursing at the red lights that conspired against me. I pulled into the parking lot with three minutes to spare, grabbed Adam, and the receptionist led us directly into the studio.

If you're wondering why I would bring a snake to a radio interview, you're about to understand.

Rhonda was talking on the air, as I stepped quietly inside, carrying Adam in his marine cooler.

She transitioned into a commercial break and turned to me. "Hey Marty, you made it just in time! You're on in two minutes."

"I'm ready. Do you have some headphones I can use?"

"Sure. In the drawer to your right." She tilted her head and smiled.

"What's in the cooler? Did you bring us some drinks?"

"No, it's Adam."

"Adam?"

"My rainbow boa snake."

She screamed!

"Sorry! I can leave him in the cooler. I bring him to radio interviews, because he tends to liven up the conversation."

"Oh, I'm sure he does!" She paused for a second. "Yes, go ahead and bring him out, but wait until I tell you to do so." She swiveled back to her microphone. "Here we go, in five, four . . . Welcome back to the *Help Me Rhonda* show. I'm Rhonda, and in the studio with me is my very special guest—author and adventurer, Marty Essen. . . ."

Following her introduction, I explained why I was in Duluth, and we talked for a bit about my book and my upcoming show for the public in the Little Theatre.

Then she nodded and said, "You walked into my control room carrying a big white cooler. At first, I thought you were going to serve us drinks or we were going to have a picnic or something. Now I know you have something very different in there."

"Yes, I brought Adam with me. He's a rainbow boa."

"What's a rainbow boa?"

"A colorful, heavy-bodied snake, native to South America."

"Is he alive?"

"Very much so."

"And he likes being cold?"

"He's in the cooler to stay warm, not cold. I have hot water bottles in there to keep him at about eighty-five degrees—similar to what he'd experience in the Amazon Rainforest."

"Can he breathe in there?"

"Snakes are cold-blooded, which is kind of a misnomer. They get their heat from their surroundings. So right now, Adam's body temperature is right around eighty-five. Since his body doesn't have to work to stay at a certain temperature, like ours does, he doesn't need to breathe as much as we do either. I open the cooler from time to time to give him fresh air, but he's good in there for many hours."

"I'm gonna have you bring him out, but as you can tell, I've been stalling." She took a deep breath. "Okay, I'm ready. Take him out."

I opened the lid, grasped Adam at mid-body, and lifted him out.
Rhonda screamed!

I lowered him back into the cooler.

"No! No!" she said. "Keep him out. I just wasn't expecting him to be
so big. How long is he?"

"A little under seven feet."

"How long will he get?"

"Technically snakes never stop growing. They just slow way down.
He's now at the point where his growth is practically unnoticeable."

"How long will he live?"

"About thirty years."

"He's beautiful. For all of you out there listening, I can best describe
Adam as orange with black markings that almost look like hearts. Oh!"
She lowered her head. "When the light hits him just right, he appears to
glow. Is that why he's called a rainbow boa?"

"Yes. His thin outer layer of skin creates that effect. It's a little difficult
to see here in the studio, but if we took him outside into the sunlight,
he'd really glow."

While I continued to hold Adam, we moved on to other topics. Over
the years, I have participated in hundreds of radio interviews on some
of the biggest radio stations in America. Rhonda Grussendorf's talent
as a host was up there with the best of them. She was engaging, curious,
and funny.

In fact, I was so into our conversation that I hadn't noticed that Adam
was in the mood for some exploring. My microphone was attached to
a scissor-arm boom—the kind with double bars, spaced roughly three
inches apart. Adam had squeezed himself between the bars and then
wound himself around the mic cable for good measure. The boom was
high quality, but not nearly strong enough to support such a heavy snake.

With one hand, I supported the microphone at mouth-level, and with
the other, I tried to disengage Adam. You're probably aware that snakes
can make themselves thin, if they want to squeeze into tight places.
You're probably unaware that they can do the opposite. To keep himself
firmly in place, Adam puffed out his body a good inch, until he was rock
hard.

The little shit!

Rhonda reached over to help support my mic, freeing up both of my hands to wrestle with Adam. For several minutes, there was chaos in the studio, as I tried to dislodge a stubborn snake without hurting either him or any radio station equipment. All the while, Rhonda and I were engaged in a delightful conversation about my world travels and trying not to crack up.

KDAL listeners never had a clue about the battle going on behind the scenes.

* * *

Pro tip: Should a snake ever get loose in your house or apartment, search first wherever you have a big tangle of cords in a tight space—like behind a desktop computer or a stereo system. Chances are good you'll find a contented snake waiting for you there.

* * *

My show that evening at Duluth East High School was a tremendous success, with some people even driving an hour south from the Iron Range to see it. Then it was on to the Twin Cities and west across South Dakota for more bookstore shows. Adam and I arrived home several days later—both human and snake happy to be reunited with our respective mates.

CHAPTER 31

Blood and Dogs

I've always had dogs in my life. Annie, a white, not quite purebred Labrador retriever that I adopted from the Bitterroot Humane Association, will likely always be my favorite dog. She and I were practically inseparable, and she stayed by my side for the entire twelve thousand hours it took me to write *Cool Creatures, Hot Planet*. She died of cancer on the day I finished the manuscript.

As much as I'd love to write a whole chapter about my beloved Annie, she already has a big part in the Canada chapter of that first book, and often it's the dogs that get themselves into the most trouble that make the best stories. With that in mind, let me introduce you to Lucy!

Like Annie, we adopted Lucy from the Bitterroot Humane Association. She was a medium-sized border collie mix—likely two years old at the time of the adoption. Officially, she was Deb's dog, because Deb picked her out as a replacement for her golden retriever, Kate, who had recently died of old age.

Lucy initially seemed to be well-behaved, and because Kate and Annie died just a few months apart, she was our only dog at the time. A week or so after the adoption, Deb and I left Lucy alone in the house while we attended an afternoon political function. Normally for such an event, we'd go in one car, but this time we drove separately, so Deb could run errands afterward.

I arrived home several hours later, climbed the steps, and entered through the door leading into the laundry room/coat room on the main floor. I felt something sticky under my feet and looked down. The white and gray tile was smeared red. I was standing in blood!

Lucy pushed against me, wagging her tail and panting. I crouched down to check her out. She didn't have any visible cuts on her body, but her front feet were caked with blood.

"What happened, Lucy?" I asked. It was a rhetorical question.

When I stepped into the kitchen, I noticed that the top of the kitchen table had deep claw marks in it. I looked to my left, and bloody paw prints led me into the great room. In there were two stories of floor-to-ceiling windows, providing a stunning view of the Bitterroot Mountains. Those tall windows weren't what caught my attention, however. Instead, my eyes focused on the two smaller, floor-level, crank-open ventilation windows. The interior screens were shredded and bloody paw prints streaked the glass. I peered into my adjacent writing room. Every screen in there was similarly shredded. I crossed to the dining room and pinpointed were Lucy had cut herself. Somehow, she had climbed onto our antique dining room table and broken a glass vase. I turned to see bloody paw prints, leading to the top floor. I ran up the steps and crossed to our bedroom. Lucy had destroyed the screens in there too.

I grabbed a phone and called Deb.

"You need to come home right now!" I demanded as soon as she answered.

"What's wrong?"

"*Your* dog has destroyed our house!"

* * *

The two of us put the house back together, and the next day I bought the sturdiest kennel I could find in the Bitterroot Valley. It was an airline-approved fiberglass crate with a metal bar door. I placed the kennel in the laundry room, and Lucy went right inside and lay down. I took that as a good sign.

We conducted a short test, locking her inside, and leaving the house for ten minutes.

A happy escapee greeted us at the door when we returned. Somehow, she had managed to pry open the kennel door.

Since Deb and I had to attend another political event in a few days, I tightened every bolt on the kennel and brainstormed on how to make it escape-proof. When the time came to leave, we put Lucy back into the kennel, gave her a bone, wrapped the kennel with bungee cords, and—just to be safe—pulled shut the pocket door between the laundry room and the kitchen. That way if she got loose, at least she'd be confined to the laundry room.

Or so we thought.

Later that night we returned to find an empty kennel—still wrapped in bungie cords—and an empty laundry room. Obviously, we were mistaken when we guessed Lucy's breed as a border collie mix. She was a purebred Houdini dog! Figuring out how to slide open the pocket door may have been her most impressive feat.

The damage she did to our house was virtually identical to her first demolition job. We cleaned up the worst of it before carrying stiff drinks outside to the front porch and collapsing in chairs.

"What should we do about Lucy?" I asked

"She obviously has separation anxiety," Deb said.

"We're still within the Humane Association's trial period. We could return her."

"I don't know. . . ." She chuckled. "At least we know why she was up for adoption."

"Yeah. Who knows how many houses she's destroyed before ours."

"We can't stay home with her all the time, and we can't let her destroy the house over and over either."

"So are you voting to return her?"

"Is that what you want to do?"

"That wasn't an answer." I took a big swallow of my drink. "Right now, I don't ever want to see Lucy again. But you know if we returned her, it would be her death sentence. We've always been animal advocates. If not us, who? We'd be hypocrites if we didn't keep her."

"I was hoping you'd say that."

"You could have said it first."

"I didn't want to force you into keeping a dog you didn't want."

"Wait a minute! She's *your* dog!"

* * *

The next day, I searched the internet and bought the strongest all-metal dog cage I could find. When it arrived a week later, I let Lucy have at it for a ten-minute test. Although that test was mostly positive, she had already bent some of the bars and likely would have broken out if given enough time.

I made a trip to the hardware store and returned with a bag full of pipe clamps and locking D-rings. Then I reinforced every bar and every joint, saving the last two locking D-rings for the cage door once Lucy was inside.

"Deb!" I called out. "Come here."

She stepped into the laundry room and burst into laughter. "I'd say that was overkill, but I know better."

"It's *Al-dog-atraz!*"

Fortunately for all, Al-dog-atraz held for the next month or so, while I kept an eye open for a permanent fix for Lucy's separation anxiety. That fix came home with me after a trip to Missoula: I bought her a puppy!

Bella was a yellow lab. Normally, I prefer to adopt dogs from animal shelters, but after Annie died, I was determined to get another dog like her. That, however, turned out to be an unrealistic expectation. Even though Bella was officially my dog, as far as she was concerned, she was actually Lucy's dog. The two were inseparable from day one. And until she was too big to do so, Bella slept on Lucy's fluffy tail—with Lucy loving every minute of it.

Four years later, we had to prepare ourselves for the end of Lucy. She and Bella were wrestling outside when Deb heard loud yelping. She raced out the door to find Lucy pulling herself along by her front legs—her hind legs dragging uselessly on the ground. I was out of town that day, so Deb had to lift Lucy into the car by herself and drive her to the veterinarian. That's when we learned that Lucy had horrible hip dysplasia and a frayed tendon that wouldn't last for six months. Once that tendon snapped she would be unable to walk. At least Lucy's hips had popped back into place, and soon she was moving around as if nothing had happened. Even so, with the combination of problems in her back end, the vet recommended forgoing surgery and simply enjoying our final months with her.

* * *

Four years after that, Lucy was still going strong, albeit with the help of a daily pain pill and glucosamine tablet. That's when a third dog, Buddy, adopted us.

I had known Buddy for most of his fourteen years. He was a cantankerous part-Saint Bernard who lived with a woman on our road. Several times over the years, he had nipped at my ankles, though he never drew blood. Then one day Buddy's life changed. The woman brought home Miley, a cute little pug puppy. Miley was full of energy, and Buddy didn't like her. He was smart enough not to hurt the puppy, but he soon tired of abruptly waking up from naps with the puppy attached to his face.

To catch a break from all that hyperactivity, Buddy started joining Lucy, Bella, Deb, and me on our evening walks. We always walked in the opposite direction of Buddy's house, but it didn't take him long to figure out that we took our walks at the same time each day. He adopted us gradually. At first, he kept his distance as we walked; then he inserted himself into the middle of the pack; later he started hanging out at our house, and finally he refused to go home.

Even when we escorted Buddy to his house, he'd only stay for a minute or so before catching up with us. That's when Buddy's owner said, "Just keep him." She was having health problems and could no longer handle a big dog anyway.

I'm sure the woman also thought Buddy was going to die soon. He was already older than most dogs his size lived to be, no longer walked well, incessantly scratched himself, and was losing hair in clumps. All in all, he was one pitiful, ugly old dog.

Nevertheless, if he was going to be our pet for his final months, and come inside our house, I had to clean him up. As I confirmed later, Buddy had never had a bath. As I confirmed at that moment, Buddy wasn't a bath kind of dog. The big old Saint Bernard cried through his entire bath but didn't bite or try to get away.

Over the next few months, we kept Buddy clean, fed him high-quality food, gave him glucosamine for his joints, and took him to the vet for his first ever rabies and distemper shots. He also got plenty of exercise via our walks and the constant company of Bella and Lucy. All of that helped transform Buddy into a version of himself that was barely recognizable. His skin problems disappeared, his fur grew back, and he had a bounce in his step. Most surprising was his temperament change. He was friendly to everyone and became my big buddy, frequently hanging out with me in my writing room.

Aside from Buddy's amazing transformation, there are two incidents with him that I will never forget. The first happened when we had a mountain lion in the area, and Buddy chased something away from our house. Other than Saint Bernard, part of Buddy's bloodline might have been hound dog, because he bellowed like one whenever he ran. I could hear him giving chase, deep into the forest. He returned a half-hour later, all proud that he had protected us. A deep slash across his muzzle confirmed his mountain lion encounter.

The second incident happened on one of our walks. The five of us were on the dirt road that descends from our house, when I looked up and spotted a mother black bear and her cub on the hill to the left of us, forty yards ahead. Deb and I gathered the dogs around us and stood there watching as the clumsy cub tried to climb a sapling. It was a beautiful moment, worthy of a nature film—until Buddy couldn't take it anymore and charged!

"No, Buddy! No!" we screamed.

He raced toward the bears, barking with every stride. As he closed in, he realized the error of his ways, slammed on the brakes, and turned.

Too late!

The mother bear swatted him across the rear end. He yelped and hightailed back toward us with the mother in hot pursuit!

"No, Buddy! No!" we screamed.

Fortunately for all, the mother bear was more interested in protecting her cub than engaging in a confrontation. She broke off her chase before reaching us, allowing Deb and me to break into laughter. Without a doubt, Buddy had set the all-time speed record for geriatric Saint Bernards.

* * *

Epilogue: Buddy lived with us for five years. Presumably, they were the best five years of his life. He had always been a wanderer, and even at the age of nineteen, he still attempted to make his rounds. Unfortunately, bowels he could no longer control and arthritic back legs he could barely walk on prevented him from reaching twenty. After I found him shivering and cold, unable to escape a shallow ditch he had tried to cross, I reluctantly put him to sleep.

Bella had similar rear end problems and developed tumors throughout her body. One day, while on a walk, she fell down and couldn't get up. I had to put her to sleep at age eleven.

As for Lucy—the dog who wasn't supposed to make it past the age of six? She's now sixteen and enjoying a nap in the great room as I'm typing this. She may not live until I finish this book, but I gave up on underestimating her many years ago.

Her life as an old dog is quite different from how it used to be. Similar to what happened to Buddy and Bella, her back legs are now quite weak. The difference with Lucy is that she uses doggy physics to figure out tricks for things such as maneuvering into a standing position or walking without much pain. Though she can no longer climb our outside stairs without help, she has a trick for that too. She puts her front paws on the bottom step and waits for me to lift her rear end and wheelbarrow her up the steps.

Overall, she is still a happy dog. When she started getting forgetful about letting us know when she had to go to the bathroom during the night, we solved that problem with some pills for her bladder and bringing Al-dog-atraz out of storage. Now she loves to sleep in the cage she once hated so much, and we seldom have to clean up after her.

Several months ago, I joked to my wife that Lucy was going into her cage so willingly because it was the only thing ever to defeat her. "Obviously, she's busy working out the physics necessary to launch an escape," I said.

Shortly after that—and I swear this is true—Deb and I had to leave the house for a few hours. Though Lucy was long past her separation anxiety days, I put her into her cage, just in case her bladder problem acted up. When we returned, she greeted us at the door with her tail wagging away. Whether I had forgotten to tighten the latch or she finally figured out how to pop it open I can't say. But this much I know for sure: Lucy had escaped Al-dog-atraz!

CHAPTER 32

Adventures in College Speaking

When I presented my digital slideshow in bookstores, I wasn't thinking of expanding it beyond that. I was just trying to do something more compelling than a traditional book reading. But as often happens with me, the industrious side of my personality kicked in. As near as I could tell, Al Gore's *An Inconvenient Truth* was the only large-scale traveling slideshow in America. While the country surely had room for more than just one traveling slideshow, Al Gore's fame guaranteed his show's success. Could I find an audience for mine without the name recognition that comes from being the vice president of the United States? Then I remembered working the college market when I was a talent agent. Colleges had budgets for entertainers and speakers, and my show might fit if I marketed myself in the speaker category. I researched that possibility and decided to go for it.

Once I made my decision, I knew that standing at a lectern with a clicker while presenting a simple slideshow of photos I'd taken on all seven continents wouldn't do. I needed to reach back to my talent manager days and work with myself as I had worked with bands to create an energetic and exciting stage show. In other words, I needed to add some rock 'n' roll-like excitement.

After buying a wireless remote that doubled as a laser pointer, I set up a makeshift performance area in the rec room of my daylight basement. I practiced for days, adding funny and educational stories as they came to me. I called the show *Around the World in 90 Minutes,* and like a front man in a rock band, I worked the entire stage—sometimes running or crawling across it. I even blocked it like a play, memorizing it until I said the same words during the same steps in each performance.

Before moving my show into the colleges, I had one final problem to address: I had stage fright. That may seem like a strange claim, considering that I grew up working in radio, had done a large number of radio and television interviews, and had already been presenting a smaller version of my show. But on radio and TV, I didn't actually see my audience, and my school and bookstore presentations were low-pressure shows performed for free. There is a big difference in expectations when a fee is involved. At colleges, I would be speaking in auditoriums filled with students while getting paid thousands of dollars for doing it.

Different people overcome stage fright in different ways. Should you ever have to give a speech and have stage fright like I did, here's my pro tip: Get the brightest light you can and shine it in your face as you practice. You'll feel like you're on stage under a spotlight. The first time I tried it in my rec room, I actually felt nervous. Then, after a few rehearsals, I relaxed. Now, after speaking in colleges for fourteen years, I still get a little nervous if I'm performing in a packed auditorium—but it's a good kind of nervous, not the kind that makes my mind go blank.

* * *

I debuted *Around the World in 90 Minutes* on October 6, 2007, at the Idaho Museum of Natural History on the campus of Idaho State University. I performed that show for free, because I wanted to see how it played on a college campus and didn't feel right about charging money for it until I knew everything would run smoothly. Then, three days later, I performed my first paid gig at Yavapai College in Prescott, Arizona.

I run my show remotely off a laptop computer and always carry two computers, in case one fails. I also bring my own headset microphone system and digital projector. Generally I use the college's projector, but every once in a while I speak at a college with old or inferior equipment. The only problem with taking all that heavy gear on the road is that I have to carry it onto airplanes. Before TSA PreCheck, I was the last person you'd want to follow through an airport security line.

Beginning with that first paid gig at Yavapai College, I have always shown up at least ninety minutes early to make sure everything works and to change into my stage clothes. At Yavapai, I learned that sometimes you just have to shrug and do your best. There, they didn't have any way to connect my laptop to their projector, and instead I had to copy my show onto their desktop computer, which was located in a different room. Things seemed to be working okay, until a few minutes into my show a message popped up on the screen, "Windows would like to install updates. Please click to continue." A technician hurried into the other room to get rid of the pop-up. Windows would not be denied, however, and continued popping up every ten minutes for the remainder of my show.

Later, I performed in a ballroom at Texas State University, where their digital projector and screen were suspended from a high ceiling. The equipment worked fine, except for one problem: the projector mount had slipped so badly that the picture on the screen was almost at a 45-degree angle. My student contact told me that they didn't have a ladder tall enough to reach the projector, and it had been that way for a long time. "Students are used to tilting their heads," she said.

I wasn't about to perform a sideways show, so I dug into my backpack and pulled out my digital projector. Since the ceiling screen was too high for it to reach, I sent the student in search of a portable screen. Apparently, the only portable screen on campus was one intended for slideshows in closets, but a small image was better than a sideways image. I made do, and the show turned out fine.

Other technical issues I've had to work around included a screen at the University of North Dakota that automatically retracted into the ceiling every fifteen minutes, and a PA amp at Brookdale College that blew up and forced me to present part of my show in an auditorium without amplification. Fortunately, I have a strong voice. The bottom line is that in all my years of speaking at colleges, I've never encountered a problem I couldn't overcome.

The show must go on!

* * *

Something memorable happens every time I'm on a speaking tour. Generally, I love being on the road, but there are exceptions. One such time was when I had to fly to Rapid City, South Dakota, on November 4, 2008. You may recognize that date, because that was when Barack Obama won his first presidential election. Deb and I had worked hard during that election cycle, and I wanted to be with her and our Democratic friends when the celebrating began. Having to celebrate via cell phone from a quiet hotel room just wasn't the same.

I didn't have a gig that night. Sometimes flying out of Missoula can be complicated, and this time airline schedules forced me to depart a day early to make my Black Hills State University performance on the evening of November 5. Following that show, I planned to get up early and drive across the state for a November 6 show at Augustana University in Sioux Falls. From there, I'd fly to the East Coast for a series of shows in New York, Vermont, and New Hampshire.

Black Hills State University is located fifty miles northwest of Rapid City, in the town of Spearfish. Because of the town's small size (population eleven thousand), it made sense for me to stay two nights in Rapid City. Therefore, late in the afternoon on the day of the performance, I left all of my clothes and toiletries in my hotel room, packed up my show gear, and departed for the easy forty-five minute drive along Interstate 90 (the main highway that crosses South Dakota).

Since the day had been sunny, I hadn't bothered to check the weather forecast, and when snow began falling a few miles outside of Rapid City, I figured it was just one of those brief fall snowstorms—nothing to be concerned about.

Suddenly the wind picked up, and a sheet of white blocked my view. I slowed way down, until a heavy gust threatened to blow my little economy car off the road. I sped up just enough to make the car feel more stable but not so fast that I couldn't avoid the snowdrifts that were already forming.

I made it to Spearfish and managed to forget about the storm while I performed my show. My worries returned when I stepped outside afterward, and the blizzard was still going strong. As I trudged across the parking lot, those worries turned to glee. A snowplow was passing by! Obviously, the people of South Dakota were well prepared for such storms. I jumped into my car and followed the plow all the way to the Interstate 90 entrance ramp. When the plow continued straight on the road, I turned onto the ramp and stopped.

I asked myself, "Do I go for it or turn around?"

My elevation was high enough that I could see a little way down the freeway, and the only car lights I saw weren't moving. Had I rented a four-wheel-drive, I probably would have gone for it. My memory of the wind tossing my economy car around earlier convinced me that risking the freeway now would be unwise.

I looked over my shoulder. Just behind me was a Best Western motel. I shifted the car into reverse and the tires spun. I rocked myself free and pulled up to the motel with my fingers crossed for a vacancy.

Luck was with me, and with a key in hand, I drove around to the freeway side of the motel and parked just outside my room door. Everything was going to be just ducky. I'd still have plenty of time to get up in the morning, pick up my stuff in Rapid City, and drive across the state to Augustana University.

Or maybe not.

When I opened my exterior door in the morning, a wall of snow greeted me that was higher than the doorknob. On the opposite side of my room was a second door that led into an interior hallway. I opened that and hurried down the hall to the front desk. There I learned that I-90 was closed all the way across South Dakota and wouldn't open for at least two days. The company that plowed out the parking lot would likely take that long to arrive too.

I was trapped.

The clerk handed me a complimentary razor, a tube of toothpaste, and a toothbrush, and I returned to my room. For the next two days, I sat there with only my laptop computer and the clothes on my back.

For a while, it was kind of fun. But once I read the entire internet and started over again, I got bored. Other guests were obviously bored too. Pot smoke wafted into the hallway from under the door of the room across from me. A gutsy move to be sure. But what were the cops going to do, make an arrest via snowmobile?

Other than the breakfast buffet, my only source of food was the restaurant next door. Somehow they managed to stay open, and despite their incredibly mediocre meals, they did quite well feeding lunch and dinner to an entire hotel of captive guests.

Early on the second day, a plow arrived to clear a path through the parking lot—and pack snow tightly against all the cars. No one could get out without additional shoveling. For that project, the motel provided a single shovel and a sign-up sheet.

I got my turn on the shovel later that afternoon. Not that it did a lot of good. Just because I could get out of the parking lot didn't mean I could get onto the freeway.

I-90 didn't open until the third morning. If snow had been the only obstacle, it would have opened sooner. The problem was all the stuck and wrecked cars littering the highway. One of those cars likely would have been mine, had I decided to go for it right after my show.

Fortunately, Augustana University rescheduled my missed engagement for a few months later, and I was able to catch a flight out of Rapid City that got me to New York in time for my East Coast shows. So other than having to buy an extra airline ticket, everything worked out okay.

* * *

People often ask me if I get bored performing the same show over and over. While I have tired of the travel and living in hotel rooms during particularly long tours, I seldom get bored on stage. That's because I feed off the energy from my audience, and I am still hoping to perform that elusive perfect show. Each time I speak, I do so for ninety minutes straight (unless I'm performing the abbreviated version, *Around the World in 50 Minutes,* which I developed to fit within a class period). Despite all my memorization work, somewhere within my performance, I will inevitably make a mistake. The vast majority of those mistakes are unrecognizable to my audience, but I know what I did.

Often my mistakes happen because my mind wanders. Even though I've become very good at thinking about other things while I'm giving a speech (perhaps I'm thinking about Donald Trump's latest vindictive act or the student by the aisle who hasn't looked up from his smartphone), it's an imperfect talent.

On the other hand, during the rare times when students are trying to screw me up, they don't stand a chance. My most memorable instance of that happened at Diné College, on the Navajo Nation, in northeastern Arizona. The college sits at seven thousand feet, and I had to drive some lonely roads to get there. I was already expecting an unusual experience, but nothing close to what actually happened.

My evening show was in a large room, and in the front row were two good-looking teenaged women. The host introduced me and dimmed the house lights. Since I'm as much a part of the show as the photos are, I always perform with some stage lights or a follow spot. I can't always see my audience, however, because sometimes those lights blind me. Here the lighting allowed me to see everyone in the first several rows.

I was less than five minutes into my show, when the two women in the front row went at it. And by "at it," I don't mean fighting. They passionately kissed, had their hands up each other's shirts, and rubbed each other's crotches. Whether the women were acting on a dare, trying to mess up my show, got off on being watched, or were just incredibly horny, I can't say. All I know is that I was determined not to let them affect my performance.

My skill of being able to give a speech while thinking about something else came in quite handy that night. Even so, if I had the opportunity to do it over again, I would pause my show, sit on the edge of the stage, directly in front of them, and say, "Your show is *much* better than mine. Proceed!" But responses like that seldom come to me until well after the moment has passed.

* * *

Until publishing my *Time Is Irreverent* series of novels, I had been relatively quiet about my thoughts on religion. Consequently, I have performed many shows at religious colleges. My show is neutral on religion anyway—except for a few sentences about evolution, which I remove at conservative institutions. I do particularly well at Catholic schools and often get asked back. Neumann University, just outside of Philadelphia, is my favorite Catholic college to perform at. The first time I was there, I set a personal record for books sold after an engagement. The second time I was there, a nun who couldn't have been taller than four-foot-six, walked up to me after my show and asked, "Do you know how old I am?"

"No," I said.

"I'm ninety-five!"

"Wow! I wouldn't have guessed you a year over eighty."

"You're a flatterer!" she said with a bright smile. "I loved your show."

"Why, thank you!"

"Can I buy you lunch?"

"Sure!"

The tiny nun, along with three standard-sized nuns, walked me to the cafeteria and, unlike meals in public places with my father, we paused for only a short silent prayer before eating.

"Do you know what I want to be in my next life?" the tiny nun asked.

"Next life?" I asked, not sure where she was leading our conversation.

"When I'm reincarnated!" she said with a mischievous grin.

"What do you want to be?"

"I want to be a wildlife biologist!" she declared.

I can't recall where our conversation went from that point, but I do remember that the three standard-sized nuns were equally delightful, though not quite as irreverent. From that day on, I've never looked at nuns the same way.

* * *

Partly because of population and partly because liberal states do a much better job of funding education, I perform roughly 70 percent of my shows in the northeast. There are both positives and negatives to this. A big positive is that I can fly into a single airport (usually Philadelphia or Newark), rent a car, and perform multiple shows before having to get on an airplane again. A big negative is that I have to deal with all the traffic.

During my many business and pleasure trips to New York City, I've always taken a taxi in from the airport each time. Though I'm accustomed to driving in major cities, doing so in New York City was something I swore I'd never do. I couldn't imagine negotiating the packed, seemingly lawless streets with everyone honking.

My GPS, "Sally," and I have experienced multiple adventures out East, such as when we took the Lake Champlain Ferry from Burlington, Vermont, to Port Kent, New York, and midway across the lake she announced, "When possible make a legal U-turn!" But by far our best adventure happened following a show in New Jersey, when I had to drive far out on Long Island, so I could stay overnight at a hotel and perform a noon show the next day at Suffolk County Community College. I had intended to take the George Washington Bridge across, but I was paying more attention to the heavy traffic around me than the nifty shortcut Sally wanted to take through the Lincoln Tunnel. When I ended up in Manhattan, I tried to make a course correction, and that only made things worse.

I looked to my left and saw the marquee for *Spider-Man: Turn Off the Dark*. My first thought was, "Shit! I'm gonna die!" Then I realized that despite the bumper-to-bumper traffic and horns blaring everywhere, it wasn't as bad as I had imagined it would be.

I chuckled and glanced at my watch. It was a little after eight, which meant it was a little after six in Montana. I pulled out my cell phone at the next stoplight and dialed my wife.

She recognized my number on caller ID and answered, "Hi Hon! You're calling early."

"Guess where I am?"

She laughed as she asked, "Where?"

"Times Square!"

"You're kidding."

"No. I took a wrong turn. When I passed the *Spider-Man: Turn Off the Dark* sign, I immediately thought of when we were here to see the show on our anniversary. I had to give you a call."

"Wait a minute! You're talking on your cell phone, while *driving* through Times Square?"

"Yes," I said sheepishly. "Oh, shit! The tall buildings are blocking my GPS. Now I have no idea where I'm going."

"Get *off* the phone! And don't call me till you get to your hotel."

"Fine," I whined.

"Goodbye!" she said with a chuckle. "I love you."

"I love you too."

* * *

Not all of my shows are at colleges. Some are at museums, nature centers, or zoos. The venues with live animals are among my favorites, because I always get behind-the-scenes tours. Over the years, those shows have allowed me to pet a bobcat, hold owls, snakes, groundhogs, and opossums, and even hand-feed ring-tailed lemurs and red pandas.

Sometimes my shows also give me the opportunity to do a little exploring. Between performances in California, I took a side trip into Death Valley. Between performances in Arizona, I explored the Petrified Forest National Park and the Mojave Desert. Between performances in the Carolinas, I explored wild areas along the coast and nearly sat on a copperhead snake.

My show at St. Thomas University in Miami Gardens, Florida, indirectly provided content for two of my books (three if you count this one). After that performance, I intentionally left open several days, so I could rent a condominium in Everglades City and explore the Everglades. The nonfiction part of that wonderful solo adventure became a chapter in my second book, *Endangered Edens: Exploring the Arctic National Wildlife Refuge, Costa Rica, the Everglades, and Puerto Rico.* Later, when I wrote the first novel in my *Time Is Irreverent* science-fiction political-comedy series, a jealous alien sends my male protagonist, Marty Mann, to the year 2056 and drops him in the middle of global-warming-flooded Everglades City.

When I write fiction, I still use real facts and real places whenever possible. Having visited Everglades City helped me accurately write that part of Marty Mann's adventure. And later, when he and my female protagonist, Nellie Dixon, embark on a road trip across America, I route them through other places I had personally visited on college tours, while adjusting those locations to reflect how I imagined they would appear under theocracy rule in 2056.

My two favorite performances—so far—have been homecoming shows. The closest college to me is the University of Montana in Missoula. It's also the college where my son, Sean, graduated. There I performed a show in the UC Theater, and despite a windstorm a little before show time that was strong enough to toss a trampoline on top of powerlines, I still managed to fill the house.

My other homecoming show was at the University of Minnesota Duluth. There my old college gave me the red carpet treatment. The chancellor, Dr. Lendley Black, held a special preshow dinner for me, which was also attended by Don Ness, the mayor of Duluth, and other local dignitaries. That evening I performed *Around the World in 90 Minutes* in the Weber Music Hall—a beautiful, almost acoustically perfect, concert hall designed by world famous architect César Pelli. In addition to the chancellor and the mayor, my full-house show included friends and teachers from Open School and people I introduced to you earlier in the book: Vern, Steve, and Luann. And if that wasn't enough, the college rented a luxury car for me and put me up in the penthouse suite at Fitger's Inn (located in a renovated building that used to house the Fitger Brewing Company).

Though I didn't know it at the time, that unique suite and hotel, which sits right on Lake Superior, would later become the setting for one of the most emotional scenes in *Time Is Irreverent*. Now that I've immortalized Fitger's Inn in that novel, I have to keep my fingers crossed that the hotel will still be there for Marty Mann and Nellie Dixon in 2056.

* * *

My college shows put me back into the agency business. During my first few years of booking myself, I spent thousands of hours on the internet compiling what is arguably the most complete college contact list in the nation. Since using that list just for me seemed wasteful, I formed Encante Entertainment, Inc., and signed performers exclusively for the college market.

Of all the jobs I've done over the years, booking college shows may be the most difficult. That's because predicting what college students want is tricky, and even if you hit it right, students two years down the line might have completely different interests. I was lucky with my show, because it's both animal- and travel-oriented. What student doesn't love animals or dream of traveling?

Initially I signed some of the musicians I had worked with during my Minneapolis talent agency days. Unfortunately, as cool as those musicians still were, college students preferred rap, hip-hop, and boy bands. Had a quality rap or hip-hop act fallen into my lap, I might have considered representing it. But a boy band? I have my dignity and would rather starve before representing such a thing!

I've had much better luck representing speakers. Among my most successful long-term clients are Emmy nominee Naomi Grossman (famous for her role as Pepper in *American Horror Story*) and civility speaker Traciana Graves (who was previously a backing vocalist for Celine Dion and Steel Pulse).

As I type this, both the COVID-19 pandemic and the Republican

Party's reluctance to fund education have fogged the future for college performers and agencies. While I hope both deterrents will soon fade away, if they don't, I will adjust—as I always have.

CHAPTER 33

Satan and the Masonic Watch

As my father grew older, his version of Christianity grew more extreme—if that was possible. His influences included Pat Robertson, whatever other charlatan happened to be on the Christian Broadcasting Network at that moment, and his local conman preacher.

My attempts to convince him to moderate his views even a tiny amount failed, as always. For a while, I enjoyed our biblical arguments, but eventually they grew too predictable. Whenever I would back him into a corner with logic and science, he'd get angry with me, declare I couldn't understand because I wasn't a Christian, or resort to the old standby: "And then a miracle happened."

Mostly he just wanted one-sided conversations where he preached to me, and I didn't question him, the Bible, or the GOP (God's Own Party). On the latter, I often wondered why God, who was supposedly all about love, would side with a political party that favored so many hateful policies aimed at minorities, health care, education, and the environment.

"I didn't raise you that way!" my father shouted during one of those phone conversations. "You changed after you married Deb. I think Satan is working through her to deceive you!"

Yeah, that went over well with me.

Unfortunately, my father had heart problems near the end of his life, and I pretty much had to let him say his piece with minimal resistance. I would have felt horrible if an argument sent him into cardiac arrest in mid-phone conversation.

With the exception of the Satan working through my wife thing, my father's indoctrination attempts rarely upset me. Instead, I reserved my anger for the Christians who took advantage of him. His local preacher, his born-again Christian third wife, various televangelists, and numerous Christian organizations all contributed to suck him dry. And he was so brainwashed into "giving 10 percent to the Lord," that when he needed financial help from me for basic necessities, I had to make him promise that he wouldn't turn around and give 10 percent of what I gave him to his church, or worse—Pat Robertson.

Ultimately, my father died virtually penniless because of those horrible human beings.

I don't remember the name of the Florida church he attended late in life, but I'll never forget when my father called me, victim of the most ingenious con job I'd ever heard of.

"Hello."

"Marty, I'm so glad you're home," my father said in a frantic voice.

"What's wrong, Dad?"

"Do you still have the Masonic Lodge watch I gave you?"

"You never gave me such a watch."

"Are you sure?"

"Yes. I'm absolutely sure. Maybe you gave it to Paul."

"Oh, boy, I have to find it. I'm sure you know that I belonged to the Masons before I gave my life to the Lord. Now I know the Masons served Satan, not Christ."

"What does that have to do with your watch?"

"Today in church, Pastor Peters* gave a sermon about demon possession. He warned us that demons can possess almost anything—especially jewelry that has been involved in divorces or other negative events. At the end of the service, he set a bucket on the altar, so people could drop in any jewelry that might be possessed. People were dropping in necklaces, rings, and watches. Pastor Peters* is going to make sure it all gets destroyed. That's when I got to thinking about the watch."

"Dad, that's b—never mind. Check with Paul."

His voice was now shaking, "Please look for it and promise me that if you find it, you will destroy it."

"I promise, Dad."

My father was less than a year away from dying when he made that call. I knew he didn't have long to live, and the genuine fear in his voice kept me from making any snarky comments.

That said, had Pastor Peters* not been all the way across the country from me, the conman preacher and I would have had one hell of a face-to-face Come to Jesus Talk—and I wouldn't have held back. I wonder how much money he made selling his congregation's "possessed" jewelry?

CHAPTER 34

Damn You Amazon!

No matter how many books I write, *Endangered Edens: Exploring the Arctic National Wildlife Refuge, Costa Rica, the Everglades, and Puerto Rico* will always be my black sheep. Essentially it was the sequel to *Cool Creatures, Hot Planet: Exploring the Seven Continents,* and it featured three adventures with Deb plus my solo Everglades adventure. The biggest difference was that I listened to comments from readers of my first book, who wanted to see more of my pictures. So while *Cool Creatures, Hot Planet* featured 85 smallish color photos in an insert, *Endangered Edens* featured 180 color photos, many of them large, and the entire book was printed on high-quality glossy paper.

Endangered Edens was an expensive book to produce. One of my favorite reviews came from a woman who wrote that she bought two copies: one for reading and one for cutting out photos to frame. The book also featured wonderful back cover blurbs from Dr. M. Sanjayan, the host of the PBS television series *EARTH: A New Wild,* Stewart Brandborg, one of the key people behind the creation of the Arctic National Wildlife Refuge, and Cindy Shogan, the executive director of the Alaska Wilderness League.

Despite everything the book had going for it, the sales were somewhat disappointing. I blame that on several factors. First, a nine-year gap between books caused me to lose my momentum. The reason for the delay was that I had put so much time and energy into *Cool Creatures, Hot Planet* that it took me a while to become excited about writing again, and then, once I regained my enthusiasm, I had to come up with a concept and finish the necessary travels.

The delay also meant that I had to put together a new national distribution deal. I should have approached Midpoint Trade again, but I made the mistake of becoming enamored with a distributor that claimed to work with a wider variety of markets. I won't name that distributor, because they don't even deserve the negative publicity I'm about to give them. In addition to pitching *Endangered Edens* to bookstores across the country, they also promised to push it to major outdoor recreation catalogs and stores. While they ultimately had some success with bookstores, they totally failed in the outdoor market.

I'm not the kind of author who sits back, waiting for things to happen, so as I had done with *Cool Creatures, Hot Planet,* I supported *Endangered Edens* with a book tour and a large number of local, regional, and national radio interviews. While that strategy worked great with Midpoint Trade, with my new distributor I could give them more than a month's notice of my bookstore events and still end up having to placate pissed-off owners and managers who had trouble getting books. In fact, one bookstore owner in New York had to buy multiple copies of *Endangered Edens* at retail from Amazon, so she'd have stock for the event.

As if that wasn't enough, when I decided to take a break from writing nonfiction and switch to fiction for a while, my distributor dropped me, claiming that I'd have to build a new following from scratch. They also sent me a bill, claiming that they had overpaid royalties. When I asked for documentation to back up their bill, they sent me another bill with a completely different figure and no documentation. Since this wasn't the first time my distributor had demonstrated an appalling lack of competence, I repeated my request for documentation. Caught and unable to provide evidence that they had done anything other than pull numbers out of their corporate asses, they never contacted me again.

That, unfortunately, was an expensive lesson learned. To this day, boxes of that beautiful book take up a wall in one of the offices in my basement. I still sell copies at my college shows and via mail order. Mostly though, I donate signed copies to liberal nonprofits that want them for fundraisers.

Should any books remain after Deb and I die, they'll be my son's responsibility. Since we already live in our dream house, the chances are good that we'll never move again. Accordingly, with Sean being our only child, unless something unforeseen happens, he's going to come out great when we're gone. Therefore, I enjoy giving him shit that his inheritance isn't going to be all roses. In addition to having to figure out what to do with any unsold copies of *Endangered Edens*, he's also going to own one of the world's largest cord collections (I'm not a hoarder, but I refuse to toss old telephone, stereo, printer, charger, and computer cords) and what was once advertised as the world's largest picture tube television. That Mitsubishi TV was the first item we purchased when we moved into our Montana house in 1996. Flat screens were available back then, but that $3,500.00, 300-pound behemoth outperformed them all. While our son now laughs at that ancient TV in our rec room, it still works as well as it did the day we bought it. So in retrospect, it was worth the outrageous price. When the time comes to haul it out, it will take three or four people to do so. But like I said—that will be Sean's responsibility!

* * *

People in the arts are notoriously independent, yet many—including me—still seek corporate approval. In the 1980s and early 1990s, I wanted nothing more than to acquire big honking record deals for my clients with labels such as A&M, Atlantic, Columbia, EMI, Geffen, MCA, Poly-Gram, RCA, and Universal. Later, as an author, I wanted to acquire a big honking publishing deal with a similarly prestigious major publisher.

Fortunately, the mindset that artistic people without corporate backing are somehow lesser talents is beginning to fade. Independent films are cool, and now many huge musical artists have bypassed the major record labels to form their own indie labels. So far, indie authors haven't received the same acceptance overall, but they're making progress.

For *Cool Creatures, Hot Planet,* as much as I wanted a major publishing deal, I wasn't willing to sell out to meet corporate specifications (still one of the best decisions I've ever made). For *Endangered Edens,* I already knew that publishers would balk at such a photo-intensive book, so I didn't even bother submitting to them.

My foray into fiction made me yearn for corporate approval again. Interfering with my goal was that I don't write mainstream fiction, and anything I'm going to dedicate thousands of hours to is going to reflect my liberal viewpoint. Sure, I like money, but far more important to me is to write books that will inspire people to become politically active and/or work to make their little corner of the world a better place.

As I soon learned from sending out *Time Is Irreverent* manuscripts, publishing companies either didn't know what to do with it or found it offensive. Was it science fiction? Was it satire? Was it political commentary? Was it religious criticism? The answer to all those questions is yes!

Reviewers have compared my fiction writing to Kurt Vonnegut and Douglas Adams. While I'm humbled to be in such company, neither Vonnegut nor Adams pushed the envelope as far as I did. I mean, people are used to over-the-top sex and violence in books, but a novel with no shoot 'em up scenes that sends its protagonists back to the time of Jesus to crash the Sermon on the Mount and suggests that Jesus's miracles were flimflam-man cons used to build a following—now that's extreme! Had my father been alive to read *Time Is Irreverent,* he would have been convinced that Satan had set up housekeeping inside my skull.

When it became apparent that mainstream publishing companies weren't going to bite on my controversial science-fiction political-comedy, I searched for alternative options and found what appeared to be the perfect opportunity. Amazon's Kindle Press had a rolling contest called "Kindle Scout." It was essentially a way to earn a publishing contract by entering a book cover with an excerpt and getting people to vote on it over a thirty-day period. That was right in my wheelhouse, because not many authors are as good at promotion as I am. I entered the contest and kicked ass. While Amazon hid the actual vote numbers, they did provide daily rankings, and during *Time Is Irreverent's* thirty-day run, no book outperformed mine.

Amazon, however, had plenty of weasel words in their contest rules, and they made it clear that votes would be only one of the factors in their decision to offer a contract. So despite my efforts, Amazon passed on publishing my novel. The one thing I did earn, as one of the top vote-getters, was a written critique. This sentence from that critique pretty much sums things up: "Also, the reality is that much of the content is deeply offensive to a lot of people, and will likely be very difficult to market successfully."

Although initially I was disappointed when the news arrived that I didn't win, I'm now thrilled about what happened. Amazon discontinued their Kindle Scout program shortly after they passed on my book, and though they promised to continue supporting their previous winners, I certainly wouldn't have wanted them to have exclusive rights to my novel under those circumstances. Later, after publishing *Time Is Irreverent* via Encante Press, LLC, I visited Amazon's website to compare my novel's sales ranking against Kindle Scout winners I recognized from my month in the contest. Every time I checked, *Time Is Irreverent* had the superior ranking.

Amazon's editors were correct about one thing: *Time Is Irreverent* did offend people. I had assumed that readers prone to becoming upset by irreverent content wouldn't buy a book with *irreverent* in the title, but what did I know? While the vast majority of the reviews for *Time Is Irreverent* have been enthusiastically positive, my first round of promotions generated more negative reviews than I anticipated. That was especially the case on Amazon's website, where numerous people were furious that I had the nerve to insert my politics into "their book." One reader declared my call for equal rights "bigoted," another called the book "liberal idiocy," another called it "left-wing propaganda," and yet another cut right to the chase and called it "pure crap." Most outrageous was a one-star review that said simply "Trump 2020."

While I generally laughed at the reviews, I had to file a complaint with Amazon when a group of obvious non-readers worked together to tank my ranking by rapidly posting a series of bogus one-star reviews. Fortunately, Amazon agreed with me and removed many of the worst offenders.

After that, I took what I learned and did a better job of targeting my marketing. I also greatly reduced the vindictive reviews by inserting a disclaimer in the book description:

Publisher's Warning: This book is intended for a liberal audience and features satirical content that may not be appropriate for Donald Trump supporters or those who are offended by views that challenge traditional religious beliefs. Common side effects include wide smiles, sudden laughter, and occasional snorts. Reader discretion is advised.

I also used the same warning for the sequels, *Time Is Irreverent 2: Jesus*

Christ, Not Again! and *Time Is Irreverent 3: Gone for 16 Seconds*, with great success.

* * *

Better reviews don't necessarily mean smooth sailing. The cover of *Time Is Irreverent* featured an uncontroversial spaceship and a 1959 Ford Thunderbird convertible. For *Time Is Irreverent 2: Jesus Christ, Not Again!* I wanted to play up the comedy side of the series (in this episode Jesus time travels to present day America, where he encounters right-wing Christians who think he should be white) and hired an artist to create a cover reminiscent of the scene where Marty Mann, Nellie Dixon, and Jesus Christ run naked with the Porcupine caribou herd in the Arctic National Wildlife Refuge. A caribou in the foreground and the positioning of arms hilariously block all of the characters' private parts, so there is no actual nudity. Nevertheless, both Amazon and Facebook refused to sell me advertising that showed the book cover because of the "perceived nudity." (Amazon does allow the cover on the regular sales page for the book, however.)

Even though I can't prove that Amazon and Facebook made their decisions based on bigotry toward snarky heathens, I'd be willing to bet that neither company would reject advertising for Sade's multi-platinum *Love Deluxe* album, which features the naked singer covering herself up much like Nellie Dixon does on the cover of *Time Is Irreverent 2: Jesus Christ, Not Again!*

Despite the many battles, I can't complain about the success of the *Time Is Irreverent* series. The Kindle versions of all three novels became Amazon #1 Best Sellers in Political Humor, and overall the series has developed a loyal following.

While it's difficult to predict the future, I assume that after I finish this book I will return to the fiction side and write more *Time Is Irreverent* novels. I will miss the characters too much if I don't. I enjoy writing both nonfiction and fiction, but the latter is especially rewarding because I'm telling myself the story at the same time I'm telling it to my readers. Unlike some authors, I don't plot out my novels ahead of time. I try to sit back and type the story as it happens—and sometimes that can get quite emotional.

For example, Nellie Dixon was supposed to be just a short-term character that poofed away in a timeline change. She didn't enter the first novel until a third of the way in. There she met my male protagonist, Marty Mann, shortly after a time-jump had tossed him into flooded Everglades City. The year was 2056, and America was a strict theocracy, where drinking alcohol, listening to rock 'n' roll, and being gay or lesbian were all illegal. I planned to send Marty Mann on a road trip across America to the liberal Canadian province of Minnesota and thought having him do so with a beautiful, snarky lesbian-on-the-run would add an interesting twist to the story. Then, when I reached the point where Marty Mann had to travel back in time to change the future, thereby eliminating Nellie, I realized I couldn't do it. From the moment Nellie entered the story, she had become my favorite character and almost certainly my readers' favorite too.

In well-written time travel novels, the author sets up the rules for time travel early in the story and sticks with them, no matter what. Therefore, I spent days thinking about Nellie's predicament and how to save her without pulling a *deus ex machina* or breaking my rules. Never before had writing affected me in such a way. The story felt so real that I got all choked up.

I must have done a good job with my solution, because out of the blue I received an email from Jeff Abugov, the story editor for the sitcoms *Cheers, Golden Girls, Rosanne, Grace Under Fire,* and *Two and a Half Men.* In his email, he included this blurb:

"Highly recommend. It's fun, clever, cool, witty, surprising, political, sexy, everything a sci-fi book should be. And as someone who's also written a sci-fi-time-travel-humor novel, I love that Marty Essen doesn't break the time rules he sets up from the start—so many sci-fi authors do, and as far as I'm concerned, that's just lazy writing. Not the case here! Yes, his characters learn and adapt and grow, but the foundation of his rules remain intact always. To repeat: fun, witty, surprising, sexy. Highly recommend."—Jeff Abugov, writer, producer, director

CHAPTER 35

Fun with Attorneys

I shut down Essen Communications Corporation in 2019. We had outlasted the vast majority of companies that resold landlines in Montana. We had even outlasted the companies we got our landlines from. Our original provider, US West, was bought out by Qwest, which was ultimately purchased by CenturyLink.

It's common knowledge that America's legal system unfairly benefits the wealthy. While I'm not poor, I certainly don't have the wherewithal to fight a large corporation in court. That unfair system is why contracts with such corporations are virtually worthless. Even if a person or small business clearly has the law on their side, big corporations can simply say, "make me," knowing that anyone taking them to court will quickly go broke.

I was well aware of that unfairness from the very first resale contract I signed on behalf of Essen Communications Corporation. Sure, I won some small battles for ECC by raising holy hell at the Montana Public Service Commission, but when CenturyLink dictatorially misbehaved on a critical aspect of our agreement and refused to correct their ongoing violation, I said to myself, "Fuck it! We're done."

That critical aspect was my company's ability to pay its reseller bill with a credit card. Like all resellers, we had to pay for services in advance. Consequently, CenturyLink received their money from us well before we received our money from our customers. A credit card gave us a thirty-day free ride, which evened everything out, and using credit cards with airline travel benefits provided a nice company perk.

I've always been obsessive about paying bills. That includes never paying a bill late, paying off our house early, and paying cash whenever Deb or I buy a new car. Therefore, even though I had a contract on my side, I still felt uneasy holding my ground when CenturyLink demanded payment. Each time they made a collection attempt, I offered to pay by credit card. When they refused, I reminded them that not only had they set a precedent by accepting ECC's credit cards for nineteen years, but also our contract required them to treat my company the same way they treat their retail customers, who can pay via credit card.

I'm sure the muckety-mucks at CenturyLink thought I would back down when they started disconnection procedures. What they didn't realize was that my company hadn't done any marketing for years, nor replaced customers we had lost (mostly due to moving out of state or dropping land lines in favor of cell phones). We were now small enough that we didn't have any employees, and Deb was back handling billing and the few customer service calls that came in. In fact, the only reason we were solvent was because Deb took only a small monthly paycheck, and I hadn't taken a paycheck for years. We let this happen largely because the two of us had moved on to projects we enjoyed more (book writing and college speaking for me, and teaching weaving and a weaving kits business for Deb). Essentially we were keeping the company going out of a sense of obligation to the couple hundred customers who loved us and stuck with us year after year. But now, unless we wanted to become a virtual charity, CenturyLink had made it impossible for us to stay in business.

So instead of backing down, I decided to hire an attorney to do the one thing even a big corporation couldn't bully me out of doing: closing Essen Communications Corporation by declaring bankruptcy.

My telecommunications attorney, Tom Orr, didn't do bankruptcies, so he referred attorney Billy Benjamin* to me. When I met with Billy the first time, he practically begged me for money before I left his office. Since I trusted Tom, and therefore his referral, I pushed aside my redlining bullshit meter and convinced myself that all bankruptcy attorneys must work in a similar manner. I gave Billy a small upfront payment and later sent him a larger retainer.

Because my new attorney knew nothing about telecommunications law, and I have always done much of my own legal work, I continued interacting with CenturyLink while sending Billy copies of our correspondence. I wasn't going to pull the plug until all our clients were safely with another telephone company and every bill other than the disputed one was paid.

Several months later, an independent attorney hired by CenturyLink called me to collect their money. After I explained to him my side of the story, and that CenturyLink's actions were forcing my company into bankruptcy, I expected him to launch into a series of aggressive threats. Instead, he said, "Why are you even bothering with bankruptcy? I've had other clients in similar situations and advised them to dissolve their corporations with the State of Montana. It's a simple process. If your attorney has any questions about how to do it, have him call me, and I'll give him instructions."

I thanked him and hung up in shock. I had just received the best legal advice in years—and it came from an opposing attorney! Yes, honest attorneys do indeed exist. From the beginning, I had hated the concept of bankruptcy, and now I could shut down ECC nice and easy without using the "B word."

I called Billy with the good news. As expected, he was unfamiliar with the method the independent CenturyLink attorney described for putting a company out of business. I asked him to contact that attorney, which he did. Then, after he confirmed the method was valid, he offered to complete the process for me.

Before saying yes, I called the State of Montana to make sure there would be no surprises afterward. From the helpful woman there, I learned that although the process was indeed simple, it required two steps and documentation only I had. Since there was no reason to dig up all that information just to give it to my attorney so he could type it on the appropriate State of Montana forms, I went ahead and entered everything myself.

This is where the story gets interesting. I had paid Billy a $2,500 retainer, which was to cover the entire bankruptcy process. By definition, a retainer is an advance on attorney's fees. Since up to that point Billy had done little other than read the emails I copied him on and have the conversation with the helpful CenturyLink attorney, he shouldn't have come close to using up my retainer.

With that in mind, I sent Billy an email, stating that I was happy to pay his hourly rate for services rendered and to please send me a final statement and a refund for the unused retainer. After a month passed without a response, I left a voice mail message and emailed a second request. Billy emailed me back, claiming he was shorthanded and would respond within a week. From that point on, he ignored my emails, letters, and voice mails.

When Billy's intentions became obvious, I called my telecommunications attorney, Tom Orr. After offering his profuse apologies for what had happened, he informed me that the State Bar of Montana offered a free arbitration service and suggested I contact the Office of Disciplinary Counsel too. I followed his advice and filed complaints with both entities.

That got things rolling. Until then, I hadn't received a single statement from Billy. Suddenly he produced for the Office of Disciplinary Counsel four monthly statements, using up all but $600 of the money I had given him.

Here's what I wrote to the Office of Disciplinary Counsel in response:

> These statements were, apparently, made up after the fact. And even if they weren't, I had no idea that Mr. Benjamin* was billing me up to $40 for listening to a voice mail or up to $60 for reading a simple email that I cc'd him on. He even billed me $40 for the introductory phone call before I hired him! Had I known of his unscrupulous billing practices in real time, I could have fired him early in our relationship, come to an agreement on such charges, or simply not left him voice mail messages or sent him cc's.
>
> I repeat: Mr. Benjamin* kept me in the dark on his billing the entire time. He has been incredibly deceptive and dishonest in his dealings with me. His offer to refund $600 of my $2,500 retainer is an insult.

Meanwhile my arbitration filing was working its way through the State Bar of Montana. I had filed for $2,000, which left room for negotiating down to my ultimate goal of half of my retainer. Considering that, and wanting to close ECC's books for good before December 31, 2019,

I sent Billy a letter offering to drop both my arbitration case and my complaint with the Office of Disciplinary Counsel if he refunded $1,250 before the end of the year.

When Billy accepted, I was quite surprised. Then again, I suspected he knew I would have kicked his ass in arbitration.

Once his check arrived, I mailed out notices of our settlement and assumed we were done. The Office of Disciplinary Counsel disagreed, however, and mailed me a letter stating that just because I dropped my complaint didn't mean that they were going to drop it too.

As I type this, the Office of Disciplinary Counsel has taken matters directly to the Montana Supreme Court, and they have asked me to testify. While I have the option of refusing, I plan to honor their request. I'm likely not the first person Billy has attempted to bilk, and considering that most people who come to him are in dire straits, who better than me to stand up for those who can't stand up for themselves? Besides, the older I get the more I relish new experiences. Although testifying before the Supreme Court wasn't on my bucket list, what a kick it's going to be to do so!

CHAPTER 36

Not Even Close to the End

When I began writing this book, my goal was to write a laugh-a-minute humorous memoir. While I hope I've succeeded in making you laugh, my guess is that doing so every minute was a bit optimistic. As I'm nearing the end (of the book, not my life!), I've retroactively updated my goal to make this a laugh-every-ten-or-so-minutes inspirational memoir. Hey, I never know where my novels are going until I write them, so why should this book be any different?

At heart, I'm a realistic optimist who enjoys life. Sure, I'd love to manage a superstar rock band. Sure, I'd love to own a big-city radio station. Sure, I'd love to write a *New York Times* #1 Best Seller. But life can be satisfying even if you don't get all the way to the top. In fact, sometimes it's better if you don't—because you may not have reached high enough. If I had compiled a list of life goals when I was twenty, I might have written, *Sure, I'd love to marry someone as beautiful and sexy as Heather Locklear.* Now I know I actually surpassed that goal. I married someone who, while certainly attractive, has an even more important quality—brains (i.e. personality, intelligence, and depth). Looks fade faster than brains. Somehow I lucked out, and the ideal woman for me just happened to walk into the room I was sitting in. Sure, it took an elaborate deception to reel her in, but that's beside the point.

I also believe that every day I get older brings me one step closer to perfecting life. Sometimes I laugh when I discover a new, more efficient way to do something I've been doing for years. Should I ever become satisfied that I've perfected life, I have no doubt that I'll die the next day. Isn't it a shame we can't all go back in time and relive our lives, knowing everything we've learned the first time around? Hmm. . . . That sounds like a plot for a time travel novel.

* * *

Deb and I haven't perfected marriage, but I think we're getting closer to perfection as we get older too. We seldom argue and overall we're happy. Part of the reason is that we are both self-employed, with offices in our house. While being around each other twenty-four hours a day would spell disaster for some couples, it works for us. That we have similar musical tastes is helpful, and that we have similar political beliefs is critical.

Our marriage could have survived one of us being a Republican in the 1980s, because back then people of differing opinions were much more likely to agree on a common set of facts. Now, if Deb began declaring Fox News "truthful" and the Associated Press "fake," believed global warming was a hoax, and subscribed to the long list of conspiracy theories spewed forth by the far right, I'd probably head for the door. Not because we disagreed on political points, but because I couldn't respect someone with the willful ignorance to believe that only ideology-tailored news sources were truthful, and that all the major, legitimate, vetted news organizations worldwide got together each day to report fake news in a unified voice. Conversely, if I was the one subscribing to The Cult of Alternative Facts, I'm sure Deb would say "buh bye" to me too.

While mutual respect is important, so is communication, physical contact, and occasionally doing something spontaneous together.

Deb and I go on a walk every evening, and a half-hour before bed, we "porch." In the summer, that means winding down and discussing the events of the day with liquid refreshments on the porch. In the winter, it means doing the same thing under dim lights in our great room.

I'm often surprised when I see married couples that never touch each other. Physical contact doesn't have to be only for sex. For us, unless one of us is on the road, a day doesn't go by where we don't kiss and hold hands.

The two of us also have a long history of doing spontaneous things together. Getting engaged after knowing each other for just four months, suddenly deciding to move to Montana, and traveling to all seven continents come to mind. One of our more recent spontaneous decisions happened when I fell in love with a genre of music called "symphonic metal." That type of music is much more popular in Europe than it is in the United States, and it's not as hard as the name implies. It merges up-tempo rock with orchestral and choral elements, and it often features a classically trained female lead vocalist. In the United States, the best-known symphonic metal band is Evanescence, and overseas, Within Temptation and Nightwish lead the pack.

I watch very little TV, but I love to stream concerts on a big screen, using my digital projector and stereo system. After discovering Within Temptation on Pandora, I bought all of their albums and searched the internet for high-quality concerts. When I found a good one, filmed in their home country of the Netherlands, I talked Deb into watching it with me. By the end of the show, she was as big a fan as I was.

"That was amazing!" she said. "I'd love to hear that wall of sound in person."

Although I knew she wasn't being literal, I couldn't pass up the opening she gave me. I brought up Within Temptation's website, found a list of upcoming concerts, and showed it to her.

"Pick one," I said.

Well, it wasn't quite that easy. I had college shows to work around, and Deb had some weaving events to work around too. After we nailed down our collective open dates, we debated on whether to see the band in the Netherlands, Italy, Sweden, or Norway. Since Within Temptation was selling out some of their shows a year in advance, we only delayed a few days before selecting their December 15, 2018, Milan, Italy concert.

Once I purchased our tickets, we had close to a year to plan the rest of our trip. That detracted a bit from our feeling totally spontaneous about flying to Italy to see a concert. Even so, when we finally did make it to the country, the wait was well worth it. We enjoyed an entire week of exploring, made some new friends, and toured the historic Tessitura Bevilacqua Velvet Weaving workshop in Venice (which Deb turned into an article for *Handwoven* magazine). And need I say that Within Temptation was awesome?

On another recent trip, we visited the Baja California Peninsula in Mexico. Though our decision to go there wasn't quite as spontaneous as deciding to fly to Italy for a concert, once we arrived, we enjoyed some unforgettable adventures. Among our favorites were swimming with sea lions in the Sea of Cortez and spending a morning playing with octopuses.

Our octopus adventure was as spontaneous as it gets. Deb and I had both read Sy Montgomery's book, *The Soul of an Octopus: A Surprising Exploration into the Wonder of Consciousness*, and became fascinated with the creatures. We were staying at a small lodge during the off-season and shared the place with just one other couple. One morning at breakfast, I inquired about octopuses. While my inquiry was unusual, a local guide knew just where to look. An hour later, we were dressed in snorkel gear, wading out to an octopus's lair—okay, "garden." (And yes, I was stuck on the Beatles' song all day.)

Before long, our guide reached in between some rocks and pulled out an octopus! All octopuses are venomous, though only a few are deadly. When he handed the octopus to Deb, venom was the last thing on her mind. She broke into a wide smile and declared, "Oh, my God. This is incredible!"

Soon I had an octopus as well, and we sat there in three feet of water, holding two of the most amazing creatures on the planet. Once the octopuses realized we weren't going to harm them, they settled down and enjoyed the heat from our bodies. In fact, my octopus climbed down my leg and curled up on my feet—apparently falling asleep.

Octopuses are intelligent and curious creatures, and we got a taste of that when we set them free. One swam to the other side of some rocks but wasn't quite ready to say goodbye. Acting almost like a submarine periscope, it manipulated its body to raise only its eyes above the rocks to look at us. If we moved the slightest bit, its eyes would go back down for a minute or so before rising once again to check us out.

We stayed with the octopuses for more than an hour before walking ashore with shouts of, "That was *sooo* cool!"

* * *

That's my life up to this point. Even though Essen Communications

Corporation is no more, and the COVID-19 pandemic and government spending cuts will likely hamper my college speaking tours for years to come, I will always have my writing and some new adventure to look forward to. Becoming bored or retiring is the furthest thing from my mind.

Hmm. . . . I wonder if Deb would like to go to . . .

AFTERWORD

I hadn't planned on writing an afterword, mostly because my books usually go from writing to proofing to editing to production to publication with very few delays. With this book, I decided to hold off on publication for several months while I investigated various publishing options and waited for blurbs to come in. A lot happened during that time.

Finding a publisher was a frustrating endeavor. This was partially because I eliminated so many publishers when I checked their catalogs and learned that the vast majority of their books were selling less than my own books. Why go with an outside publisher if giving them a cut wouldn't result in more sales? That obviously wouldn't be the case if I signed with one of the big five publishers, but those companies require literary agent representation, and the agents open to memoirs all seemed to be looking for life stories of minorities rising up against all odds. I'm not complaining about that or crying reverse discrimination. Agents have a right to go for what's currently hot. I did get one offer from a medium-sized publishing company, but I turned them down when a second look at the popularity of their previously published books convinced me that I would be better off on my own. So once again, I'm publishing on Encante Press, LLC.

* * *

As I read this book one more time before publication, I was shocked by how many dead people are in it. I had mentioned my father, my sister, Mark Alan, Buck Reeves, and Lenny, but they aren't the only ones. Others include my mother, Tom Simpson, the woman we acquired Buddy from, Elvira Patterson*, Chester Webster* and two players from my Victor/ Corvallis Mud Hens baseball team. And remember my attorney Billy Benjamin*? He died suddenly, shortly before I was to testify against him in front of the Montana Supreme Court.

I'm also sad to tell you that our Houdini dog, Lucy, finally reached the point that her back legs couldn't carry her anymore. I hauled her around for a week, hoping she might rally. When that rally didn't happen, Deb and I reluctantly put her to sleep. She was a happy dog to the very end.

I started searching for another dog several months before Lucy died and continued for another month afterward. My patience was rewarded when Deb and I stopped by the local animal shelter and fell in love with a newly arrived stray that had yet to be put up for adoption. We placed dibs on her and picked her up a few days later, after she had been spayed and ID chipped.

We named the newest member of our family Nellie, after the snarky female protagonist in my *Time Is Irreverent* series of novels. The name fits her to a T. She looks almost like a black Lab, but a DNA test revealed her to be one-half golden retriever and one-half Australian cattle dog. Nellie was skinny and roughly nine months old when we adopted her. That she had to fend for herself for a significant amount of time was obvious. Even months later—as a healthy dog that put on nearly fifteen pounds of muscle and has the shiniest black coat I've ever seen—she still can't resist eating insects and digging up mushrooms. We're working diligently to break her of her shroom habit!

Nellie is also the smartest dog we've ever had. Although she's still young, her understanding of the English language is off-the-charts. With a little work, I think I could train her to retrieve a beer for me out of the refrigerator. Of course, persuading her to shut the refrigerator door afterward would be a different matter. But rather than teaching Nellie tricks, we're simply enjoying her company and laughing at her antics. Deb claims that we're more like grandparents to Nellie than parents. We spoil her and let her get away with things we would have never let our other dogs get away with. But how can anyone be angry with that cute, innocent face, looking up from whatever she's chewing that she shouldn't be chewing? Yeah, Nellie has stolen our hearts.

* * *

Do you remember the story about me asking comedian Karen Pickering out on a date and then canceling after I met Deb? I debated whether to use Karen's real name in the story or make one up. Finally, I decided to contact Karen and let her decide. Since we hadn't spoken in thirty-six years, I was surprised she remembered the incident as clearly as I did. She was a great sport about what I wrote and even provided me with a nice blurb for this book. While I'm most definitely a heathen, I do believe in a series of forks in the road that affect everyone's life. In Karen's case, she met the man who would become her husband just one week after our cancelled date. Perhaps nothing would have changed had we gone on that date. But what if it did? Fortunately for both of us, we ended up on the correct fork.

* * *

I started writing *Hits, Heathens, and Hippos* at the beginning of the COVID-19 pandemic, and as I write this now, in late November 2020, the pandemic hasn't let up. While the election of Joe Biden and vaccines on the horizon give me hope for a better 2021 for everyone, Deb and I have adapted quite well to the current situation.

My college speaking gigs ceased when the pandemic hit. Then Portland State University contacted me to see if I could perform a show for them via Zoom in early June. I quickly said "yes" and then scrambled to figure out how I could pull it off. My first step was to buy a broadcast-quality webcam, but there had been a run on webcams like there had been on toilet paper. I ended up having to pay three times the retail price to get a good one. After that, I had to re-choreograph my show to accommodate an up-close, stationary camera.

Everything worked out fine, and following that first show, more college Zoom gigs flowed in. Soon I had a nice fall speaking tour that never left my house. The same thing happened for Deb with her weaving guild workshops. With Zoom eliminating her travel expenses, she put together an impressive schedule that included many guilds that could have never afforded her in person.

To accurately display all the colors Deb weaves with, she bought a set of high-quality studio lights. Consequently, I share my webcam with her, she shares her lights with me, and we have to make sure our bookings don't overlap. Not too long ago, I performed a Friday night show in my basement studio for a college in Connecticut, and as soon as that was over, Deb had to rush all the equipment upstairs to her weaving studio to prepare for an early Saturday morning workshop in Maryland.

In all, the ongoing theme of adjusting our lives to accommodate the next fork in the road continues. I guess I'd better publish this book before I have to write an afterword to my afterword!

PLEASE REVIEW THIS BOOK

Reviews are important! That's especially the case for indie authors. If you enjoyed *Hits, Heathens, and Hippos*, please post a review on the website of the retailer where you purchased this book. Thank you.

ABOUT THE AUTHOR

Marty Essen grew up in Minnesota and resides in Montana. In addition to being an author, he is a talent agent and a college speaker. Since 2007, Marty has been performing *Around the World in 90 Minutes* on college campuses from coast to coast. *Around the World in 90 Minutes* is based on his first book, *Cool Creatures, Hot Planet: Exploring the Seven Continents*, and it has become one of the most popular slide shows of all time.

The author before going on stage
at Eastern Arizona College

Please check out all of Marty Essen's books:

- *Cool Creatures, Hot Planet: Exploring the Seven Continents*
  Winner of six awards. Features 86 photographs.
- *Endangered Edens: Exploring the Arctic National Wildlife Refuge, Costa Rica, the Everglades, and Puerto Rico*
  Winner of four awards. Features 180 photographs.
- *Time Is Irreverent*
  Amazon #1 Best Seller in Political Humor, Humorous Science Fiction, Parodies, and LGBT Science Fiction
- *Time Is Irreverent 2: Jesus Christ, Not Again!*
  Amazon #1 Best Seller in Political Humor
- *Time Is Irreverent 3: Gone for 16 Seconds*
  Amazon #1 Best Seller in Political Humor

For information on Marty Essen's speaking engagements and for signed copies of his books, please visit www.MartyEssen.com. For beautiful nature photography and biting political commentary, please visit www. Marty-Essen.com.

Readers are welcome to write the author at Marty@Marty-Essen.com or to send him a Facebook friend request at www.facebook.com/marty. essen.

CPSIA information can be obtained
at www.ICGtesting.com
Printed in the USA
FSHW011647030221
78199FS